Rooted and Grounded in Love

DISTINGUISHED DISSERTATIONS
IN CHRISTIAN THEOLOGY

Series Foreword

We are living in a vibrant season for academic Christian theology. After a hiatus of some decades, a real flowering of excellent systematic and moral theology has emerged. This situation calls for a series that showcases the contributions of newcomers to this ongoing and lively conversation. The journal *Word & World: Theology for Christian Ministry* and the academic society Christian Theological Research Fellowship (CTRF) are happy to cosponsor this series together with our publisher Pickwick Publications (an imprint of Wipf and Stock Publishers). Both the CTRF and *Word & World* are interested in excellence in academics but also in scholarship oriented toward Christ and the church. The volumes in this series are distinguished for their combination of academic excellence with sensitivity to the primary context of Christian learning. We are happy to present the work of these young scholars to the wider world and are grateful to Luther Seminary for the support that helped make it possible.

Alan G. Padgett
Professor of Systematic Theology
Luther Seminary

Joy J. Moore
Associate Dean for African American Church Studies
and Assistant Professor of Preaching
Fuller Seminary

www.ctrf.info
www.luthersem.edu/word&world

Rooted and Grounded in Love

Holy Communion for the Whole Creation

TIMOTHY REINHOLD EBERHART

PICKWICK *Publications* · Eugene, Oregon

ROOTED AND GROUNDED IN LOVE
Holy Communion for the Whole Creation

Distinguished Dissertations in Christian Theology 14

Pickwick Publications
An Imprint of Wipf and Stock Publishers
199 W. 8th Ave., Suite 3
Eugene, OR 97401

www.wipfandstock.com

PAPERBACK ISBN: 978-1-4982-0961-8
HARDCOVER ISBN: 978-1-4982-0963-2
EBOOK ISBN: 978-1-4982-0962-5

Cataloguing-in-Publication data:

Names: Eberhart, Timothy Reinhold, author.

Title: Rooted and grounded in love : holy communion for the whole creation / Timothy Reinhold Eberhart.

Description: Eugene, OR : Pickwick Publications, 2017 | Series: Distinguished Dissertations in Christian Theology 14 | Includes bibliographical references and index.

Identifiers: ISBN 978-1-4982-0961-8 (paperback) | ISBN 978-1-4982-0963-2 (hardcover) | ISBN 978-1-4982-0962-5 (ebook)

Subjects: LCSH: Ecotheology. | Human ecology—Religious aspects—Christianity. | Economics—Religious aspects—Christianity. | Lord's Supper. | Consumption (Economics)—Religious aspects—Christianity.

Classification: BT695.5 .E24 2017 (print) | BT695.5 .E24 (ebook)

Manufactured in the U.S.A.   06/01/17

To Becky, for your friendship, patience, and solidarity, and to Henry, Frederick, and Audrey, for your daily gifts of affection and joy.

Contents

Preface

I GREW UP IN South Dakota, a rural farming state in a part of the country people call the "Breadbasket of the World," the "Farm Belt," or the "Wheat Belt." Both of my parents, Emil Eberhart and Penny Kramer, were raised on farms and in small farming communities near Eureka, South Dakota, which for many years was known to be the "Wheat Capital of the World." Since my parents are both ordained elders in the United Methodist Church, most years growing up, in the first part of June during their Annual Conference, my older brother, sister, and I would spend a week or two out at my grandparent's or my uncle's farm up near Eureka. I have warm memories of helping out with farm chores, getting itchy playing king of the hill on stacks of hay bales with cousins, and, at the end of the day, cleaning up and sitting down around the farm table—usually a spread of German pork sausage, Grandma's homemade pickles, fried dumplings, and potatoes. What I remember in those early years, during the mid- to late-70s, were small farming communities still getting by okay. I remember the youthful faces of my aunts and uncles, who were still making a viable living on their small family farms.

After four years of college in Minnesota at St. Olaf, where I majored in religion, and a year in D.C. working for State Senator Thomas Daschle, I moved back to South Dakota to serve as a United Methodist pastor in two small, rural communities out on the open prairie—Doland (pop. 297) and Frankfort (pop. 166). This was just over twenty years ago. Going down to the coffee shop, paying visits to parishioners, I heard countless stories about the good old days, when Main Street was buzzing with a hardware store and two cafes and the school had its own football team and the church pews were filled with grandparents sitting next to grandchildren sitting next to parents sitting next to neighbors. Like most of the rural areas in our country, these two communities were devastated by the farm crisis of the 80s. Higher costs for newer and bigger farm equipment leading to more and more debt, decreased prices for agricultural products, and massive governmental subsidies given to large, corporate factory farms led to a wave of bankruptcies and foreclosures on small family farms, along with a spike in suicides, alcohol, drug, and gambling addictions, and domestic abuse amidst the collapse not only of rural communities but an entire way of life. Since I was the son of two ministers, pastoral care came pretty naturally to me, and so I spent a good deal of time listening and caring during my time at Doland and Frankfort. I also officiated at many funerals. Almost all of the deaths were due to cancer, and although no one openly spoke of it, I think most folks were aware of the connection between the pesticides and herbicides being used on the crops and the unusual number of people dying of cancer in our rural areas. So there I was, doing what I could as a pastor to care for the souls of these dear people, without any sense at all of how to address what was happening in their communities and, ultimately, to their bodies. That disconnect and the dissonance it created in me had a significant impact on the kind of questions I brought to my research as a divinity and then doctoral student in theological education, much of which is reflected in this book.

Introduction

A SOWER WENT OUT to sow wheat in central North Dakota. His farming operation, though twelve times larger than the one-hundred-and-sixty-acre homestead his great-grandparents settled in the late 1880s, is considered small. In May, he purchased seeds from Agripro Wheat, a subsidiary of Advanta, the sixth largest seed company in the world. In early April, with his John Deere tractor and Case IH seed drill, he planted two thousand five hundred bushels of wheat across a thousand acres of land, burning approximately a gallon of diesel fuel per acre and contributing carbon emissions to the atmosphere.[1] Over the course of the growing season, he applied a combined total of a hundred pounds of nitrogen (Terra Industries) and phosphorous (The Mosaic Company) per acre and sprayed thirty-two ounces per acre of an herbicide, twenty-five ounces per acre of a rust fungicide (Bison), and another twenty-five ounces per acre of a scab fungicide. Each spring, the fertilizer runoff from his fields drains into the Missouri river, which flows through the Mississippi and down into the Gulf of Mexico, creating dead zones in the marine ecosystem.[2] The chemicals he applies have been directly linked to rises in asthma, allergies, attention-deficit disorder, fibromyalgia, and cancer in both farmers and consumers.[3] In August, he used his John Deere Combine to harvest the wheat, which he loaded onto his Ford grain truck for transport to the grain elevator. On that particular day, the market price for wheat was $4.80 a bushel. With input

1. Industrial agriculture worldwide is a primary cause of climate change. Lin, "Effects of Industrial Agriculture on Climate Change," 2.

2. Raloff, "Dead Waters," 360.

3. Moore, "Hidden Dimensions of Damage," 130–47.

costs (including land rent, seed, fertilizer/chemical, fuel, machine repair, marketing, soil sampling, and loan/interest costs) running about $210 per acre, and with wheat yields averaging around forty bushels an acre, he netted around $18 an acre, or $18,000 total. By the time the grain companies, millers, food retailers, and marketers were paid, the wheat farmer made approximately five cents on a $2.00 loaf of bread sold at the grocery store.[4] Although he continues to work between seventy and eighty hours a week and despite farm payments that subsidize his planting of commodity crops like wheat, soybeans, and corn, one year of unfavorable weather, market fluctuations, or a health crisis in the family could lead to his bankruptcy.[5]

There was a landowner who planted a vineyard in Chile's Copiapo . Valley. Following General Augusto Pinochet's bloody military coup in 1973 and as part of the liberalization of the Chilean economy, counter-agrarian reforms were implemented by the Pinochet regime whereby lands that had been subdivided and given to peasant farmers by previous administrations were returned to wealthy plantation owners. Central to these reforms was the opening of Chilean society to the global market economy by way of a series of societal "shocks" recommended by the University of Chicago economist Milton Freidman.[6] Throughout the 70s and 80s, governmental subsidies supporting cash crop agriculture and foreign investments from the U.S. encouraged large landowners to shift from traditional domestic crops such as wheat, milk, and sugar beets to grapes and other fruits for export. As a result, wealthy landowners who planted vineyards in Copiapo Valley flourished under Pinoche's government, which from 1973 to 1990 tortured its citizens, "disappeared" political dissidents, and assassinated over three thousand Chileans, including many peasant leaders. Since 1990,

---

4. Presbyterian Church (U.S.A.), "We Are What We Eat."

5. It should be clear that the burden of ecological degradation and public illness does not fall primarily on farmers themselves. As Frederick Kirschenmann, distinguished fellow at the Leopold Center for Sustainable Agriculture at Iowa State University, says, "Farmers, for the most part, are caught in a system that we've all helped to create." Although the gross income of farmers have increased sixfold over the last fifty years, their total expenses have also risen sixfold. "So farmers have had to use all of their increased gross income just to pay the bills, just to pay the expenses. And of course, predictably, their net income has remained flat for that 50 years. So what does this tell you about what farmers have to do? Farmers have to each year increase their units—more animals, more acres—just to pay last year's bills. As long as they're in that situation, we cannot reasonably expect them to do the kind of agriculture that we, and they, know that we need to do" ("Reflections, Encouragement, and Inspiration for Iowa Agriculture," 2).

6. See Klein, *Shock Doctrine*.

Chile's democratically elected governments have tried to temper the massive social inequities caused by export agriculture with tariffs and wealth redistribution programs, but the benefits of economic growth have continued to flow primarily toward large-scale landowners. As a result, more and more small-scale farmers have lost their land to financial insolvency and been forced to sell their labor as temporary workers during fruit harvest, as industrial laborers in Santiago's *maquiladoras,* or as undocumented low-wage workers in kitchens, fields, and hotels in the United States.[7] Since the 90s, Chile has been the leading exporter of fresh fruit in the Southern Hemisphere and a major exporter of wines, grape juice, and grape concentrate.

On a Sunday morning in the United States, a congregation of Protestant Christians is gathered to participate in the sacrament of Holy Communion. Following the confession of sins and a litany of thanksgivings, a pastor raises a loaf of bread—bread baked with flour ground from North Dakota wheat—then breaks it, and, recounting Jesus' words to his disciples at the last supper, says, "Take, eat. This is my body which is given for you. Do this in remembrance of me." And then, lifting a cup of wine—wine fermented from grapes crushed in Chile—the minister continues, "Drink from this, all of you. This is my blood of the new covenant, poured out for you and for many for the forgiveness of sins. Do this, as often as you drink it, in remembrance of me."

Holy Communion in an Unholy Economy

How should this meal be described? Is it holy? Do the many elements and relationships gathered together, blessed, and consumed make this a holy communion?

One of the central claims of this book is that God's invitation to join in the love feast of Holy Communion resounds at the very heart of the Christian faith and life. Come and eat. Taste and see. Drink from this. Take and eat. Do *this* in remembrance of me. In accepting this summons, we discover the true purpose and end of all creation, which is fullness of life in God. The God who is Father/Mother,[8] Son, and Holy Spirit is love, and the love of God is perfect, complete, whole—it is holy. God's holiness is God's perfect

7. Gwynne and Kay, "Agrarian Change and the Democratic Transition in Chile."

8. I refer to the first person of the Trinity as the Father/Mother to affirm, in accordance with the Scriptures, both the fatherly and motherly nature of God the Creator.

love shared with the world that all might enjoy life in complete abundance (John 10:10). Holy Communion is thus the feast of wholly loving life together, and the invitation is simply this: "Come, for everything is prepared" (Luke 14:17). *The Host invites everyone with gracious love. The Spirit of the feast joins all together in convivial love. The Bread and Cup nourish every body as love enfleshed. Guests are assembled in mutual love. And the Head of the banquet blesses its commencement through creative love.* Faithfully accepting God's call means participating in the divine love actively gathering the whole of creation into the abundant life of Holy Communion.

The communion that presently binds much of the earth and its inhabitants together is founded not upon the holiness or the fullness of God's love, however, but on a distorted, deficient form of love leading to the diminishment of life in almost all its forms.

Today's global economy joins participants from around the world in a social and ecological web of relations woven through with the myopic energies of self-interested love. The institutions, practices, and relational dynamics, which constitute the worldwide market economy, are all based in the affirmation that self-interest is the most powerful and efficient force in the universe. At the heart of modernity's reigning economic paradigm is the belief that an economy held together by self-interested love inherently leads to abundance for all.[9] As the founder of modern economics, Adam Smith, famously wrote:

> Man has almost constant occasion for the help of his brethren,
> and it is in vain for him to expect it from their benevolence only.
> He will be more likely to prevail if he can interest their self-love in

9. No philosophical or religious worldview has impacted the shape and tenor of modern existence more than neoclassical economic theory. Neoclassical economics portrays the economy as a network of rational, self-interested individuals—both consumers and firms—who "maximise their utility" through voluntary exchanges in markets that, when freed from the external interferences of governmental influence, produce an efficient equilibrium. This economic paradigm is often referred to as the Austrian tradition, because of the influence of Austrian economist Alfred Marshall (1842–1924), who recovered and expanded upon Adam Smith's understanding of the constructive power of human self-interest by way of the utilitarian tradition's doctrine of hedonism. Marshall's approach signals a turning point from economics as a form of moral philosophy to being a discipline dominated by mathematical calculus. See Canterbery, *A Brief History of Economics,* esp. 121–43. For a contemporary articulation, see Wheelan, *Naked Economics: Undressing the Dismal Science*: "Economics starts with one very important assumption: Individuals act to make themselves as well off as possible . . . Individuals seek to maximize their own utility . . . Economists don't particularly care what gives us utility; they simply accept that each of us has his or her own 'preferences'" (6).

his favor . . . [For] it is not from the benevolence of the butcher, the brewer, or the baker that we expect our dinner, but from their regard to their own interest. We address ourselves, not to their humanity but to their self-love.[10]

The global spread of this logic—referred to today as "neo-liberalism," "free market capitalism," "laissez faire capitalism," or "unfettered capitalism"[11]—has resulted in a worldwide web of social, economic, and ecological relationships knit together by self-interested love. The problem is not that love for self is necessarily incompatible with the divine love, but that self-love *alone*—apart from the holiness or wholeness of God's love—is incomplete, partial, and myopic. By itself, self-love is ultimately unholy. The promise of the modern global economy is therefore undermined by inevitable contradiction. *While some prosper in opulence, many are denied access to the basic means of life. As the exchange of goods binds more people and places together, social and ecological bonds are torn asunder. While financial wealth is gained, real wealth is destroyed. Through the consolidation of corporate–state partnerships, egalitarian governance is undermined. And with the unfettering of markets comes the expansion of corporate domination.* To participate in today's global economy is to share in an unholy communion held together with the distorted energies of insular self-love.

God's call to share in the abundant life of loving communion is given, of course, in the form of a meal invitation. So, too, the unholy nature of modern economic life together is centrally embodied in a meal—the agro-industrial meal. Since the processes involved in the production, distribution, and consumption of food traverse economic, ecological, political, historical, cultural, and personal spheres, the defining structures and characteristics of a society are revealed in how it gathers together to eat. Eating is one of the most basic processes binding us together with others and with

---

10. Smith, *The Wealth of Nations*, 12.

11. The underlying ideology that each of these names describes, all of which are based in a neoclassical economic perspective, is that free markets, based in open competition and driven by the self-interest of both producers and consumers, are the most efficient way of organizing the distribution goods and services throughout a society. Whereas governments are overburdened by bureaucratic inefficiencies and corruption, and whereas centralized control stifles individual freedom, open markets provide the conditions in which the innovation and creativity of free individuals automatically generates economic growth, growth that ultimately benefits the whole of society through Smith's "invisible hand of the market." Therefore, markets need to be freed from governmental regulation so that every aspect of society can be privatized and organized according to the principles of market exchange.

the world. As such, if our eating is disordered, much else will be disordered as well. In fact, nowhere is the unholy nature of the global market economy more evident than in our modern food system. The story of our present agro-economy, when fully told, includes coerced land enclosures, the decimation of small communities, the degradation of natural ecosystems, the commodification of seeds and plant genes, and the enormous concentration of socio-political power and wealth in a handful of transnational agribusiness corporations. Precisely because all of these processes are bundled up in the consumption of our daily bread, the seemingly innocuous act of gathering to eat entails a partaking in an unholy socio-political, economic, and ecological communion. Although the ties binding the church and its members to the political economy governing contemporary existence are innumerable, our "daily bread" and "common cup" is a uniquely representative site of Christian participation in unholy communion. By focusing on food and eating through the lens of Holy Communion, it is possible to see, in a very concrete and immediate way, how Christians are presently participating, in nearly all areas of daily life, in the unholy communion of the modern global market economy.

How, then, are Christians faithfully to gather in the love feast of Holy Communion amidst an unholy web of social and economic relationships held together by the destructive energies of insular self-interested love? My claim is that Christians are called to join today in the perfect love of God by participating in charitable and just modes of economic life, beginning with holistic agro-economic practices that share in the holiness or wholeness of God's love. In a holistic economy aligned with the holiness of God's love: *The earth is a commons accessible to all. The exchange of goods fosters social and ecological health. Productive activities are integrated into nature. Neighborly partnerships are localized in cooperative communities. And people are free to enjoy directly the fruit of their labors.*

The Holiness-Communitarian Tradition

This proposal for the participation of Christians in holistic modes of economic life as a faithful sharing in God's perfect love draws upon resources from two primary traditions: the holiness-communitarian Christian tradition and the agrarian-ecological economic tradition. The holiness[12]-

---

12. Holiness churches are typically identified as those denominations claiming to stand in direct succession to John and Charles Wesley and the early Methodist

communitarian[13] tradition includes the Wesleyan movements, German Pietism, the English Dissenters, the Left-Wing of the Reformation, medieval lay monastic groups, and medieval mysticism. In particular, the pre-modern holiness-communitarian figures I draw upon include John Ruusbroec (1293–1381), Johannes Tauler (1300–1361), Geert Grote (1340–1384), the fourteenth-century author of *Theologia Germanica*, Thomas à Kempis (1380–1471), Thomas Müntzer (1489–1525), Michael Sattler (1490–1527), Hans Hergot (d. 1527), Andreas Karlstadt (1486–1541), Johann Arndt (1555–1621), Jacob Boehme (1575–1624), Gerrard Winstanley (1609–1676), Phillip Jakob Spener (1635–1705), August Hermann Francke (1663–1727), Gottfried Arnold (1666–1714), Nicolas Ludwig von Zinzendorf (1700–1760), and John Wesley (1703–1791). The modern figures I draw upon include Johann Christoph Blumhardt (1805–1880) and his son Christoph Friedrich Blumhardt (1842–1919), Leo Tolstoy (1828–1910), Eberhard Arnold (1883–1935), Dietrich Bonhoeffer (1906–1945), Frederick Herzog (1925–1995), and Jürgen Moltmann (1926–).[14]

movement, including, for example, the Free Methodists, the Church of the Nazarene, the Church of God (Anderson, Indiana), the Salvation Army, and many of the revivalist groups associated with Charles G. Finney and Phoebe Palmer. The unifying doctrinal emphasis of these churches is the doctrine of Christian perfection or entire sanctification, which, historically, has been embodied in active participation in abolitionism, the inclusion of women in teaching and preaching roles, ministries with and for the poor and oppressed, radical critiques of money/privilege and existing social structures, consistent emphases upon peace and non-violence, and affirmations of simplicity of lifestyle. See Dayton, "The Holiness Churches: A Significant Ethical Tradition," 197–201. The use of "holiness" in this book includes these specific traditions, while also encompassing a broader identification with those ecclesial and theological traditions that have stressed the importance of being transformed by the grace of God in this life, of becoming *holy* in the *whole* of life. For example, Thomas à Kempis, who influenced John Wesley's understanding of entire sanctification, says that "whoever desires to understand and take delight in the words of Christ must strive to conform his *whole life* to Him . . . Lofty words do not make a man just or holy; but a *good life* makes him dear to God . . . At the Day of Judgment, we shall not be asked what we have read, but what we have done; not how eloquently we have spoken, but how *holily* we have *lived*" (*The Imitation of Christ*, 27, 31).

13. My use of "communitarian" is meant to be descriptive of certain ecclesial traditions (i.e., monastic orders, the Waldensians, Beghards/Beguins, Friends of God, the radical communities of the reformation, Spener's schools of piety, Wesleyan societies/classes/bands, the Blumhardts' village life at Bad Boll, the Bruderhof communities, Catholic Worker houses, etc.) and not the political philosophy associated with a republican view of society—though certain themes, such as subsidiarity, cooperation, collectivity, co-membership, etc., no doubt overlap.

14. While this is by no means a complete or even comprehensive genealogy, these particular figures and movements give voice to a set of theological affirmations and ecclesial

In identifying these various figures and movements as a distinct tradition of Christian thought and practice, I am not implying that important differences do not exist among them. For example, several key modern figures, including the Blumhardts, Bonhoeffer, Herzog, and Moltmann, articulate a theological vision that is more overtly public, political, and global in nature than that of many, though not all, in the pre-modern period. Likewise, the relationship of different figures and movements to the Lutheran-Reformed tradition varies, with Müntzer and Sattler offering a much starker contrast than Bonhoeffer or even the German Pietists. Moreover, whereas several in the holiness-communitarian tradition uncritically appropriate certain dualistic tendencies from Gnosticism and/or Augustinian Neo-Platonism, others seek to overcome depictions of holiness that sharply distinguish between notions of interiority/exteriority, spirit/body, private/public, and worldly/otherworldly.

What holds these diverse figures and communitarian experiments together as a tradition is not complete uniformity, therefore, but an organic unity made up of a set of shared theological emphases and ecclesial practices recognizable over time in a variety of contexts.[15] As in any tradition, this unity can be traced through a lineage of influence and inspiration tying disparate figures and movements together across time and space. For example, Ruusbroec and Tauler were contemporaries who visited one another at Ruusbroec's religious community in Groenendaal.[16] Ruusbroec's writings and model of communal life were the primary source of inspiration to Geert Grote, the founder of the Brothers and Sisters of the Common Life (*Devotio Moderna*).[17] One of the earliest members of the *Devotio*

---

practices that are deeply representative of what I am calling the holiness-communitarian tradition. Moreover, as I draw upon these diverse figures throughout this work, I do not attempt to reference them in any kind of equal or balanced manner, but instead utilize their respective voices wherever or however they contribute to a constructive theological vision of Holy Communion for our time.

15. In identifying this set of common themes and practices, I should emphasize that I am *critically appropriating* this tradition for the sake of offering a constructive theological-ecclesial proposal for our time and place. In doing so, I necessarily highlight certain tendencies in this tradition while de-emphasizing others—the criteria being the applicability or inapplicability of certain themes and practices in addressing our present social, political, economic, and ecological context, as well as, ultimately, my assessment of the fidelity or infidelity of these themes/practices to the God witnessed to in Scripture as Father/Mother, Son, and Holy Spirit.

16. See Schmidt's "Introduction" to Tauler, *Johannes Tauler Sermons*, 9.

17. See Van Engen's "Introduction" to Van Engen, ed., *Devotio Moderna: Basic Writings*, 7.

Moderna, as well as the chief biographer of Grote, was Thomas à Kempis.[18] Both German mysticism and the medieval lay apostolic communal life with which it was associated deeply shaped the egalitarian socio-political vision of many of the radical reformers,[19] who in turn influenced Gerrard Winstanley's project for a socially "leveled" England.[20] Johann Arndt and Jacob Boehme, who both drew upon the work of Tauler and other mystical and monastic figures,[21] were key influences upon nearly all of the German Pietists, including Spener, Francke, Arnold, and Zinzendorf.[22] John Wesley's familiarity with nearly every preceding figure and movement in this tradition, including especially á Kempis, the English Dissenters, and German Pietism, was foundational both to his doctrine of Christian perfection and his promulgation of lay religious societies.[23] Multiple strands of pietistic influence in the Württemberg region of southern Germany shaped the Blumhardts' theological vision and communal life at Bad Boll, including the works of Boehme, J. A. Bengel, and F. C. Oetinger and communitarian experiments like Zinzendorf's Moravian *Brudergemeinde* at Herrnhut.[24] The Blumhardts in turn deeply influenced Bonhoeffer's theology and the communal form of seminary life he directed at Finkewalde,[25] as well as Moltmann's theology of hope[26] and his recovery of historic free church or congregational traditions.[27]

18. See Sherley-Price's "Introduction" to Thomas à Kempis, *The Imitation of Christ*, 20–22.

19. See McGinn, *The Harvest of Mysticism in Medieval Germany*; and Kautsky, *Communism in Central Europe in the Time of the Reformation*.

20. See Kenny's "Introduction" to Winstanley, *The Law of Freedom in a Platform or, True Magistracy Restored*, 19–23.

21. See Erb's "Introduction" to Arndt, *True Christianity*; and Erb's "Introduction" to Boehme, *The Way to Christ*.

22. See Erb's "Introduction" to Erb, ed., *Pietists: Selected Writings*.

23. See Rack, *Reasonable Enthusiast: John Wesley and the Rise of Methodism*; and Heitzenrater, *Wesley and the People Called Methodists*.

24. See Macchia's excellent text, *Spirituality and Social Liberation: The Message of the Blumhardts in the Light of Wurttemberg Pietism*.

25. See Eller's "Introduction" to Blumhardt and Blumhardt, *Thy Kingdom Come: A Blumhardt Reader*, xv.

26. See Collins and Goodwin Heltzel, "Before Bloch There Was Blumhardt."

27. What I am identifying as the holiness-communitarian Christian tradition is strongly influenced by Moltmann's constructive recovery of these strands throughout his theological corpus. As early as 1975, Moltmann was turning to "experiences of the ancient congregational churches," such as "the Waldensian congregations, the Mennonites

The theological and ecclesial emphases that tie these diverse figures and movements together into a distinctive tradition are many, including a criticism of theologies detached from everyday Christian life, a commitment to peace and non-cooperation with violence, an insistence upon the inseparability of doctrine and ethics, a preferential focus upon the poor and oppressed, an affirmation of the priesthood of all believers, a dedication to lay education/formation, a commitment to communicating "plain truth for plain people" (Wesley), an avowal that the Christian life is life together in community, and the offering of concrete proposals for ecclesial reformation in each new age. At the heart of these emphases is the shared theological perspective that God's love constitutes the essence of God's being and work, that God calls and empowers us to be holy as God is holy in the whole of life, and that the primary locus and aim of holy living is loving communion with others. My proposal that Christians are called to participate in holistic modes of economic life together as a faithful sharing in God's perfect love is organized around five key affirmations constructively appropriated from this central theological orientation of the holiness-communitarian tradition:

1. **Following the Way of Jesus Christ:** Drawing on á Kempis' *Imitatio Christi*, Bonhoeffer's *Nachfolge* and Herzog's *God-Walk*, I affirm that in Jesus Christ, God's holiness is revealed for us as the incarnate way of gracious love.

2. **Abiding in the Sanctifying Bonds of the Spirit:** With Ruusbroec's spirituality of interpersonal love, Wesley's doctrine of Christian perfection, and Moltmann's theology of *perichoresis*, I affirm that through the Holy Spirit, the holiness of God is present with us in living relationships of convivial love.

3. **Worshipping the Creator in the Whole of Life:** In alignment with the *Devotio Moderna's* piety expressed through manual labor, Hergot's spiritual transformation of the people in village life, and Oetinger's theology of embodiment, I affirm that from the Father/Mother, the holiness of God is given to us in the form of enfleshed love.

---

and the Moravian Brethren" (*The Church in the Power of the Spirit*, xiv). In his later work in pneumatology, Moltmann draws heavily on German Pietism, early Methodism, and medieval mysticism. See especially *The Spirit of Life: A Universal Affirmation*. Although he does not explicitly weave these various theological and ecclesial strands together into a unified tradition, as I do, the threads are implicit.

4. **Conforming to the Triune God within Local Assemblies:** Consonant with Tauler's Beghard/Beguine communities, Spener's *Collegia Pietatis*, and Zinzendorf's image of the triune family of God, I affirm that out of the communion of the Father/Mother, Son, and Holy Spirit, the divine holiness is shared among us as mutual love.

5. **Accepting Freedom to Live Now as Citizens of God's Kingdom:** With Münzter's rebellion against feudalism, Winstanley's commonwealth platform, and the Blumhardt's *Christus Victor*, I affirm that by the inbreaking power of the Lord God, the divine holiness is active through us as creative love.

Taken together, these five affirmations form the substantive content of the claim that we are invited to be holy as God is holy in the whole of life by participating in—i.e., following, abiding, worshipping, conforming, obeying—the perfect nature of God's love as gracious, convivial, enfleshed, mutual, and creative.

The Agrarian-Ecological Tradition

The second tradition this proposal principally draws upon, especially in its agro-economic focus, is the agrarian-ecological tradition.[28] This tradition includes such social critics, environmental reformers, and political visionaries as Robert Owen (1771–1858), John Ruskin (1819–1900), Henry David Thoreau (1817–1862), William Morris (1834–1896), John Muir (1838–1914), Peter Kropotkin (1842–1921), the late nineteenth-century Prairie Populists and early twentieth-century Southern Agrarians, Liberty Hyde Bailey (1858–1954), Rudolf Steiner (1861 1925), Ralph Borsodi (1886–1977), Mohandas Gandhi (1869–1948), Gustav Landauer (1870–1919), Sir Albert Howard (1873–1947), Martin Buber (1878–1965), Scott Nearing (1883–1983) and Helen Nearing (1904–1985), Aldo Leopold (1887–1948), J. I. Rodale (1898–1971), Rachel Carson (1907–1964), E. F. Schumacher (1911–1977), Jane Jacobs (1916–2006), Murray Bookchin (1921–2006), Bill Mollison (1928–2016), Elinor Ostrom (1933–), Wendell Berry (1934–), Wes Jackson (1936–), Joel Kovel (1936–), David Korten (1937–), Herman Daly (1938–), John Jeavons (1942–), Frances Moore Lappé (1944–), Alice

---

28. Among the many historical and contemporary influences that continue to shape and overlap with this tradition are "Anarcho-Communitarianism," "Eco-Socialism," "Gandhian Economics," "Communitarian Economics," "Economics for Life," "Local Living Economies," and "Economic Democracy."

Waters (1944–), Frederick Kirschenmann (1935–), Carlo Petrini (1949–), Richard Heinberg (1950–), Vandana Shiva (1952–), José Bové (1953–), David Holmgren (1955–), Michael Pollen (1955–), Joel Salatin (1957–), Bill McKibben (1960–), the contemporary Zapatistas in Chiapas, Mexico, and participants in food and land sovereignty movements around the world.[29]

The agrarian-ecological tradition can be characterized by a variety of foundational emphases, including an affirmation of the close bonds between human culture and cultivation of the earth; the uniqueness of farming, gardening, husbandry, forestry, and craftsmanship among human endeavors; the importance of conservation and care of the land through sustainable practices, communities, and economies; the virtues of self-sufficiency, humility, patience, and neighborliness; the integration of all aspects of life, including economic, political, and moral/religious spheres; local economy/community as a balance between the extremes of capitalistic individualism and centralized communism; the importance of living attentively and responsibly within one's local place/space; and a just distribution of land and its resources within a society. My proposal that Christians are called to participate in charitable modes of economic life, beginning with holistic agro-economic practices, draws upon 5 chief affirmations that I develop from this tradition:

1. **Ensuring Common Access to the Land:** Inspired by Bailey's *Holy Earth*, Muir's National Park Bill, and Ostrom's theory of collective-ownership of property, I affirm that the earth's resources are a commons to be enjoyed by all in peace.

2. **Weaving Diverse Parts into a Whole:** Whether patterned after Mollison's Permaculture principles, Salatin's Polyface Farm, or the Fair Trade movement, I affirm that the diverse elements, processes, and participants of our economy are to be interwoven in synergistic relationships that nurture health.

3. **Integrating Human Economy into the Economy of Nature:** With Berry's depiction of the Great Economy and Daly's Steady-State Economy, I affirm that the earth with its rhythms, needs, and limits is the material ground of all human economic activity.

---

29. As in the holiness-communitarian tradition, the level of successive inspiration across and mutual influence among most of the figures in the agrarian-ecological tradition is extensive.

4. **Cooperating Together in Worker-Owned and Governed Enterprises:** Following Owen's cooperative movement, Buber's *Paths in Utopia*, and Korten's local-living economies, I affirm that the economic foundation of a genuinely egalitarian and neighborly society requires that workers share ownership over the means of production and govern the workplace through democratic processes.

5. **Acting Directly to Create a New World:** Whether in the form of the Nearings' homestead, guerilla gardening, or the Zapatista uprising, I affirm the transformative power of direct action by individuals, groups, and movements in bringing about a new and more just social order.

Together, these five affirmations represent the kind of concrete economic practices and social reforms I believe Christians are called to participate in today, precisely because they are more closely aligned with the perfect—i.e., gracious, convivial, enfleshed, mutual, creative—nature of God's love.

Although I have identified the holiness-communitarian and agrarian-ecological traditions as two distinct traditions, it is important to note the thematic and praxiological connections between the two.[30] Much of this is due to the mutual ties and sympathies between figures of both traditions. To give just a few examples: The various models of worker-owned cooperative industries promoted by Robert Owen, Peter Kropotkin, and other first-generation anarcho-socialists were all deeply influenced by the work of John Bellers (1654–1725), a Quaker theorist who was himself part of the long Christian communitarian tradition of worker mutualism (e.g., Anabaptists, Taborites, Beghards/Beguines).[31] Indian agrarian activist Vandana Shiva models her Navdanya agricultural movement on Gandhi's non-violent struggle against the British Empire,[32] which was itself inspired by the pacifism and agrarian communalism of Leo Tolstoy,[33] who drew in-

30. One of my underlying intentions in authoring this work, in fact, is to make these mostly hidden connections much more visible and explicit, in order to encourage Christians to embrace the affinity that exists between the logic of certain Christian theological affirmations and the practical socio-economic proposals of the agrarian-ecological tradition. It is possible that non-Christian agrarians or environmentalists may also discover that the logic of the holiness-communitarian Christian tradition is aligned with many of their deepest convictions and practices.

31. See Polanyi, *The Great Transformation: The Political and Economic Origins of our Time*, 105–10; and Kautsky, *Communism in Central Europe*, esp. chap. 5.

32. See Shiva, *Earth Democracy: Justice, Sustainability, and Place*, 183.

33. See Gandhi, *An Autobiography: The Story of My Experiments with Truth*. Looking

spiration from Gottfried Arnold's radical pietism in southern Germany.[34] The foremost agrarian writer of our time, Wendell Berry, is a self-avowed Baptist Christian, who has long argued that an ecological vision is both supported by the scriptures[35] and exemplified in Christian communitarian traditions like the Amish and Shakers.[36] And Jürgen Moltmann's theological project, from at least *God in Creation* (1985) forward, has been profoundly shaped by an ecological consciousness and commitment to environmental advocacy.[37]

At the heart of this affinity between the holiness-communitarian and agrarian-ecological traditions is a shared holistic perspective. By holistic, I mean in general the rejection of the particularly modern approach to understanding a unit, part, or thing isolated from its relation to the whole and the affirmation that "the whole is greater than the sum of its parts." A holistic perspective seeks to understand the ways in which any particular action, episode, entity, or concept functions within a broader system—or set of overlapping systems—and how the dynamic processes of the whole impact the particular. As Wendell Berry writes, "everything happens *in concert*; not a breath is drawn but by the grace of an inconceivable series of vital connections joining an inconceivable multiplicity of created things in an inconceivable unity."[38] To think holistically, then, requires understanding that any particular problem is connected to a variety of other dynamics, such that solutions will need to interconnected as well. Theologically, I use the word "holistic" similarly, while drawing upon the intimate connections between the meanings of holiness, healing, and wholeness. As Jürgen Moltmann writes, "since holy and whole belong so closely together, what is holy is that which has become whole again . . . We can then describe 'holistic

---

back upon the influence of Tolstoy's *The Kingdom of God Is within You*, Gandhi later wrote: "Before the . . . profound morality and the truthfulness of this book, all the books. . . seemed to pale into insignificance" (99).

34. See Tolstoy, *The Kingdom of God is within You*. Tolstoy refers to Arnold's book, *Die Erste Liebe*, as a "remarkable . . . little known" work (49). It's not incidental to my present argument that in this book, Arnold locates the pristine era of the church's "first love" for its Lord in pre-Constantinian Christianity and describes the early love feasts as central to the early church's loving fellowship and ministry to the poor.

35. See, for example, "Christianity and the Survival of Creation," in Berry, *Sex, Economy, Freedom, and Community*.

36. See, for example, "The Use of Energy," in Berry, *The Unsettling of America*.

37. Moltmann, *God in Creation*.

38. Berry, *Home Economics*, 117–18.

thinking' as 'healing thinking,' because it takes account of the wholeness of that which has been separated, and tries to restore that wholeness."[39] What is holy is whole, which means that unholiness is a state of separation, division, fracture, or woundedness caused by human sin. Unholiness, like sickness and disease, is therefore defined by the diminishment or loss of health and wholeness. "For the body does not consist of one member," as Paul says, "but of many" (1 Cor 12:14). This holistic perspective, as shaped by both the holiness-communitarian and agrarian-ecological traditions, forms the basis of my 5 primary criticisms of a global market economy driven by the sin of self-interested love:

1. **Enclosure of the Commons:** An economy based in the ongoing severance of people from direct access to the earth is operating opposite God's gracious love.

2. **Fragmentation of Bonded Communities:** An economy dependent upon the ongoing fracturing of ecosystems and human communities is working against God's convivial love.

3. **Detachment of Financial Accumulation from Earthly Existence:** An economy rooted in the abstraction of monetary wealth from corporeal-material realities stands against God's enfleshed love.

4. **Centralization of Power Among an Elite Few:** An economy that results in an amassment of the world's financial resources and political power by a global elite operates counter to God's mutual love.

5. **Expansion of Corporate Dominionship:** An economy marked by the ongoing penetration of corporate ownership over more and more spheres of personal, social, and even biological spheres of life is oriented against God's creative love.

In claiming that Christians are called to join in the holiness of God in the whole of life, in particular by participating in loving modes of economic life together with others, I am attempting to articulate, with the help of the agrarian-ecological tradition, a holistic understanding of Holy Communion for our time, in contrast to the unholy—i.e., exclusionary, divisive,

---

39. *The Spirit of Life,* 175. Moltmann, in particular, has done much to emphasize a holistic theological perspective in affirming the dynamic, non-dualistic relationship between body and soul, the church and the cosmos, the cross and the resurrection, the head and all its members, this age and the age to come, the Holy Spirit and the Spirit of Life, transcendence and immanence, justification and sanctification, the personal and the political, and the theoretical and practical.

false, unjust, imperious—nature of a global economy woven together by sinful self-love. Wendell Berry states the challenge this proposal seeks to address:

> You cannot know that life is holy if you are content to live from economic practices that daily destroy life and diminish its possibility. And many if not most Christian organizations now appear to be perfectly at peace with the military-industrial economy and its "scientific" destruction of life . . . Probably the most urgent question now faced by people who would adhere to the Bible is this: What sort of economy would be responsible to the holiness of life? What, for Christians, would be the economy, the practices and the restraints, of "right livelihood"? I do not believe that organized Christianity now has any idea. I think its idea of a Christian economy is no more or less than the industrial economy—which is an economy firmly founded on the seven deadly sins and the breaking of all ten of the Ten Commandments. If Christianity is going to survive as more than a respecter and comforter of profitable iniquities, then Christians are going to have to give workable answers to those who say we cannot live without this economy that is destroying us and our world, who see the murder of Creation as the only way of life.[40]

It is my claim that by drawing deeply upon the theological and ecclesial resources of the holiness-communitarian tradition, in concert with the agrarian-ecological economic vision, Christians today will be equipped to give workable, livable, and restorative answers to the social, economic, and ecological crises facing us today.

Methodology: Critically Appropriating the Holiness-Communitarian Tradition

My claim that Christians are called to participate in holistic modes of economic life together as a faithful sharing in God's love is based in four methodological suppositions influenced by the holiness-communitarian tradition. I begin with the premise that the being and work of God alone determines the nature of a truly holy communion. A communion (*koinonia*),[41] in the most basic sense, simply means an association, or an

40. Berry, "Christianity and the Survival of Creation" in *Sex, Economy, Freedom & Community*, 99–100.

41. The centrality of communion (κοινωνία) in understanding the fundamental

interconnection of two or more relations woven together through a common bond. To be in a communion is to be joined together in a partnership with others. In the active sense, to commune with another is to participate or partner with her in a common endeavor or shared reality. There is nothing necessarily propitious about communion per se. We might enter into beneficial or deleterious associations with others. Paul especially cautions that we not "participate [*koinonei*] in the sins of others" (1 Tim 5:22) or be "partners [*koinonous*] with demons" (1 Cor 10:20).[42] What then makes a communion truly *holy*? The holiness of a particular communion does not reside in the efficacy of a prescribed set of religious practices, in the

---

nature and work of the church has been articulated most recently by Orthodox theologian John Zizioulas. In his influential *Being As Communion*, Zizioulas argues that the key theological advances of the patristic period concerning the nature of Christ, the triune God, and human personhood were existentially grounded in the primitive church's experience of communion. In particular, Zizioulas contends that the orthodox development of a fundamentally relational ontology, a metaphysics of communion, is only understandable in the context of the eucharistic gathering of the people of God—precisely because of the fundamentally theological nature of ecclesial existence. The church, he says, is not simply an institution but a "mode of existence" or a "way of being" that, as eucharistic, participates in God's very "way of being" as a triune communion of free persons (15, 18).

42. The Greek word κοινωνία and its related forms is used by New Testament writers to convey a variety of interconnected meanings: 1) The early church depicted in Acts portrays the first Christians as being devoted "to the apostles' teaching and *fellowship*, to the breaking of bread and the prayers" (Acts 2:42, NRSV); and "all who believed were together and had all things in *common*" (2:44). κοινωνία in this sense describes the material life of the gathered community in the sharing of possessions, which is intimately connected to the teaching of the apostles, the sharing of meals, and prayer. 2) In Gal 2:9, Paul recounts how James, Peter, and John recognized his mission to the Gentiles by giving him "the right hand of *fellowship*." Here, κοινωνία is used to express the legitimizing union between the established Jerusalem church and newer, developing churches. 3) Referring to the financial collection for the poor saints in Jerusalem, Paul writes that "Macedonia and Achaia have been pleased *to share* their resources" (Rom 15:26). κοινωνία is used here in relation to care for the poor. 4) To the church at Philippi, Paul appeals: "If then there is any . . . *sharing* in the Spirit . . . be of the same mind, having the same love, being in full accord and of one mind" (Phil 2:1–2). κοινωνία is understood here as unity. 5) Paul concludes 2 Corinthians with the blessing of "the *communion* of the Holy Spirit" (13:14). Here, κοινωνία is used to convey the gift of fellowship with and in the Spirit. Paul also speaks of κοινωνία in direct relation to the eucharistic meal: "The bread that we break, is it not a *sharing* in the body of Christ? Because there is one bread, we who are many are one body" (1 Cor 10:16–17). κοινωνία here signifies a shared mutuality or reciprocity in which all members, though different, are valued participants. 6) Finally, κοινωνία is often used in the negative sense: "For what *partnership* is there between righteousness and lawlessness? Or what *fellowship* is there between light and darkness" (2 Cor 6:14); and "Do not *participate* in the sins of others; keep yourself pure" (1 Tim 5:22). Here, κοινωνία is used to convey an association/participation in the sins of others.

moral rectitude of the individual participants, or in the liminal presence of a transcendental mystery. Holiness is *of* God and not inherently of human beings or anything else in the created world. "There is no one holy like the Lord" (1 Sam 2:2); none, whether in heaven or on earth, "like the Lord, majestic in holiness" (Exod 15:11). A properly theological account of holiness, then, starts not with traditional notions of religiosity, customary norms of human morality, or even "numinous" encounters with a "fearful and fascinating mystery" (Otto).[43] Rather, since God alone is inherently holy—"hallowed be thy name"—only God determines the nature of a truly *holy* communion.

At the same time, to approach the theological task from a specifically Christian perspective is to avow that God does not withhold Godself from us, as if the divine holiness were a privately guarded possession. The God who is Father/Mother, Son, and Holy Spirit is a God who generously shares the divine holiness with, among, and for us. Even more, God invites us to "be holy as I am holy" (Lev 19:2), which is a summons *from* God to share *in* that which is *of* God. My proposal that Christians are called today to participate in holistic modes of economic life together is based, then, in the affirmation that a communion is truly holy to the extent that it participates in the holiness of God. And because the holiness of God, who is Father/Mother, Son, and Holy Spirit, is the wholeness of God's perfect love, a truly holy communion is synonymous with a wholly loving life together. Moreover, it is only on the basis of an understanding of and participation in the holy nature of God's love that we are able to recognize that which is unholy. My claim that Christians are bound up in the unholy communion of a global market economy woven through with sinful self-love is based in the affirmation, then, that an unholy communion is one that is oriented against the holy purposes of God's perfect love.

My second methodological premise is that one of the most important tasks of Christian theology is to discern whether the church is faithfully gathering together in the divine bonds of Holy Communion in the whole of its life. The work of theological reflection is focused here on critically examining the concrete relations that constitute Christian life together in specific social contexts to determine if those called to follow Jesus Christ, in the Spirit, for the sake of God's creation are faithfully participating in the divine holiness that is actively knitting all things together in loving communion. Here, the primary question for theology is not how we are

43. Otto, *The Idea of the Holy.*

to interpret or translate the church's theological claims so that they might appear "reasonable" to non-Christians or to "educated laity" in light of contemporary philosophical, scientific, or cultural logics. Much of modern theology, including especially Protestant liberal theology in the United States, has rigorously attended to this question, with the result that the concrete dynamics of ecclesial life together in specific contexts have often been ignored in contemporary theological discourse. Although the tasks related to apologetic theology are important and not necessarily incongruent with this second premise, the question that must be addressed first and foremost by the Christian theologian is whether the church of which s/he is a member is gathering together in ways that are consonant with the God whose being and work is love.

A third premise is that the gathering together that constitutes ecclesial existence is centrally embodied in the meal of Holy Communion, such that discerning whether a particular Christian community is faithfully participating in God's holiness involves examining the very specific ways in which it should join together to eat. Since the time of the Second Vatican Council, and following upon the work of the ecumenical and liturgical movements, there is increasing concurrence across the theological spectrum that the Eucharist constitutes the essential nature and work of the Christian Church in the world.[44] Orthodox theologian John D. Zizioulas (Metropolitan of Pergamon) affirms that "for Orthodoxy, the church is in the Eucharist and through the Eucharist," because "the eucharistic community is exactly the same as the whole Church united in Christ."[45] Catholic theologian William T. Cavanaugh claims that "the Eucharist is God's imagination of the church," a liturgical space and time where "the Kingdom of God challenges the reality and inevitability of secular imaginations of space and time."[46] And feminist theologian Letty M. Russell, a Mainline Protestant minister, offers the metaphor of "church in the round" to describe the feminist vision of the church as "a household where everyone gathers around the common table to break bread and to share table talk and hospitality."[47] Although I build upon this theological and ecclesial concurrence, my focus, as influenced by the holiness-communitarian tradition, includes a critical and

---

44. See Flannery, ed., *Vatican Council II, Volume 1: The Conciliar and Post Conciliar Documents*, esp. 106–7.

45. *Being as Communion*, 149.

46. *Torture and Eucharist*, 272–73.

47. *Church in the Round*, 42.

reforming stance toward not only the meaning but also the praxis of Holy Communion. In other words, although a great deal of recent theological reflection has focused upon recovering, revising, or even re-conceiving the various meanings inherent in the practice of the Eucharist—how Christians are to *think* about the holy meal—much less attention has been given toward reflecting critically upon whether the eucharistic practices themselves—what Christians actually *do* in being gathered together for the holy meal—truly substantiate the fullness of those respective meanings. The theological task of examining the concrete relationships that constitute congregational life together in a particular context, then, especially those gathered together in an ecclesial meal, is especially aimed at discerning whether or not the many elements and relationships joined together in our communion meals are consonant with the holiness of God's perfect love.

The final premise that informs my claim that Christians are called to participate in holistic modes of economic life together as a faithful sharing in God's love in the whole of life is that the work of theology is not ultimately fulfilled in critical reflection alone but properly culminates in concrete proposals for the reformation of the church in light of its calling to share fully in God's Holy Communion. Here, the theologian must venture across disciplinary distinctions between doctrine, ethics, spiritual formation, pastoral care and counseling, and even ecclesial polity to identify the practical implications for daily Christian life of any particular theological affirmation. In one of the most important articulations of a distinctively Protestant—in particular, free-church or communitarian ecclesiology—in our time, *After Our Likeness: The Church as the Image of the Trinity,* Miroslav Volf writes:

> I look mainly inside, at the inner nature of the church; the outside world and the church's mission are only in my peripheral vision. Moreover, even as I look inside, I concentrate on the formal features of the relation between persons and community, rather than on their material character. What does it mean for the church to embody and pass on the love of Christ and "the righteousness and peace and joy in the Holy Spirit" (Rom. 14:17)? How should it fulfill its most proper calling to participate in God's mission in the world? What is the nature of the relation between the churches and the societies they inhabit? How is participation in the life of the church—how is *being* a church—related to the plausibility of the Christian way of life?[48]

48. Volf, *After Our Likeness,* 7.

In many ways, the theological approach this book takes up is precisely the attempt to concentrate on the material features of the relationship between persons and community in the context of a global market economy, and to propose concrete ways of how the church might more fully participate in God's being and work by embodying and passing on the peace of Christ, the love of the Holy Spirit, and the mission of God the Father/Mother through truly holy ways of life together in and for the world.[49] In this sense, my theological approach closely follows the logic of Paul's exhortation to the gathered community at Corinth to "examine yourselves" by "discerning the body"—because when you join together, you may not actually be eating the Lord Jesus' supper—an appeal that culminates in specific instructions concerning how to "come together to eat" (1 Cor 11:28–29, 20, 33).

Contemporary North American Protestant Theology

As I have already indicated, the set of contextual concerns, theological affirmations, and methodological suppositions that are constitutive of my approach are not entirely absent from North American Protestant theology today. Two of the more prominent strands in contemporary theological reflection—Protestant Liberal-Liberationist Theology and Protestant Postliberal Theology—communicate important aspects of the kind of holiness-communitarian perspective I am seeking to express. In particular, my approach is consonant with Liberal-Liberationism's *holistic* emphasis, exemplified by Sallie McFague, on the radical interconnectedness of bodily life, on the socially and ecologically destructive nature of life within the global market economy, and on the need for Christians to re-orient their lifestyles toward the flourishing of the whole creation. My argument is also aligned with Postliberalism's *communitarian* emphasis, exemplified by Stanley Hauerwas, on theology's responsibility to attend to the dynamics of ecclesial existence, on the church as a particular social-political body set apart by its unique practices, and on the Eucharist as the central embodiment of the church's politics. Whereas the problem with much of Liberal-Liberationist theology in the United States is its failure to attend substantively to concrete local churches as the primary site for social and political transformation, the problem with much of Postliberal theology, in turn, is its failure to attend fully to the social, political, economic, and

---

49. To be clear, I am not arguing that these are the only important tasks of theology in our time, but they are the ones I am undertaking here.

ecological dynamics within which North American Christians live, work and worship. The theological tradition that has most successfully maintained both emphases—the extensive call to holiness in the whole of life *and* an intensive focus upon the church as a concrete community embedded in and for the world—is the holiness-communitarian tradition. The North American Protestant theologian who has best articulated the dual affirmations of this tradition in our time, and whose methodological approach is closest to my own, is Frederick Herzog.

Protestant Liberal-Liberationist Theology: Sallie McFague

McFague's ecological liberation theology "for life," intentionally situated within the context of North American society and focused on the ecological and human crises caused by our contemporary economic way of life, represents an important articulation for our time of the nature, scope, and demands of Christian *holiness*. The defining moral issue of our time, McFague claims, concerns the globally pressing question of whether or not we and other species will live. In an age of nuclear power, the devastation of species and ecosystems, and climate change, theology must take seriously the reality that human beings have acquired the power not only "to destroy ourselves and other forms of life,"[50] but to destroy the very possibility of planetary life itself.[51] McFague locates the problem ultimately in the modern worldview undergirding our social, political and economic systems, a worldview that she argues is atomistic, dualistic, hierarchical and objectifying.[52] Theology in our context must therefore not only critically reject this worldview, she claims, but incorporate a more holistic "way of thinking of bodily unity and differentiation that stresses the radical interrelationship and interdependence of all bodies as it underscores their radical differences."[53] In this holistic paradigm, she says, "nothing is itself taken alone. Things are because of their interrelations or interconnections."[54]

50. McFague, *Models of God*, 15.

51. "We have never before been in the position of potential 'uncreators' of life, of being able to prohibit birth, but it is precisely imagining the extent of this power and feeling deeply what it means to live in a world where this is possible that is part of the new sensibility required for Christian theology" (ibid., 5).

52. McFague, *Life Abundant*, especially chap. 4.

53. McFague, *The Body of God*, x.

54. McFague, *Models of God*, 4.

Moreover, because "we middle-class Westerners are primarily responsible" for the multiple economic and environmental crises facing us today because of our consumerist lifestyles,[55] theology done in our context, she argues, must attend to "the concrete activities of *our* daily lives."[56] Theological reflection, then, "is not an end in itself" but needs to be oriented toward "the purpose of right action," for its goal "is functional, that is, to actually work in someone's life."[57]

McFague's orienting concern for the human and non-human victims of contemporary global political and economic structures, her embrace of a holistic perspective, and her practical calls for the reformation of North American Christian lifestyles all align closely with the holiness-communitarian tradition's affirmation that loving relationship is at the heart of holy living. Methodologically, her theological approach overlaps with my assertions that the primary context of contemporary Christian existence is a socially and ecologically destructive global economy and that theological reflection must ultimately culminate in concrete proposals for the reformation of Christian life together.

What is absent from McFague's work is sufficient attention to the local ecclesial *community* as a vitalizing center from which alternative modes of economic and ecological life together might emerge. Christian political responsibility for McFague, as for many liberal-liberationist thinkers, is realized primarily through the work of *individual* Christians seeking to transform larger social structures in ways that are detached from or unrelated to the political-economic practices of particular ecclesial communities. "We love God by loving the world," she says, "but such loving can only be done in public, political, and economic ways."[58] As postliberalism has properly identified, however, by circumventing the ecclesial body in advocating for national and global structural change, Liberal-Liberationist thought often

---

55. McFague, *Life Abundant*, xii.

56. McFague, *The Body of God*, 9–10.

57. McFague, *Life Abundant*, 15.

58. Ibid., 151. It should be noted that in two of her later books, *Super, Natural Christians* and *Life Abundant*, McFague urges North American Christians to adopt a "cruciform way of life" that will be liberating to others and to the earth. The primary emphasis in both books, however, is upon *individual* lifestyle changes and not upon a reform of embodied communal life in the church. Not surprisingly, therefore, when McFague speaks of the kind of life Christians are to emulate, she consistently points to individual saints: e.g., Dietrich Bonhoeffer, John Woolman, Sojourner Truth, Dorothy Day, and Mohandas Gandhi.

reduces Christian political witness to being an immaterial, "spiritualized" presence within the realm of the state's exterior governance of the body. The result—unintended, no doubt—is a disembodied church, which is incapable of effecting social-political change *as the church*, precisely because the ecclesial community is granted no discernible body of its own.

One of the contributing problems is that many of McFague's theological claims reflect the attempt, common among most Protestant Liberal theologians, to translate the particularity of Christian doctrinal affirmations into a universally accessible and applicable framework detached from the concrete dynamics of ecclesial existence. For example, the unique particularity of the story of Jesus is for McFague "paradigmatic . . . of the Christian understanding of the God-world relationship."[59] Jesus is not God enfleshed in the history of a specific Jew from Nazareth but rather is a "parable" of how God is universally manifest in the world.

> The scandal of uniqueness is absolutized by Christianity into one of its central doctrines, which claims that God is embodied in one place and one place only: in the man Jesus of Nazareth . . . But the scandal of uniqueness is perhaps not the central claim of Christian faith . . . The model of the world as God's body might, for Christians, be understood in "shape" and "scope" through the Christic paradigm. That is, from the story of Jesus of Nazareth and his followers we can gain some sense of the forms or patterns with which Christians might understand divine immanence.[60]

Within this framework, McFague describes Jesus' "scandalous table fellowship," where outcasts are welcomed and the hungry fed, not as a distinctively ecclesial way of life together but as a "central symbol" pointing toward the kind of universal political structures Christians ought to help form in the world at large.[61] As such, although the world is envisioned as the universal "body of God," for McFague, the particular communal body of Christ is only a cipher for a more egalitarian political order. The result is a theological project that is rightly aimed, with the holiness-communitarian tradition, toward the interrelated and corporeal peace of the whole of creation, beginning with the suffering poor and afflicted earth, but which fails to account for the ways in which Christian communities, participating in

59. McFague, *Models of God*, 46.
60. McFague, *Body of God*, 159–60.
61. McFague, *Models of God*, 51–53.

holistic economic practices aligned with the holiness of God's love, might both embody and effect such restorative transformation.[62]

Protestant Postliberal Theology: Stanley Hauerwas

No recent Protestant theologian, especially in the United States, has focused more upon the socio-political significance of ecclesial life than Stanley Hauerwas. Hauerwas' principal claim that the Christian church today is called to embody a tangible social alternative to the violent practices of the modern nation-state through its own distinctively peaceable politics represents an important recovery of the holiness-communitarian tradition's "political" focus on the locally assembled *community*. Like McFague, Hauerwas is highly critical of the contemporary social order, though for somewhat different reasons. He argues that the modern nation-state and contemporary economic order that presently govern the everyday lives of Americans, including Christians, was founded on the Enlightenment's attempt to create a universal morality centered in individual rationality and "freed" from the constraints of religious tradition.[63] Politics, he says, ceased being an ongoing and collective conversation, embedded within a tradition, about those goods we share in common, and became simply a coercive "means necessary to secure cooperation between" isolated individuals "who share nothing in common other than their desire to survive."[64] According to Hauerwas, theological liberals-liberationists are unable to address the fundamental source of the violent nature of our present economic way of life because their demands for "equal rights" and "justice" are dependent upon the competitive assumptions and structures of modernity itself.[65]

---

62. In the concluding pages of *Life Abundant*, McFague offers a rather different emphasis, suggesting that "we are now at a time when the churches should recall their origins prior to the Constantinian establishment; they were then fringe groups, sects, counter-cultural voices . . . This is the counter-cultural mission of the Christian churches: the promulgation of a different view of the abundant life . . . We must individually and collectively devise alternative ways of working, eating, cultivating land, transporting ourselves, educating our children, entertaining ourselves, even worshipping God" (198). Building upon *this* vision of ecclesial life-together—with the help of the holiness-communitarian and ecological-agrarian traditions—is a central aim of this book.

63. Hauerwas, *The Peaceable Kingdom*, 8–10.

64. Hauerwas, *After Christendom*, 29.

65. Ibid. "So in the interest of working for justice, contemporary Christians allow their imaginations to be captured by the concepts of justice determined by the presupposition

Moreover, Hauerwas says, in order for church and state to "peacefully" co-exist in modern societies, it was deemed necessary to relegate religion to the realm of private opinion so that the state might maintain absolute control over the bodily conduct of all its citizens. As a result, "Christian belief gets located in an interior, asocial sphere," allowing for a public space in which "a counterfeit form of 'religion'" has emerged as the shared, national way of life.[66] Therefore, the theological and ecclesial task before us, he says, is to reform the church "as a body" in order to resist the body of the modern nation-state, and in order to do this, the church must rediscover the "practices" through which it is constituted.[67] For Hauerwas, the central practices that constitute the church's politics are the sacraments of baptism and eucharist. "They are the essential rituals of our politics," he argues. "These liturgies *are* our effective social work."[68] In the eucharistic meal, in particular, "we become part of Christ's kingdom" through "God's continuing presence that makes possible a peaceable people."[69]

For the most part, my theological approach shares Hauerwas's concern with the disembodiment of the church in contemporary societies and his insistence that the primary locus of the church's "politics" ought to begin with the upbuilding of a peaceable social community. In this respect, his ecclesiology is closely aligned with the holiness-communitarian tradition's affirmation of the church as a concrete social body and resembles my methodological assertions that theology is to be oriented toward the concrete dynamics of ecclesial existence in particular contexts and attentive to the particular ways Christians are gathering together to eat.

Missing from Hauerwas's perspective, however, is an expansive enough recognition of the economic and ecological implications involved in affirming the church's call to participate in the *holiness* of God in our context. Hauerwas does not recognize how fundamentally entwined most North American Christians are in an economic web of global relations—in an unholy communion—constituted by violence and the destruction of bonded communities. In this sense, his characterization of the Eucharist as

---

of liberal societies" (ibid., 63).

66. Hauerwas, *In Good Company*, 210.

67. Ibid. "What we Christians have lost is just how radical our practices are, since they are meant to free us from the excitement of war and the lies so characteristic of the world . . . Salvation is being engrafted into practices that save us from those powers that would rule our lives, making it impossible for us to truly worship God" (ibid., 8).

68. Hauerwas, *Peaceable Kingdom*, 108.

69. Ibid.

a self-contained practice that exemplifies an isolatable alternative to modern social existence fails to account for the social and ecological fracturing-dismembering woven into nearly *every aspect* of life in the modern world, including the assembled life of Christians. Precisely because the church, as Hauerwas himself affirms, is called to manifest the implications of God's kingdom of peace, not only through its ritual actions, but also "by a relentless questioning of *every aspect* of her life,"[70] involving such everyday matters as "what to wear, how to eat, how we are to entertain ourselves,"[71] it is imperative to recognize just how embedded most North American Christians presently are in the violent habits of the modern world—in and through their clothes, recreation, and food. In other words, a church that gathers together in the eucharist meal, while ingesting wheat grown with cancerous pesticides and grapes picked by exploited laborers, is not yet a social body manifesting the divine call to holiness in every aspect of her existence. To maintain, in our context, that Christians are called to participate in God's work of reconciling peace in and through their communal practices requires, I argue, an even broader recovery of the holiness-communitarian tradition than Hauerwas provides, especially in affirming the call for Christians to pursue holiness in the whole of their economic and ecological lives with others. The theological approach needed to accomplish this recovery in our present context, moreover, must include more than calls for Christians to engage more vigorously in the church's existent practices but concrete proposals for the re-imagination of these practices in light of God's invitation to share fully in the divine love at work in and for the world.

Protestant Holiness-Communitarian Theology: Frederick Herzog

The contemporary Protestant American theologian whose theological approach is most directly aligned with my own is Frederick Herzog. Although Herzog's work does not include the kind of concrete economic proposals for holy living that I believe are necessary in our context, it otherwise closely models an approach to theological reflection—theo-centered, ecclesially and contextually focused, praxiologically, holistically and communally oriented, eucharistically grounded—that I adopt in this book.

70. Ibid., 132.

71. Hauerwas, *Sanctify Them in the Truth: Holiness Exemplified*, 125.

God-Centered Theology: What is the Nature of God's Work in the World?

My first methodological premise includes the assertion that a theology of Holy Communion must be rooted in the nature and work of God's holiness, which I affirmed is not withheld from us but is shared that we might participate in the divine love active in and for the world. The problem, according to Herzog, is that much of modern theology following in the wake of the Enlightenment has attempted to speak of the reality of God "conceptually" by way of metaphysical speculation abstracted from, even indifferent to, the concrete dynamics of ecclesial fidelity/infidelity in particular contexts of social struggle. Often, the theological starting point, he says, is the supposed problem of God's "concealment" in history, as if we are "dealing with some dark impenetrable depths when we think of God."[72] The principal task of theology, thus, becomes that of trying to *think* the possibility of God's uncertain existence in relation to the perceived stability of one modern worldview or another.[73]

For Herzog, the true starting point for Christian theology is not a "metaphysical conundrum," however, but the triune God's "unconcealment" in history in and through what he calls the "divine praxis" or "God-walk," which "is always in the center of the historical process" as a "vigorous movement we need to fall in line with and find our cues in."[74] The problem is not that God is shrouded in hiddenness or inaccessible mystery, he says, but that humanity, beginning with Adam and Eve, continually hides from the "embodiment of the heart of God" in history.[75] For God does "not hide the divine life," Herzog affirms, but rather the divine praxis "is unconcealed in relationship to all humankind."[76] The theo-praxis of God the Creator in particular is present in the divine love that bears the whole of creation, suffering with brutalized creatures and degraded nature, and working for justice and restoration for all. "God is grasped as the creator as we see God

---

72. Herzog, *Liberation Theology*, 30.

73. Particularly in the United States, Herzog says, Paul Tillich's philosophical theology is the representative model of a "theological starting point too much determined by the needs of the modern mind." The question is, "will theology persist in turning to the creative self-interpretation of man in culture or will the social self-contradiction of the church be its major concern?" (Herzog, *Theology from the Belly of the Whale*, 123–24).

74. Herzog, *God-Walk*, 55.

75. Ibid., 82.

76. Ibid., 64.

making justice prevail in the midst of strife."[77] Theology that takes as its starting point the unconcealment of God the Creator will therefore seek to make clear where the creativity, love and justice of divine praxis are at work in nature and human history amidst all that stands opposed to the wellbeing of God's creation.

So too, in the incarnation, Herzog affirms, "God is unconcealed."[78] And God has become concrete in the visible Word, he says, not primarily to resolve humanity's problem with divine mystery but to disclose the problem of humanity to itself. In Jesus Christ, "we are no longer confronted with a new possibility for speculative philosophy, but with a contradiction of existence." In other words, "he protests how we *live*,"[79] and he does so by embodying, in his whole person, a truly human life. Herzog here speaks of God's activity in the world being revealed in the "basic shape" (*Gestalt*) of Jesus' ministry or what he calls "christo-praxis." What we are confronted with, he says, is the decision to accept or reject, not a speculative proposal concerning what ultimately concerns us in the abstract, but the concrete particulars of Jesus' life. "We are confronted first of all with a particular praxis, the christo-praxis that coincides with theo-praxis."[80] Theology that takes God's unconcealment in the incarnation as its starting point, therefore, must continually seek to clarify precisely where such confrontations between the public activity of Jesus' "christo-praxis" and the social structures of human existence exist today.

Not only in theo-praxis and christo-praxis, Herzog affirms, but also in "spirit-praxis" is the love and justice of the triune God at work in the world. Herzog describes the workings of the Holy Spirit in history as "that activity of God through which, in a 'networking' of spirit, God draws all human beings together . . . and expresses special solidarity with all those who are suffering and oppressed."[81] In and through the Spirit, he says, God creates environments in which human beings are empowered to strive toward the realization of divine love and justice for neglected human beings and the neglected earth.[82] Once again, Herzog insists that the problem is not that the work of the Spirit is concealed in history but that we choose

77. Ibid., 74.
78. Herzog, *Liberation Theology*, 31.
79. Ibid., 46.
80. Herzog, *God-Walk*, 101.
81. Ibid., 170.
82. Ibid., 177.

not to participate in what the Spirit is doing. In fact, the activity of the Spirit always involves "concreteness and even earthiness," Herzog claims.[83] "In spirit-praxis the way to God is based on concretion. It is always God's own concretion and self-realization." In this sense, Herzog says, "there is no way to God but God . . . God is the way."[84] Theology that takes as its starting point the unconcealment of God in the Holy Spirit will therefore seek to identify the many ways in which our everyday lives are bound up in relationships of injustice, oppression, and ecological degradation, while lifting up movements for peace among humans and peace in nature.

A theology that begins with the praxis of God, Herzog says, depicts God's redemptive activity in the world not in the categories of "emanation," in which all things are understood to be part of God's "effulgent being." Such categories reflect a theoretical approach to God's relationship to the world.[85] Instead, Herzog says, God's active presence leads to the captivation of followers, participants, co-laborers. "In God-walk, we are motivated to see the world moving toward purpose," he says, which means that "the model is not emanation, but *concurrence*."[86] God's concurrence with the world, for the sake of the world's redemption, evokes our concurrence with what God is doing, such that we are taken up into the divine work in and for the world.

Ecclesially Focused Theology: Is the Church Gathering Together Faithfully?

My second methodological claim is that one of the most important tasks of Christian theology is to discern whether the church is being faithful to its mission to be gathered together in the loving bonds of Holy Communion. Similarly, at the center of Herzog's attempt to fashion a distinctively North American theology of liberation is his contention that the focus of Christian theology should be primarily directed toward the dynamics of Christian life together. Following his theological mentor, Karl Barth, Herzog argues that "the conflict of faith with unfaith in the church" is far more pertinent to the work of theology than "the irrelevance of faith to the unfaith

---

83. Ibid., 178.

84. Ibid., 252.

85. Ibid., 86.

86. Ibid., 86.

of the world."[87] As such, the primary "addressee" of Christian theology is the Christian community.[88] Especially among the many North American Christian "minds" who are publicly committed to the liberation of the poor and oppressed, he says, there is "a generally freewheeling notion" that Christian struggles for social justice at large can happen apart from specific denominational struggles over the concrete structures of ecclesial life—in other words, apart from our own "church struggle" (*Kirchenkampf*). Moreover, precisely because "the church framework" for social liberation in our context is "practically nonexistent"[89]—apart from a few small "lights" in a "vast darkness," i.e., the Catholic Worker, Sojourners, Jonah House[90]—the primary focus of theological reflection today decidedly "*cannot* bypass our churches"[91] but must attend all the more closely to the concrete relations constituting ecclesial existence in North America.

Contextually Rooted Theology: What are the Social Dynamics within which the Church is Embedded Today?

Included in my second methodological premise is the assertion that the theological work of discerning whether the church is truly gathering in Holy Communion involves examining the dynamics of congregational existence in specific social contexts. So too, Herzog's theological focus on the church is not an insular one. As a liberation theologian, he affirms that the theological task of reflecting on the life of ecclesial communities must be done in light of the particular social locations in which church bodies are embedded. As such, the work of theology, or "accountable teaching" within and for the church, as he often describes the theological task, must include "an awakened analysis of our context."[92] For Herzog, the chief purpose of engaging in contextual analysis of certain socio-political, cultural, or economic structures is not to ensure theology's relevance in the world at large but to help discern whether or not the church is faithfully participating in the "divine agenda" in and for the world.[93] This is the sense in

---

87. Herzog, *Theology from the Belly of the Whale*, 64.

88. Herzog, *Justice Church*, 5.

89. Herzog, *God-Walk*, 19.

90. Ibid., 259.

91. Ibid., 1.

92. Ibid., 191.

93. Ibid., 151.

which to understand Herzog's insistent claim that "we need to develop a North American vision of our own, a genuine North American model" of Christian dogmatics, "whatever the cost."[94]

According to Herzog, the primary social reality that contemporary theological reflection in the United States must learn to analyze and engage—in addition, and intimately connected, to the structures of racism, sexism, militarism, and neocolonialism—is the socioeconomic system of global capitalism. In closely examining the "internal activities" of nearly all North American churches, it is undeniably apparent, Herzog says, that "we are so tightly woven into the fabric of the economic global power called 'money' that we appear . . . to be *money-woven* rather than *God-woven*."[95] In spite of countless denominational pronouncements and resolutions expressing the incompatibility of the gospel of Jesus Christ with social inequity, war, and ecological genocide, an honest assessment of the material resources of most churches in the United States reveals their utter dependence upon global economic structures that are driven by the incessant pursuit of financial gain at the direct expense of the exploited poor and degraded earth. "American churches hardly suspect that in merely participating in the economic system they might be living in apostasy."[96] As such, one of the principal tasks of Christian theology, in this particular context, is to make clear to the church that it "no longer controls its own life,"[97] because "there are principalities and powers that own our lives."[98] Said another way, within the "belly" of the "American empire"—which, according to Herzog, is constituted by the corporate dominance over all life, including the political, cultural, and religious spheres—the American church has become thoroughly captive to the idol of money, which means that "the first task of dogmatics is to show the illusory nature of the idol and to smash it."[99] Because, for Herzog, the clash between the "gospel of Jesus" and the "gospel of profit" is so absolute, all theological teaching today "which is not explicitly also a critique of the present economic system *eo ipso* also becomes a justification of the system, and opium for the people."[100]

94. Ibid., 203.

95. Herzog, "Full Communion and the Eucharist," in *Theology from the Belly of the Whale*, 292.

96. *Justice Church*, 96.

97. Ibid., 20.

98. *God-Walk*, 44.

99. Ibid., 204.

100. Herzog, "United Methodism in Agony," in *Theology from the Belly of the Whale*, 183.

Praxiological Theology: What is God Calling the Church to Do Today?

My fourth methodological supposition is that the task of examining the concrete relations that constitute Christian life together in specific social contexts must culminate in concrete proposals for the reformation of the church in light of its calling to share fully in God's Holy Communion. So too, Herzog calls for a fundamental change in theological discourse toward a more holistic paradigm focused on the particulars of everyday life. A "complete restructuring of theology is called for, orienting it radically in the concrete—where theology functions as praxiology."[101] Perhaps the primary metaphor used in the gospels to depict the faithful human response to God's theo-praxis in history, Herzog says, is that of "walking" (*peripatein*), which is often translated as "following," "leading a life," or "conducting oneself" as an entire "way of life."[102] This is the fullest meaning of Christian discipleship. "What counts is to act in the body, in the totality of our being, in response to God's unconcealment" as the Creator, Redeemer, and Sustainer.[103] Methodologically, this requires shifting the "concern syndrome" from "ultimate concerns to bodily concern" as the focal point of theology.[104] Said another way, "in theology we can no longer argue a separate point, say, man's knowledge of God, without relegating it immediately to a particular lifestyle."[105]

Moreover, because the way of life that God the Creator instigates, that Jesus embodies in his public ministry, and that the Spirit empowers is aimed at the "full sharing" of humanity, the "*koinonia* of persons" in the whole of creation, according to Herzog, the mode of theology as praxiology he proposes is likewise oriented toward the divine intention of "full communion."[106] For Herzog, "full communion" contains two meanings.

---

101. Herzog, "Liberation Theology or Culture-Religion?," in *Theology from the Belly of the Whale*, 136.

102. *God-Walk*, xxxi.

103. *Liberation Theology*, 59.

104. Herzog, "Theology at the Crossroads," in *Theology from the Belly of the Whale*, 127.

105. Herzog, "Theology of Liberation," in *Theology from the Belly of the Whale*, 89. In emphasizing praxiology, Herzog is seeking to go beyond what he understands to be Barth's narrow focus on doctrinal clarity. "For Barth it was possible for the church to be church on account of good theology. What is missing for the North American situation is the discipleship moment. We cannot tie the continued existence of the church just to theology revitalized" (*God-Walk*, 203).

106. *God-Walk*, 20.

First, amidst the manifold ecological crises facing us today, one of the great temptations, he says, is to allow the "dulling of our moral sensibility toward creation as a whole."[107] In this regard, the task of theology involves providing a broader picture of "how things hang together" by helping North American Christians see the direct correlation between their lifestyles and "God's creatures whom we are hurting . . . the natural elements we are thoughtlessly poisoning." Accountable teaching, here, involves not only an awakened analysis of ecclesial life together within our particular social location but also "our place in the whole cosmos."[108] Second, because our identity as Christians, he says, is rooted not in speculative concept, propositional doctrine, or existential feeling[109] but "in God's *interaction* with us, God's will to be corporate, to incorporate us into the divine body,"[110] the theological work of serving God's "full communion" in the world entails recalling the people of God to their true identity in charitable community. In fact, according to Herzog, in order for meaningful social liberation to take place in our time and place, a new Christian community has to emerge, because "solutions to such vast socio-anthropological dilemmas" as we now face will "never come in sheer theory" but only, if at all "in bands and groups of people who *communally* seek to *embody* a new way of life."[111] The problem, he says, is that "the church has failed and is failing," in the context of North American society, "in making community real," such that "our task is to discover how God's reality can break through to the people of God so that a new community will be built."[112]

Eucharistically Grounded Theology: Are We Truly Eating and Drinking the Lord's Supper?

My third methodological premise is that the gathering together that constitutes ecclesial existence is centrally embodied in the meal of Holy Communion, such that discerning whether the church is faithfully participating in

107. Herzog, "Who Speaks for the Animals?," in *Theology from the Belly of the Whale*, 257.

108. *God-Walk*, 191.

109. Herzog here is referring, of course, to the respective theological approaches typified by Tillich, Barth, and Schleiermacher.

110. *God-Walk*, 18.

111. Herzog, "Full Communion Training," in *Theology from the Belly of the Whale*, 283.

112. Herzog, "God: Black or White?," in *Theology from the Belly of the Whale*, 70.

God's holiness involves examining the very specific ways in which it should join together to eat. So too, the various emphases that shape Herzog's theological approach, including his concern with the fidelity of the church in particular social contexts, his avowal of the triune God's unconcealment in theo-praxis, christo-praxis, and spirit-praxis, and his affirmation of the holistic life of discipleship in community, are ultimately centered in what he calls the "realpresence" of God in the eucharistic praxis of God. He writes:

> It cannot be stressed enough how little the liberation dynamic has made an impact on the North American scene . . . We usually do not even understand the minimum that tough social analysis would compel us to acknowledge about our North American situation . . . [We begin with] what historically is mediated to us—a precious historical configuration of the lowly shape of Jesus' public ministry that offers us a new insight into reality. Here is the corporate selfhood that bends low toward each threatened creature, which at the same time erupts in opposing empire, the oppressive power that threatens human dignity and the dignity of every creature. So we raise the question time and time again: Is there sacred space in reality where we can rediscover the dynamics of this historical configuration? It is especially at the eucharist that this question arises most compellingly.[113]

Herzog argues that one of the most important tasks for contemporary theology is to promote a more holistic understanding of the Eucharist for the contemporary church. In the Eucharist, he says, God's action in history is joined with the faithful response of the community of followers in a "concentrated way." "There is Messiah Jesus together with the gathered community, and there is Messiah Jesus *as* community (the body of Christ) . . . It is full communion, communion in every aspect of Christian life."[114] The early church, he says, had a much clearer understanding of this intimacy between God the Creator's communing activity in the world, Jesus' public ministry, and the ongoing impact of his life in the Spirit's formation of a new humanity in the eucharistic meal. "In primitive Christianity the meal was the center of the new reality Messiah Jesus had brought," a reality manifest not as a cultic act cut off from the realm of the everyday but as an entire way of life shared in the corporate body.[115] It is this holistic understanding of the Eucharist—as "the realpresence of God in history

113. *God-Walk,* 241–42.
114. Ibid., 109.
115. Ibid., 138.

in terms of Christian community"[116]—that Herzog says theology needs to help reconstruct for our context today.[117]

Although he doesn't ultimately offer concrete proposals for how to relate God's presence in the eucharistic gathering to an alternative economic way of life for Christians, Herzog does provide a suggestive framework for what a more holistic communion praxis might look like in the context of North American society. First, he argues that ecclesial communities embedded within the "belly" of the American empire need to begin actively discerning just how to confront the principalities and powers of this present age "in the political act of worship in the *body* language of the Eucharist" in ways that manifest "a sociopolitical structure other than the world's."[118] The problem, he says, is that for most worshipping Christians, the gathering together that takes place in the eucharist meal "is still a strange cultic act" with its own internal dynamics completely unrelated to their everyday socio-political and economic lives.[119] What would it look like, he asks, for a substantive socio-political alternative to arise out of the daily lives of Christians brought together in the Eucharist? Ultimately, he says, this is not a question that can be answered by way of "theoretical discussion" alone but only through an ongoing interchange between theological reflection and concrete experiments in communal praxis. Second, Herzog proposes that ecclesial communities in our context should explore ways in which the church's eucharistic praxis can truly become a "*justice meal,* in which nature and neighbor receive their due."[120] Because both human and natural history are joined together in the eucharist meal, in the elements of the field and the dynamics of shared human life, "full communion" entails a willingness of the Christian community to be immersed in "life as a whole and to stand where Jesus stands in all walks of life," especially in intimate and just relationship with the suffering poor and the injured creation.[121] For "one cannot take bread and wine on Sunday at the Lord's Supper," he writes, "and on Monday poison the soil," because when "bread and wine

116. Ibid., 10.

117. In this regard, Herzog affirms Geoffrey Wainwright's attempt to offer a systematic theology written from the perspective of Christian liturgy in his book, *Doxology,* but argues that what is needed is to push "the issue one step back to the genesis of Christian thought in christo-praxis as social location also of worship," *God-Walk,* 212.

118. Herzog, "Why We Can't Wait," in *Theology from the Belly of the Whale,* 14.

119. *God-Walk,* 129.

120. Ibid., 5.

121. Ibid., 10.

are no longer produced responsibly, celebrating the Lord's Supper does not make sense."[122]

A Holistic Communion Praxis for Today

That the North American church's daily and eucharistic bread and wine are *not*, for the most part, produced, distributed, or consumed responsibly is indicative of the problem I am seeking to address, which is the unfaithful gathering together of church communities within the unholy communion of the global market economy. In claiming that Christians are called to join in the perfect love of God in the whole of life by participating in holistic modes of economic life together, I am building upon Herzog's methodological approach of affirming the active presence of God's work in history, which captivates and compels us to engage as participants, of directing accountable theological teaching toward church communities, of providing an analysis of our global economic context for the awakening of Christian conscience, of identifying the immediate practical implications of any doctrinal affirmation for daily Christian life, and of promoting a more holistic understanding and practice of Holy Communion for the church today.

One of the predecessors to liberation theology in Latin America, Camilo Torres, a Colombian priest who died a guerilla, believed it was ultimately impossible to celebrate the Eucharist in a society as structurally violent and unjust as Colombia. "I took off my cassock" and gave up celebrating mass, he said, "to be more fully a priest."[123] Gustavo Gutierrez has written that, for many Latin American Christians, participation in the Eucharist "appears to be an action which, for want of the support of an authentic community," has become "an exercise in make-believe."[124] The theological question that the church in North America has yet fully to ask itself is whether it is possible to join together in the full communion of the Lord's Supper while enmeshed in a political economy as socially divisive and ecologically destructive as contemporary global capitalism. What I propose is not for North American churches to cease gathering together in the Holy Communion meal in order to participate in what might appear to be a more revolutionary type of action. In fact, just the opposite, I am urging North American Christians to embrace a more holistic understand-

---

122. Ibid., 139.

123. Cited by Forrester, *Christian Justice and Public Policy,* 244.

124. Ibid., 245.

ing *and* practice of Holy Communion as the focal center from and toward which new, life-serving forms of political economy might emerge in our time and place.

Herzog himself continually looked to the Pietist tradition, exemplified for him in the holistic theology of Friedrich Christoph Oetinger, as a fertile source of inspiration for imagining what ecclesial renewal might look like in our time and place.[125] In an essay surveying the new experiments in holy Christian living that appeared in eighteenth-century Protestant Europe, Herzog describes the pastorate of pietist Jean-Frédéric Oberlin, whose ministry to impoverished parishioners in a mountain village southwest of Strasbourg included "teaching them how to improve their soil" and "how to raise better vegetables."[126] Rejecting suggestions that he build a poorhouse or an orphanage as the way to aid the poor, Oberlin—who was directly influenced by the communitarian life of the Moravians at Halle—instead focused on transforming the socioeconomic conditions of his parishioners through the formation of agricultural societies, schools of practical instruction, and a type of bank where members of the church could offer and receive loans from one another. Following Oberlin's lead, factories in Germany were built on the model of Christian cooperation between employer and employee.[127] In Hamburg, Johann Hinrich Wichern founded the *Rauhe Haus*, where vagrant boys were educated in the practical arts of shoemaking, tailoring, and baking. Wichern, Herzog says, "expected the church to be concerned with the 'whole' man, to save the people bodily as well as spiritually."[128]

With Wichern, Herzog, and others in the holiness-communitarian tradition, I share the expectation that the church today might faithfully participate in the holy nature of divine love actively redeeming the whole of God's creation. It is toward this end that the following chapters are directed.

---

125. See Herzog, *European Pietism Reviewed*, 105–8. Oetinger was also a source of inspiration for Bonhoeffer, who regularly quoted Oetinger's affirmation that "the end of all God's ways is embodiment."

126. Herzog, "Diakonia in Modern Times," in *Theology from the Belly of the Whale*, 35.

127. Ibid., 38. As Herzog points out, Oberlin had a direct influence on Robert Owen, one of the founders of modern anarcho-socialism, in particular of the cooperative movement. He quotes Beyreuther in this regard, who writes that "historical research sees in Puritanism the beginning of capitalism, in German Pietism the beginning of socialism" (37).

128. Ibid., 40.

A Map

Each of the five ensuing chapters follows a common format based upon the methodological approach I have described, as well as the key affirmations I have drawn from both the holiness-communitarian and ecological-agrarian traditions. Each chapter includes a theological examination of the holy nature of divine love and unholy nature of sinful self-love, a biblical exposition of the Holy Communion meal, a critical assessment of the unholy nature of today's global agro-economy driven by self-interested love, and a constructive proposal for the participation of Christians in a set of holistic agro-economic practices as a sharing in God's Holy Communion. The overarching theo-logic in each of the chapters is that the holiness of God's perfect love leads to abundant life whereas the unholiness of insular self-love leads to its diminishment, that God's loving response to the sin of unholiness is to make the creation whole, and that we become holy as God is holy by joining together in bonds of wholly loving communion in the whole of our life together with others. For a summary chart of each chapter, see Table 1 below.

In chapter 1, I affirm that in Jesus Christ, the divine holiness is revealed as wholly gracious love, which leads to peaceable life. The unholy nature of self-interested love is thereby revealed in the exclusionary enclosure of that which God has made available to all, which requires violence. In response, God in Jesus Christ works to reconcile those who have been excluded by restoring their access to the basic means of life. Holy Communion, in the way of Jesus Christ, is wholly inclusive life together, which means we participate in God's holiness by following in the way of Jesus' gracious meal practices given "for me" and "for many" for the common welfare of all. In an agro-economic context rooted in the ongoing enclosure of the lands that God has made available for all, Christians are called to eat and drink "in remembrance of Jesus" by participating in a more inclusive food economy, in which all people have access to productive land, beginning with those presently cut off from direct access to daily sustenance and livelihood.

In chapter 2, I affirm that in the Holy Spirit, the divine holiness is present as convivial love, which fosters healthful life. The unholiness of self-love is thus present in the divisive fragmentation of that which God has knit together in love, which results in sickness. In response, God in the Holy Spirit works to heal that which sin has divided. Holy Communion, in the presence of the Holy Spirit, is wholly harmonious life together, which means we participate in God's holiness by abiding in the fellowship of the Holy Spirit so that as we eat or drink, all that we do is done in love. In an agro-economic context dependent upon the fragmentation of local communities and bonded ecosystems, Christians are called to dine in the Spirit of loving relationship by participating in a more harmonious food economy, in which the many elements and participants in our food system are interwoven in ways that nourish social and ecological wellbeing.

In chapter 3, I affirm that the divine holiness from the Father/Mother is offered to us as enfleshed love, which nourishes our earthly life. The unholy nature of self-love is thus operative in the false abstraction of certain goods from the inherent unity of God's earthly creation, which entails transgression. In response, God the Father/Mother is at work in the embodiment of truth revealed in Jesus Christ and present in the Holy Spirit. Holy Communion, in praise of the Father/Mother, is wholly integrated life together, which means we participate in God's holiness as we worship the Creator by presenting our bodies as living sacrifices for the flourishing of the earth and her many creatures. In an agro-economic context in which the wellbeing of the creation is abused for the sake of financial accumulation, Christians are called faithfully to consume the bread and cup that the Father/Mother has provided by participating in a more integrated food economy, in which the production and consumption of our daily bread is grounded in the limits and needs of creaturely existence on earth.

In chapter 4, I affirm that in the Holy Trinity, the divine holiness is shared as mutual love, which empowers us to upbuild a more neighborly life. The unholy nature of self-interested love is thereby manifest in the unjust hoarding of resources by an individual or group, which results in oppression. In response, God the Father/Mother, Son, and Holy Spirit uplifts the lowly and brings down the mighty. Holy Communion, patterned after the triune God, is wholly cooperative life together, which means we participate in God's holiness by conforming ourselves to the triune community in the way we serve one another with mutual affection as co-equal table companions. In an agro-economic context in which fewer and fewer transnational agribusiness corporations control nearly every aspect of food production and distribution, Christians are called to assemble as neighborly members of one another by participating in a more cooperative food economy, in which decentralized food cooperatives embedded in local communities and bioregions share control over the production and distribution of our daily bread.

Finally, in chapter 5, I affirm that already in this age, the reign of the Lord God's eternal holiness breaks forth as creative love, which is the well-spring of all that is genuinely new. The unholy nature of self-love is thus evident in the imperial conquest of expanding spheres of existence, which leads to bondage. In response, the Lord God breaks into the world to redeem those held in captivity to sin. Holy Communion, in obedience to the sovereign God, is wholly liberated life together, which means we participate in God's holiness by obeying the Lord God's decree to begin the eternal feast of love here and now in the midst of this present age. In the context of an agro-economy in which a few dominant agribusiness corporations are acquiring ownership over the basic structures and processes of plant and animal life, Christians are called to celebrate the Lord God's joyous banquet by participating in a more liberated food economy, in which people are set free to grow, harvest, share, and enjoy the fruits of God's good earth.

"That you . . .
may become participants of the divine nature . . .
as you are being rooted and grounded in love . . .
filled with all the fullness of God"

(2 Pet 1:4, Eph 3:17, 19).

God's	Jesus Christ	Holy Spirit	Father/Mother	F/S/HS	Lord God
Holy Love	Gracious Love	Convivial Love	Enfleshed Love	Mutual Love	Creative Love
Leads to Life	Peaceable Life	Healthy Life	Earthly Life	Neighborly Life	New Life
Unholy Self-Love	Exclusionary Enclosure	Divisive Fragmentation	False Abstraction	Unjust Hoarding	Imperious Conquest
Leads to Death	Violence	Sickness	Transgression	Oppression	Bondage
God Makes Whole	Reconciles Excluded	Heals Wounds	Embodies Truth	Uplifts Lowly Brings Down Mighty	Redeems Captives
We Participate	Follow	Abide	Worship	Conform	Obey
In Holy Communion	Inclusive Life Together	Harmonious Life Together	Integrated Life Together	Cooperative Life Together	Liberated Life Together
Love Feast	Everyone is Invited *"Do This in Remembrance"*	All are Joined Together *"Let All Be Done in Love"*	Bread and Cup is Offered *"Present Your Bodies"*	Guests Are Companions *"Serve One Another"*	The Banquet Begins *"Put New Wine Into Fresh Wineskins"*
UnHoly Communion	Exclusionary/Violent Economy	Divisive/Unhealthy Economy	False/Transgressive Economy	Unjust/Oppressive Economy	Imperious/Enslaving Economy
Holistic Communion	Inclusive/Peaceable Economy	Harmonious/Healthy Economy	Integrated/Earthly Economy	Cooperative/Neighborly Economy	Liberated/New Economy
Wholly Loving Meal	Food Commons	Healthy Food	Real Food	Food Coops	Food Movement

Table 1. Summary of Chapters.

Jesus Christ Invites All

GOD IN JESUS CHRIST invites all people to the feast of life. As the divine Host, Jesus Christ welcomes everyone, for the "Holy One of God" (John 6:69) excludes no one from sharing in the life that is abundant. God's holiness is God's perfect love, and in the fullness of divine love, all things are made whole. In Jesus Christ, the divine holiness in which the creation comes alive is revealed as *gracious love*, which is "given for you and for many" as the way that leads to peaceable life. Faithful acceptance of God's call to participate in Holy Communion, then, includes faithfully following the Host's lead in actively welcoming all people to the festal banquet of life. "Do this in remembrance of me" (Luke 22:19). Holy Communion, in the way of Jesus, is wholly inclusive life together.

But how are Jesus' followers to participate in the gracious love of God in the midst of an economy founded on self-oriented love? Cut off from the wholeness of God's love, self-love is inherently exclusionary, for it fixates on private gain at the expense of others. Modern economic life together is thus marked by a distorted social dynamic in which the financial flourishing of some is dependent upon the exclusion of others from the most basic means of life. Within the modern food economy in particular, the primacy given to self-gain as the determining factor in economic matters has resulted in the ongoing exclusion of more and more people from access to the land. In this context, following the gracious love of Jesus Christ in economic life—and thus participating more fully in the divine holiness—will entail striving to ensure that all people have access to the necessary means for life, including especially the land, which God has made available for the common flourishing of all.

The Wholly Gracious Love of God in Jesus Christ

To profess that God is revealed to us in Jesus Christ is to affirm that God does not exclude God's holiness from us. Rather, in Jesus Christ, we are given gratuitous access to the holy Life that is the source of all life. In our search for God, we are not aimless wanderers, as Bonhoeffer says, because with God we seek "what has already been found."[1] The perfect love of God is shown to us in just this way (1 John 4:9)—"the eternal life that was with the Father . . . was revealed to us" in the Son, who "we have heard" and "seen with our eyes" and even "touched with our hands" (1 John 1:1–2). We are not excluded from the divine holiness, then, as if it were a sequestered property guarded from others. For God made himself completely available through his holy life lived among us (John 1:14). Jesus Christ is God become wholly *accessible*, the "Holy One of God" who has graciously opened to us the sacred "holy of holies."

God's holiness is made accessible in Jesus Christ, moreover, *for us*. As the father of German Pietism Johann Arndt affirms, God did not reveal Godself in Jesus Christ "for his own sake but for ours."[2] We who are the beneficiaries of God's disclosure do not gain access to the divine holiness through any kind of merit or tenure fee we might offer in return. There is no compulsory need driving God's self-disclosure, as if God has become available in order to extract tribute *from* others. God's revelation in Christ is oriented entirely by God's gracious love *for* others—"for God so loved the world . . . " (John 3:16). "Christ is Christ," Bonhoeffer writes, "not for himself, but in relation to me. His being Christ is his being for me, *pro me*."[3] In Jesus Christ, the perfect nature of divine love is shown in God becoming graciously accessible for our sake.

But just *how* is the divine holiness made charitably available in Jesus Christ? Does Jesus bestow true knowledge of God to us? Are we presented in Jesus with a repeatable set of proper religious practices? Does Jesus display for us the perfect consciousness of or desire for God? One of the prominent images the New Testament writers draw upon in describing Jesus' availability to us is "the Way." Throughout the Scriptures, the symbol of the way, or the path, denotes an entire *way of life* lived in relation to God, others, and the whole of creation—the "way," which the Lord provides the people

1. Bonhoeffer, *Christ The Center*, 32.
2. Arndt, *True Christianity*, 65.
3. Bonhoeffer, *Christ the Center*, 47.

of Israel through the Mosaic Torah (Exod 18:20-23); the Psalmist's entreaty to the Lord to "teach me thy paths" (Ps 25:4); Wisdom's embodiment as the "path of life" (5:6), which stands in contrast to "the ways of those who gain by violence" (1:19). All such references encompass an interconnected complex of social, political, economic, and even ecological aspects of existence that is either consonant with or opposed to the divine life. To avow that Jesus is "the way, the truth, and the life" (John 14:6) is to affirm that Jesus' whole way of life is itself the holy Way of God that truly leads to abundant life. Christ's "life is our Way," as Thomas à Kempis says, for he has revealed to all people "the true and holy way" of God with us.[4] We have access to the holiness of God, then, not primarily through a concept, practice, or feeling deposited by Jesus for our sake, but through the more encompassing way of Jesus' holy life made manifest among us.

In accord with the gracious nature of God's self-disclosure, Jesus' holy way of life can be characterized as the incarnation of God's *gracious love for all*. The way of God that Christ embodies throughout the whole of his life is neither factional nor partisan, for God's perfect love is universally gracious to all. As the fourteenth-century mystic John Ruusbroec so strikingly affirms:

> Christ went out to all in common in his love, his teaching, and his admonitions; in the way he tenderly consoled and generously gave; and in the way he kindly and mercifully forgave. His soul and body, and his service to others were and are common to all . . . Christ never took any nourishment or anything else to satisfy the needs of his body without intending it to be for the common benefit of everyone . . . Christ possessed nothing properly his own, but had it all in common: his body and soul, his mother and disciples, his cloak and tunic. He ate and drank for our sake . . . He gave himself completely to all in common, does so still, and will do so for all eternity, [for] he was sent to earth for the common benefit of all.[5]

Not only can we speak of Jesus as "the man for others" (Bonhoeffer), but even more remarkably, he is "the man for all." Throughout the full story of his life with us, Jesus reveals a God who "shows no partiality" (Rom 2:11). Whether he heals the leprous outcast, unbinds the possessed soul, reproves the self-righteous, teaches the crowds, or sends the rich away saddened,

---

4. Thomas à Kempis, *The Imitation of Christ*, 116.

5. Ruusbroec, *The Spiritual Espousals and Other Works*, 106-7.

Jesus' orientation toward all people is for their ultimate good in concert with the well-being of others. To gaze upon his holy life, as the brothers and sisters of the Modern Devotion enjoined, is to see enfleshed "the common love that God has for all humankind without distinction."[6] For what is freely given to us in Jesus Christ is the perfection of God's love as a holy way of gracious living for the common gain of all.

Not only in life, but also through his death, Jesus reveals to us the holy way of God's charitable grace available for all. At the heart of the New Testament witness about Christ is the affirmation that he died for "all people" (John 12:32), "for everyone" (Heb 2:9), "for all" (2 Cor 5:14–15, 1 Tim 2:6). For Paul in particular, this is the central truth of the Gospel, that "we have obtained *access* to God's *grace*" through the justifying death of "our Lord Jesus Christ" (Rom 5:1–2) apart from any prior merit, status, or achievement of our own. Precisely because, as Paul declares, Christ died for us "while we were yet sinners," that manifestly proves God's perfect love *"for us"* (5:8); and because "all have sinned" (3:23), we are provided assurance that the loving grace of God, which Christ displays to us on the cross, is given *"for all"* (5:18). To say that we are "justified" by God through the death of Jesus Christ, moreover, is to affirm that there is *nothing* in the whole of created existence, including distinctions of ethnicity, gender, or social estate (Gal 3:28), that can "separate us from the love of God in Christ Jesus" (8:39). Our justification is founded in the perfection of God's gracious love that is manifest in Jesus' holy life and death for all.

The holy way of divine love for all people is precisely the way that leads to *peace*. Justified by divine grace, as Paul says, "we have peace with God through our Lord Jesus Christ" (Rom 5:1). The biblical vision of peace or "shalom" encompasses a rich variety of meanings, including the negative absence of agitation or discord but also the more affirmative promise of wholeness, completeness, welfare, safety, soundness, tranquility, fullness, rest, harmony, and prosperity. To be at peace is to be wholly alive in the gracious love of God. This is the life that is abundant. To avow, then, with the New Testament writers, that Jesus is "the Prince of Peace" (Isa 9:6) is to affirm that the full scope of his life and death—for us, for all—is given to us as the determinative revelation of the enlivening way "that makes for peace" (Rom 14:19). Although "all men want peace," as á Kempis says, "all do not seek those things that bring true peace."[7] Only the way of being gra-

---

6. Peter in *Devotio Moderna: Basic Writings*, ed. Van Engen, 218.

7. Thomas à Kempis, *The Imitation of Christ*, 127.

ciously oriented *for* the good of each person, without distinction, which is the way of divine holiness, is the path that ultimately leads to the abundant life of wholeness, harmony, welfare, and even material prosperity for all.

If the divine holiness that Jesus Christ incarnates is gracious love for all, then sin is revealed in this case as the *exclusionary enclosure* of that which God has made available for all. To enclose is to restrict entrance or to cut off access by erecting boundaries—material or immaterial—around that which had been open to all. Jesus' holy way of life, graciously given for the sake of all others, reveals that it is unholy to exclude anyone from access to those shared gifts that God has freely bestowed for the common use of everyone. Driven most often by the covetous pursuit of individual or sectarian gain, the sin of enclosure entails an inherent demarcation between those who henceforth possess exclusive control over goods previously held in common and those now cut off from free, unhindered access to such goods. In other words, whereas common grace fosters peace, the private enclosure of common goods requires *violence*. Both in the distinction made between included and excluded, and in the subsequent force needed to ensure the preservation of boundaries, whether physical, legal, or cultural, violence is intrinsic to the exclusionary possession of the common goods of God. Of course, over time, as enclosures become codified into "the order of things," the various forms of violence are also naturalized into the "way things are." Here, the universal "mercy of our God" revealed in Christ "to guide our feet into the way of peace" (Luke 1:78–9) simultaneously acts to set into relief, and therefore disclose, the reality that the unholy way of those "greedy for gain" at the expense of others is a way filled with "bloodshed" (Prov 1:11–19).

In the face of sinful enclosures, the holiness of God in Jesus Christ is manifest in the full *reconciliation* of those cut off from access to that which God has made common to all. Whenever there is an unholy exclusion or separation, God graciously seeks out the excluded to bring them back into the sphere of full access to those goods and resources needed for the abundant life. Whether seeking out enslaved laborers and providing them with a land flowing with fecundity (Exod 3:8), finding lost sheep and returning them to safety of the flock (Ezek 34:11–16), or restoring broken bodies to full health (Luke 4:40), God reconciles those separated from the means of life. Where sin divides and makes life together unholy, the gracious love of God re-unites and makes whole. To affirm that the divine holiness is revealed in Christ as God's gracious love common for all, then, is not to ignore Jesus' "preferential" orientation toward the poor, sick, and those deemed sinners, or to disregard his judgment of the religious elite and socially powerful. In fact, it is precisely the universal nature of God's grace that is revealed in Jesus' seeking out the sick, the abandoned and the lost, as well as in his condemnation of the "righteous" and "those who are well" who relate to others as if they do not deserve full access to the gracious love of God (Luke 5:27–31). The reconciling work of Christ breaks down the divisive boundaries erected by those who wish to enclose that which God has given to all. Precisely in this holy way of gracious love, then, "he is our peace," for "through him all of us have access in One Spirit to the Father" (Eph 2:14,18).

God does not incarnate the way of inclusive charity in Jesus Christ only to reveal the divine nature and demonstrate the reconciling power of holiness in the face of sin. Even more, the holiness of God is manifest for us in the gracious way of Jesus' life and death so that all might participate in the holiness that is God's. "That which is to be made holy must be made holy through God and with God," Arndt says.[8] We become holy as we share in the gracious love made available in Jesus Christ, and we do so by following in the "Way" of his life with us. "In a word," Arndt states, "this is the whole of Christianity, to follow Christ."[9] Throughout the gospel narratives, the disciples are those who literally follow after him along his way as he heals the sick and welcomes sinners throughout Judea, teaches along the sea of Galilee, and enters the city of Jerusalem. Later followers are identified as those "belonging to the *Way*, men or women" (Acts 9:2) who have been "instructed in the *Way* of the Lord" (18:25–26). "This is the goal," Pietist August Hermann Francke affirms, "for which Christ came into the world, for which he became a man," and "for which he suffered," that "we might follow the Lord Jesus" in the holy way of life he revealed.[10]

Faithfully responding to the divine summons to "be holy as I am holy" means following after Jesus in the way of gracious love for all. In fact, precisely because God has not made Godself available to us in Christ in order to extract a "return of investment" from us, but is purely oriented toward us for the common good of all, we most fully share in the perfect love of God by offering ourselves to others in this divine way. Although "God does not

8. Arndt, *True Christianity*, 66.

9. Ibid., 95.

10. Francke, "Following Christ," in *Pietists*, ed. Erb, 139.

need our service in the slightest," as Arndt says, "our neighbor does."[11] By serving the concrete others whom we encounter in our immediate midst, we encounter and enter into the very being of the God who is holy.

Sharing in the divine life by being for others in the holy way of Jesus means charitably serving *all* others without selective partiality. To "be perfect as your heavenly Father is perfect" is graciously to love both "the evil and the good," "the righteous and the unrighteous" (Matt 5:48, 45), for a love that extends only to a select few is incomplete, partial. Selective love is ultimately rooted in self-interest, for it is oriented only toward those whom it is easy to love, in particular those who love in return (Matt 5:46). In this regard, partial love is unholy, because it is a distortion of the wholly inclusive nature of the divine love. We more fully participate in the holiness of God, then, as our love graciously extends to all in common.

Precisely because the love of God is universally inclusive, however, faithfully responding to God's invitation to share in the divine holiness involves following in the reconciliatory way of Jesus' "preferential" love for those cut off from the common goods of God. This is the "ministry of reconciliation," which Christ has given us (2 Cor 5:18)—actively to seek after the excluded and break down the barriers preventing them from full access to the necessary means of abundant life. The difference between selective and preferential love is that, whereas the former is rooted in an exclusive, self-interested impulse, the latter shares in the inclusive, other-oriented nature of God's love in Jesus Christ. This work of reconciliation is the gracious way of Jesus given that we might know how to "pursue what makes for peace" (Rom 14:19) and therefore participate in the enlivened wholeness of God's love. "Peace I leave with you; my peace I give to you" (John 14:27).

God invites us to share in this inclusive, reconciling "existence for others," moreover, throughout the entirety of our lives. We are called to be holy in the whole of life, not simply within the internal, personal, or religious spheres. To participate faithfully in the holiness of God, "one must follow in the whole walk of Christ . . . in every way," as Francke says, which includes the "external matters" of our public, social life with others.[12] There is no dimension of life in which the Lord of peace does not seek to make the creation whole. Only by wholly following after the gracious love of God manifest in Jesus Christ in every aspect of our life do we fully participate in God's aim to give us "peace at all times and in every way" (2 Thess 3:16).

---

11. Arndt, *True Christianity*, 130.

12. Francke, "Following Christ," in *Pietists*, ed. Erb, 137.

To summarize: God's holiness is God's perfect love, and in the gracious way of Jesus Christ, the perfect love of God is revealed as wholly accessible and inclusive love, which leads to peace. The unholy nature of self-interested love is revealed in the exclusionary enclosure of goods that God has made available to all in common, which requires violence. God's holiness makes whole, and in the face of sinful enclosures, God in Jesus Christ works to reconcile those who have been excluded by restoring their access to the necessary means of life. We faithfully participate in the divine holiness by following Jesus Christ, who leads us in the way of God's gracious love for all people, especially the excluded, in every aspect of life.

The Wholly Inclusive Communion Meal

Holy Communion, in the way of Jesus Christ, is wholly inclusive life together. The gracious nature of God's perfect love is manifest in Jesus that we might "be holy as God is holy" in our social, relational existence with others. To accept God's invitation to Holy Communion is to participate in a way of life for others that welcomes all people to the common means of life, including especially those who have previously been denied access. This is the path to peace, for wholly accessible, inclusive life together is the way that leads to social, relational wholeness for everyone. All this is given to us in the Holy Communion meal, of which Jesus Christ is the Host and to which we are invited as participants.

The gracious love of God enfleshed in Jesus Christ for our sake is especially manifest in the particular importance of meal gatherings in Jesus' holy way of life. "The Son of Man came eating and drinking" (Matt 11:18), as the gospel narratives all affirm. Like the way of Wisdom, who sets her table and says "come, eat of my bread and drink of the wine I have mixed," (Prov 9:5), Jesus' entire way of life, which is the true way that leads to life abundant, is embodied in the shape of his meal practices. "Wisdom is vindicated by her deeds" (Matt 11:19), and Jesus' revelatory deeds are uniquely concentrated in his holy ways of eating and drinking with others. The gracious nature of God's perfect love is revealed in just this way, that the divine holiness is given to us not in the form of an esoteric religious practice or hidden knowledge, available only to an elite few, but in the commonplace event of a meal gathering. God is not disclosed in the form of a supernatural spectacle, moreover, as if God's principal intention were to draw gaped, reverential attention to Godself. In Jesus Christ, God is made wholly, humanly accessible, for our sake, around a common, everyday table.

The gracious love of God for all people is concretely manifest in the wholly inclusive nature of Jesus' table fellowship. In the stories of the feeding of the multitudes, the gospels affirm that Jesus hosts a meal in which *"all* ate and were filled" (Matt 14:20, 15:27; Mark 6:42, 8:8; Luke 9:17; John 6:11). In each case, the disciples initially advise Jesus to "send the people away" that they might go and "buy something for themselves to eat" (Mark 6:36). Faced with the enormous size of the crowds, the disciples propose a meal practice marked by the scattering of participants to their own self-interested pursuit of sustenance. Distinctions between those who have access to much, and those with little, would be readily apparent, as would partisan groupings based on kinship or geography. This way of eating, rooted in the fear that there is not enough food for all to eat and be satisfied, is "the yeast of the Pharisees and the yeast of Herod," which Jesus later warns his disciples to avoid (Mark 8:14–15). In its place, Jesus instructs his disciples to gather up the gifts of food that have been made available, arranges the guests to sit together on level ground, and after avowing that every gift of sustenance comes from God alone, orders his disciples to divide the food "among them *all*" (Mark 6:41). The result is a holy feast overflowing with abundance. Not only does everyone have enough to eat; the disciples gather baskets of surplus afterward. As host, Jesus presides over a common meal in which the perfect love of God is embodied in the gracious inclusion of all people as the way that leads to abundant life together.

The gracious nature of divine love in Jesus' inclusive meal practices discloses the sinful nature of the enclosed table. Few other spheres are as constitutive of society, of common life together, as the meal gathering. To dine with others is to dwell within a particularly concentrated nexus of interpersonal acceptance, cultural identity, social status, and of course, material belonging.[13] By being included in a meal together with others, a person is granted access to a whole set of social goods that are unavailable outside the meal. Consequently, to be excluded from table fellowship is to be denied access to one of the most generative sources of value, both immediate and potential, in society. The closed meal gathering, which requires boundaries between included and excluded, is perhaps one of the most effective ways a group establishes social identity and standing. Those gathered around an exclusive table possess a power, both patent and symbolic, over the unin-

---

13. See Douglas's classic article, "Deciphering a Meal."

vited. Whereas an inclusive table is one that nurtures a fellowship of peace, in which essential resources are made available for the common wellbeing of all, the closed table necessitates a certain kind of violence in cutting off those deemed unworthy or ineligible for commensality.

Though the meals Jesus shares in are made available to all in common, he particularly seeks out fellowship with those typically excluded from the goods embedded in commensality. In so doing, he manifests the holiness of God's perfect love in the reconciliation of those cut off from access to that which God has made common to all. Herein lies the importance of Jesus sharing meals with the socially marginalized. The Pharisees and scribes are astonished to find Jesus joining in a banquet at a tax collector's home, with "a large crowd of tax collectors and sinners sitting at the table with them" (Luke 5:29), precisely because in this context, the religious and social elite do not customarily dignify "tax collectors and sinners" with their presence at a shared meal. Jesus responds by saying that "those who are well have no need of a physician," but rather "those who are sick" (5:31). Those who already have access to commensality do not need Jesus' attendance at their tables, but those who suffer the wounds of being excluded from social belonging, do. Where sin divides and makes life together unholy, the gracious love of God re-unites and makes whole. And in the face of enclosed meal gatherings, the love of Jesus Christ actively reconciles the marginalized, those who suffer lack of access to the means of life abundant, in and through his gracious table fellowship with them.

Precisely because we are justified before God, not because of any racial, moral, or social status, but because of the wholly gracious love of God, our fidelity to the "truth of the gospel" (Gal 2:14), as Paul says, is at stake in whether or not others enjoy access to our table fellowships. Paul confronts Peter's "hypocrisy" for separating himself from eating with Gentiles, precisely because Peter had already recognized that God makes no distinction between Jew and Gentile. By removing himself from fellowship with Gentiles, out of fear of those who insist upon a closed table, Peter acts to rebuild the very barriers to a wholly inclusive communion that he had once torn down (2:18). According to Paul, this very act of participating in enclosed commensality is an "effort to be justified in Christ" through the "works of the law," which reveals Peter to be a sinner (2:16–17). For if our justification comes through the law, that is, through our own socio-moral identity and standing, "then Christ died for nothing" (2:21). But we know, Paul says, that a person is made holy to the extent that she faithfully entrusts her life to the wholly inclusive love of God revealed in Jesus Christ (2:16).

Jesus invites his followers to participate in his gracious love for all people—to be holy as God is holy—by faithfully sharing in his inclusive way of eating with and for others. In the final meal he shares with his disciples, Jesus breaks a loaf of bread, and says, "This is my body, which is given *for you.*" After the supper, he takes a cup and says, "This is my blood, which is poured out *for many.*" By identifying the loaf with his body and the cup with his blood, Jesus conjoins his very life, made graciously available for us, with his charitable way of eating and drinking. *"This"* is Jesus' wholly inclusive way of life with others enfleshed in his holy meal practices, which are graciously given *"pro me"* and "for many" for the common wholeness, welfare, and flourishing of all. To *"do this in remembrance"* of Jesus is to share in his graciously loving way of offering the goods of inclusive table fellowship for others and for all. We participate in the divine holiness by following Jesus in inviting "everyone you find to the banquet" of wholly loving communion, including "both good and bad" (Matt 22:9–10), but especially "the poor, the crippled, the lame, and the blind" (Luke 14:13). In so doing, we join in the perfect and perfecting love of God actively gathering the whole of creation together in Holy Communion.

Exclusionary Communion: Severance from the Commons

Proponents of modern capitalism portray our present global economy as if it were an inclusive web of partnerships open to anyone seeking access to the abundant life. Through the seemingly peaceable coordination of society's individual members, the free market is supposed to produce prosperity for all who join in the cohesive bonds of self-interested gain.[14] The reality, however, is that, as more and more of the world's people are brought into the global web of market exchange, countless individuals are simultaneously excluded from direct access to the basic means of livelihood

14. See Mankiw, *Principles of Macroeconomics.* "In a market economy, no one is looking out for the economic well-being of society as a whole. Free markets contain many buyers and sellers of numerous goods and services, and all of them are interested primarily in their own well-being. Yet despite decentralized decision making and self-interested decision makers, market economies have proven remarkably successful in organizing economic activity to promote overall economic well-being" (10). See also Lindblom, *The Market System,* esp. chap. 3.

and daily sustenance, while fewer and fewer enjoy the fruits of economic growth. In the modern agro-economy, in particular, the primacy given to self-gain as the determining factor in economic matters has resulted in the ongoing expulsion of more and more people from direct access to the land.

Self-love is a remarkably potent force, and the harnessing of its power within the modern economy is undoubtedly responsible for many of the more stunning material and technological advances in the modern age, including increased agricultural yields. By itself, however, self-love is incomplete apart from the holiness or wholeness of God's love, for it fixates on private gain to the exclusion of other people and other goods. Though a powerful and even cohesive force, insular self-love is ultimately destructive of a genuinely charitable and inclusive society. To participate in the modern global economy, therefore—in particular through our daily bread—is to share in an unholy communion knit together with the exclusionary force of unmitigated self-love.

The beginnings of modern capitalism can be traced to the enclosure of lands that, starting in sixteenth-century England, began the uniquely modern process of severing the majority of humans from direct access to the means of their daily sustenance. Based in arguments for the potential of increased productivity, expanded possibilities for the accumulation of profit, and ultimately, the "improvement" of both nature and human existence, the ongoing enclosure of commons is one of the most defining marks of modern economic life, effecting a "complete transformation in the most basic of human relations and practices" and rupturing "age-old patterns of human interaction with nature."[15] But as Indian physicist and agrarian activist Vandana Shiva maintains, the process of enclosing the commons, which began in England with land use and continues today with the enclosure of water rights, the use of seeds, and intellectual "property," has not led to universal human progress and ecological improvement, however, but the "growth of privilege and exclusive rights for a few and dispossession and impoverishment for the many," including most non-human life forms.[16]

In almost all pre-capitalist societies, the multitude of people—those whom the New Testament texts identify as the *ochlos* (the common people, the poor, those opposite the ruling classes)—subsisted through an immediate relationship to the earth and the fruits of the earth.[17] As Karl Polanyi

15. Meiksins Wood, *The Origin of Capitalism*, 69.

16. Shiva, *Earth Democracy*, 20.

17. To be sure, the exploitative relationship between direct producers and

writes, "traditionally, land and labor are not separated; labor forms part of life, land remains part of nature." Thus, "life and nature form an articulate *whole*."[18] In England, prior to the enclosure movement, for example, although most lands were owned either by landlords or the Crown, common law dictated that commoners had customary use rights of the land. For the majority of the population, such access to the commons served as the fundamental basis of both livelihood and self-governance. Shiva writes:

> The commons, which the Crown of England declared wastelands, were really productive lands providing extensive common pastures for the animals of the established peasant communities; timber and stone for building; reeds for thatching and baskets; wood for fuel; and wild animals, birds, fish, berries, and nuts for food. These areas supported large numbers of small peasants through common rights of access to these resources.[19]

The first surge of land enclosures in England took place in the sixteenth century during the Tudor reign, when large landowners drove peasants off the land in order to use the open fields for the increasingly profitable pasturing of sheep.[20] Although the *overall* productivity of such lands was significantly greater when supporting entire village populations, the sale of wool to the textile industry produced much higher *financial* returns for the landlords than collecting land-use rents from commoners. Through a process of fencing off properties with hedges, ditches, or other barriers to free passage, challenging the land-use rights of the commoners, and, over time, redefining legal conceptions of "property" to mean not only private but *exclusive* possession/use, English landowners unilaterally set about the "improvement" of the English countryside at the direct expense of the multitudes, including countless well-established villages. The second wave of English enclosures emerged in the eighteenth century and involved,

---

appropriators is not new to capitalist economies. In pre-capitalist societies, the appropriation by exploiters of the producers' surplus occurred by way of taxation, rents, and the use of direct coercion based in military, judicial, and political power. What is new with capitalism is that the dominant mode of appropriation is grounded in the dispossession of the producers from the land, such that their only access to continuing sustenance is by selling their own labor power in exchange for wages. As a result, the means of coercion used by appropriators is now almost entirely economic—and therefore largely hidden. Wood, *Origin of Capitalism*, 69–70.

18. Polanyi, *The Great Transformation*, 178.

19. Shiva, *Earth Democracy*, 23.

20. Wood, *Origin of Capitalism*, 83.

through direct pressure from commercial interests on public officials, the Parliamentary ratification of continued enclosures, the official extinguishing of common rights to land use, and the transferring of public lands into private ownership for commercial use.

This widespread severing of the majority of people from direct access to the land—what Marx referred to as the "original sin" of modern political economy[21]—was by no means "natural," "inevitable," or "peaceful," as many proponents of unfettered capitalism claim. As Polanyi writes, "some of this was achieved by individual force and coercion, some by revolution . . . some by war and conquest, some by legislative action, some by administrative pressure, some by spontaneous small-scale action of private persons over long stretches of time."[22] In other words, the coercive process of enclosing the commons and thereby cutting the multitudes off from the basic means of daily sustenance—a relentless process which transformed not only the English countryside but ultimately the socio-political structures of modern society worldwide—was itself grounded in original acts of direct *violence*.[23]

The enclosing of the commons and dispossession of the multitudes, as Shiva points out, inevitably creates "surplus" or "disposable" people.[24] In early modern England, for example, the enclosure of lands led to the formation of a class of "vagabonds," "beggars," and "masterless men" who aimlessly roamed the countryside seeking alternative sources of

21. See Marx, *Capital*, esp. part VIII, "The So-Called Primitive Accumulation." In chap. 26, he writes: "In the history of primitive accumulation, all revolutions are epoch-making that act as levers for the capitalist class in course of formation; but above all, those moments when great masses of men are suddenly and forcibly torn from their means of subsistence, and hurled as free and 'unattached' proletarians on the labor market. The expropriation of the agricultural producer, of the peasant, from the soil, is the basis of the whole process" (365).

22. Polanyi, *The Great Transformation*, 179–80.

23. "As an example of the method obtaining in the 19th century, the 'clearing' made by the Duchess of Sutherland will suffice here. This person, well instructed in economy, resolved, on entering upon her government to effect a radical cure, and to turn the whole country, whose population had already been, by earlier processes of the like kind, reduced to 15,000, into a sheep-walk. From 1814 to 1820 these 15,000 inhabitants, about 3,000 families, were systematically hunted and rooted out. All their villages were destroyed and burnt, all their fields turned into pasturage. British soldiers enforced this eviction, and came to blows with the inhabitants. One old woman was burnt to death in the flames of the hut, which she refused to leave. Thus this fine lady [the Duchess of Sutherland] appropriated 794,000 acres of land that had from time immemorial belonged to the clan" (Marx, *Capital*, 370).

24. Shiva, *Earth Democracy*, 20.

livelihood or new common lands on which to live. Not surprisingly, the response of the landed classes to such "upstart intruders" was to accelerate further enclosures. "The poor increase like fleas and lice," a seventeenth-century British landowner wrote, "and these vermin will eat us up unless we enclose."[25] Ultimately, the only remaining option for the landless and dispossessed was to migrate to the urban centers—London, in particular—where their singular means to gain livelihood was by selling their labor to those who owned the means of production (i.e., the capitalist class) and work within the brutalizing, exploitative factories of industrial production.[26] As Polanyi writes:

> Before the process had advanced very far, the laboring people had been crowded together in new places of desolation, the so-called industrial towns of England; the country folk had been dehumanized into slum dwellers . . . and large parts of the country were rapidly disappearing under the slack and scrap heaps vomited forth from the "satanic mills."[27]

This process of severing the multitudes, often violently, from the commons—enclosing public or shared spaces/resources for private commercial use, dispossessing people from direct access to their livelihood, forcing self-sufficient communities to sell their labor for exploitative wages—was central to the political economy of British colonialism in the Americas, Africa, and Asia. Shiva points out that in India, for example, prior to British colonial rule, up to one half of certain provinces were considered "wastelands," on which peasants possessed usufruct rights to food, fuel, and the grazing of livestock on common lands. In the colonial period, however, such lands were rapidly enclosed to corporate monopolies—the East India Company being the largest—for the purposes of growing exportable crops, such as rice, wheat, sugar, and cotton. According to Shiva, this "erosion of peasant communities'" rights to their forests, sacred groves, and "wastelands" was the "prime cause of their impoverishment."[28]

25. Pseudomismus, *Considerations concerning Common Fields and Enclosure* (1665), quoted in Hill, *The World Turned Upside Down*, 52.

26. "Separated from the means of production with which they were accustomed to sustain themselves, the newly proletarianized workers had to sell labor power in order to obtain the necessities of life" (Kloppenburg, *First The Seed,* 23).

27. Polanyi, *The Great Transformation*, 39.

28. Shiva, *Earth Democracy*, 26.

The violent sundering of settled communities from the land was central, as well, to the colonization of America. It is not by chance that Wendell Berry begins his modern agrarian classic, *The Unsettling of America*, with an accounting of the brutal displacement and mass slaughtering of the original native peoples to this land. "The first and greatest American revolution, which has never been superceded," he writes, "was the coming of a people who did *not* look upon the land as a homeland."[29] From the start, the "dominant tendency in American history," according to Berry, was to view land-nature-geography, not as a dwelling place for human communities or a generous fund of human livelihood, but as an exploitable source from which to extract economic gain. In pursuit of this kind of "progress"—in the search for gold, by exploiting the Indian fur trade, through the expropriation of vast tracts of Native American lands given over to railroad corporations—the colonists eventually expelled approximately 75 million native people from the Americas through direct enslavement, the intentional spread of fatal diseases, and outright massacre.[30] As geneticist and farmer Wes Jackson says, the native peoples who inhabited the Americas had, in fact, attempted to instruct the European conquerors how to live harmoniously on the land. Instead, they were viewed as surplus people—"redskins," "heathens," "primitives"—designations that "validated killing them off or moving them off, making their land available for *our* settlement."[31]

Over time, as both Jackson and Berry point out, the descendents of the first settlers—many of whom represented a counter tendency in American history to establish settled agricultural communities and to "stay put"—became themselves surplus people ultimately cut off from the land and forced into industrial labor. "Generation after generation, those who intended to remain" closely wedded to a place, to a geographical region, "have been dispossessed and driven out . . . exploited by and recruited into industrial society . . . by those who were carrying out some version of the search for El Dorado."[32] In the 1930 agrarian manifesto, *I'll Take My Stand*,

---

29. Berry, *The Unsettling of America*, 4.

30. See Zinn, *A People's History of the United States*, chap. 1.

31. Jackson, *Becoming Native to This Place*, 14. Berry also writes: "What appeared to the eyes of the discoverers was not one of the orders of Creation that required respect or deference for its own sake. What they saw was a great concentration of 'natural resources'—to be used according to purposes exterior to them. That some of those resources were human beings mattered not at all" (*Unsettling*, 54).

32. Berry, *Unsettling*, 4–5.

the "Twelve Southerners" warned against the impact of a technologically myopic and profit-driven economy on America's farming population. "A fresh labor-saving device introduced into an industry does not emancipate the laborers in that industry so much as it evicts them." Although the owners of industry may reap enormous financial rewards for such technological "advances," they wrote, "applied at the expense of agriculture, for example, the new processes have reduced the part of the population supporting itself upon the soil to a smaller and smaller fraction."[33]

Profit-driven technologies, of course, have revolutionized American agriculture over the past eighty years, with the result that the percentage of those earning their livelihood from the land in the United States has drastically plummeted. With the advent of the "Green Revolution" in the 1940s and the promise of increased food production, the practice of farming in the United States was fundamentally transformed by the use of fuel-intensive heavy machinery, pesticides, synthetic nitrogen, irrigation projects, and plant varieties developed specifically both to absorb increased levels of nitrogen/pesticides and to adapt to machine-intensive, monocropped fields. In the process, mostly self-sufficient farming families began "outsourcing" much of their work—i.e., producing fertilizer, developing and saving seeds, cleaning the harvest—to external industries. Initially, this enabled such "progressive" farmers to increase commodity production, and therefore profits, but as neighboring farmers transitioned to higher output production as well, crop prices quickly fell. Before long, off-the-farm industries, or the corporate "agribusiness" sector, such as fertilizer/pesticide and seed companies, processing and packaging businesses, and farm implement dealers were receiving a far greater percentage of the typical food dollar than those actually growing the food.[34] As Brian Halweil writes:

---

33. Twelve Southerners, *I'll Take My Stand,* xlix. On the infusion of scientific and technological "advances" into agriculture, Marx had written that, "if agriculture rests on scientific activities—if it requires machinery, chemical fertilizer acquired through exchange, seeds from distant countries, etc. . . . then the machine-making factory, external trade, crafts, etc. appear as needs for agriculture . . . Agriculture no longer finds the natural conditions of its own production within itself, naturally, arisen, spontaneous, and ready to hand, but these exist as an industry separate from it . . . This pulling-away of the natural ground from the foundations of every industry, and this transfer of the conditions of production outside itself, into a general context—hence the transformation of what was previously superfluous into what is necessary, as a historically created necessity—is the tendency of capital" (Marx, *Grundrisse,* quoted in Kloppenburg, *First the Seed,* 19).

34. "A corollary to the shifting mix of purchased and non-purchased inputs has

Ironically, then, as farms became more mechanized and more "productive," a self-destructive feedback loop was set in motion: over-supply and declining crop prices cut into farmers' profits, fueling a demand for more technology aimed at making up for shrinking margins by increasing volume still more. Output increased dramatically, but expenses (for tractors, combines, fertilizer, and seed) also ballooned while the commodity prices stagnated or declined. Even as they were looking more and more modernized, the farmers were becoming less and less the masters of their own domain.[35]

Faced with shrinking profit margins, and in the name of "efficiency" and "economy of scale," farmers were urged—or rather, forced, through public policy decisions that favored large-scale agriculture—to "get big or get out." As Secretary of Agriculture Earl Butz declared in 1955, "Adapt or die; resist and perish . . . Agriculture is now big business. Too many people are trying to stay in agriculture that would do better some place else."[36] Consequently, the only way to survive in farming was to purchase more and more land from neighbors whose farms had "failed," a process that led eventually to larger and larger agribusiness corporations owning an increasing amount of arable land in the United States. Ultimately, therefore, although the United States was founded as a "nation of farmers," today less than 1 percent of the American population is engaged in farming the land,[37] and that number is expected to drop. Frederick Kirschenmann writes:

In Iowa, for example, it is now being suggested that farms of the future will consist of 225,000-acre industrial complexes. It is being argued that it will be necessary to consolidate farms in to such

---

been the historical rise of agribusiness. Farmers no longer produce their own seed corn; they buy it from Pioneer Hi-Bred or Northrup King. They no longer use mules, oxen, or horses for their motive power. None of these creatures can compete with the well-known mechanical ungulate now found on every farm; after all, 'Nothing runs like a Deere'—or a Ford, or an International Harvester. And those tractors and combines run not on home-produced hay but on petroleum products from Mobil and ARCO. Fields are spread not with manure from the farm's livestock but with ammonium nitrate from W.R. Grace or superphosphate from Occidental Petroleum. And these inputs are paid for with money that is itself a purchased input obtained from Bank of America or Continental Illinois. Produce does not go direct to the consumer after processing on the farm, but to Heinz, or General Foods, or Cargill, or Land O'Lakes" (Kloppenburg, *First the Seed*, 32).

35. Halweil, *Eat Here*, 63.

36. Quoted in Kloppenburg, *First the Seed*, 136.

37. Ibid., 61.

industrial behemoths to gain access to markets and to negotiate effective prices with input suppliers. This transformation would reduce the number of 'farms' in Iowa to 140 . . . As with other industrial complexes, labor will consist largely of minimum wage earners.[38]

The exportation of industrial agriculture through developmentalist policies and free-trade agreements, culminating in the globalization of the food system, has resulted in the commensurate divorce of an increasing number of Two-Thirds world people from the land. In her first book, *The Violence of the Green Revolution*, Vandana Shiva describes how the Green Revolution was spread to developing nations through the pressure of the World Bank and the International Monetary Fund (IMF),[39] private American foundations like the Ford and Rockefeller Foundations,[40] and the United States government. With the promise of reducing poverty in so-called "underdeveloped" areas of the world, the World Bank, backed

38. Kirschenmann, "The Future of Agrarianism: Where Are We Now?," 4.

39. The World Bank, along with the International Monetary Fund (IMF), are often referred to as the "Bretton Woods" institutions. In 1944 at a Conference in Bretton Woods, New Hampshire, First World leaders established the World Bank and the International Monetary Fund with the mandate to aid in postwar reconstruction. The stated role of the IMF was to regulate the economies of countries facing fiscal deficits, while the stated role of the World Bank was to promote development in "underdeveloped" areas. In the 1950s and 60s, the Bretton Woods institutions implemented a "developmental" approach of lending billions of dollars to countries in Africa, Asia, and Latin America to assist them in creating the infrastructures and institutions that would enable them to become more like Western economies. The term "developmentalism" is one used to describe a set of political and economic policies that First World nations, through the World Bank and IMF, have urged "Third World" or "developing" countries to adopt in their societies—i.e., eliminating all barriers to free trade (e.g., tariffs, quotas, labor, or environmental regulations), by privatizing all sectors of society, and by inviting capital investments from transnational corporations into their societies.

40. "The possibilities of what came to be known as the Green Revolution were first explored in a meeting between U.S. vice president Henry A. Wallace and Rockefeller Foundation president Raymond Fosdick in 1941. It was thought that a program of agricultural development aimed at Latin America in general and Mexico in particular would have both political and economic benefits . . . It was this volatile mix of business, philanthropy, science, and politics that marked the Green Revolution . . . A series of international agricultural research centers (IARCs) was established in the Third World, with funding coming from an international consortium of donors from the advanced capitalist nations . . . The IARCS are not only a mechanism for encouraging capitalist development in the Third World countryside, they are also vehicles for the efficient extraction of plant genetic resources from the Third World and their transfer to the gene banks of Europe, North America, and Japan" (Kloppenburg, *First the Seed*, 158–61).

by strong compulsion of the U.S. government,[41] provided massive loans to countries that industrialized their agriculture by opening their economies to foreign investments in capital-intensive agribusiness industries (i.e., fertilizer, pesticide/ herbicide, seed companies), which the Ford and Rockefeller Foundations had developed. Moreover, under the economic principle of "comparative advantage,"[42] regions and even entire nations were encouraged to specialize in singular "cash crops" to be bought and sold on the international market. As trade was liberalized throughout the 90s as part of World Bank and IMF structural adjustment programs,[43] countries around the world were pressured to allow private agribusiness corporations to acquire massive areas of their agricultural lands, with the rationale that they would be able to cultivate "more efficiently" cash crops for the global market. The result, of course, has been a massive migration of rural populations to the urban centers of developing countries.

> The industrial system has . . . in virtually every area of the globe, "enclosed" farmland, forcing subsistence peasants off the land, so that it can be used for growing high-priced export crops rather than diverse crops for local populations. The result of enclosure continues to be that untold millions of peasants lose their land, community, traditions, and most directly their ability to grow their own food—their food independence. Removed from their land and means of survival, the new "landless" then flock to the newly industrialized cities where they quickly become a class of urban poor competing for low-paying jobs and doomed to long-term hunger or starvation.[44]

41. In India, for example, "the occurrence of drought in 1966 caused a severe drop in food production in India, and an unprecedented increase in food grain supply from the US. Food dependency was used to set new policy conditions on India. The US President, Lyndon Johnson, put wheat supplies on a short tether. He refused to commit food aid beyond one month in advance until an agreement to adopt the Green Revolution package was signed between the Indian agricultural minister, C S Subramaniam and the US Secretary of agriculture, Orville Freeman" (Shiva, *The Violence of the Green Revolution*, 31–32).

42. The principle of comparative advantage, first articulated by Adam Smith and refined by Ricardo, states that countries ought to specialize in the goods or services that they are best at producing and exchange them for goods and services from other nations.

43. Due to the increasing indebtedness of Two-Thirds World nations and the failure of earlier loans to eradicate poverty, refinanced loans were offered to debtor countries with the condition that they would liberalize their economies.

44. Kimbrell, *The Fatal Harvest Reader*, 7.

According to the promise of global capitalism, access to prosperity is made available to all who join in the market's seemingly peaceable coordination of individual self-interests. What an "awakened analysis" of our context (Herzog) reveals, however, is that access to the basic means of livelihood—the land in particular—continues to be enclosed through multiple forms of violence and exclusion. Seen in the light of God's holiness, an economy based in the ongoing severance of people from direct access to the earth is operating opposite the inclusive nature of God's gracious love. Whenever Christians join together to share in the elements of an agro-industrial meal, therefore, they do so as participants in an unholy communion marked by violence and exclusion.

Holistic Communion: Inclusive Access to the Land Commons

If Holy Communion, in the way of Jesus Christ, is wholly inclusive life-together, how are Jesus' followers to participate in the gracious love of God for all people in the midst of an economy knit together by the exclusionary, and often violent, force of self-interested gain? More specifically, in an agro-economic context rooted in the ongoing enclosure of arable lands, how are Christians faithfully to eat and drink "in remembrance of" Jesus— that is, in ways that are faithful to his gracious meal practices given "for you" and "for many" for the common wholeness, welfare, and flourishing of all? Those seeking to follow in the holy way of Jesus' gracious love are being called today to participate in inclusive modes of economic life together that ensure that all people have access to the sustaining means of life. In particular, this will include the involvement of Christians in the emergence of a more inclusive food economy, in which all people have access to productive land, beginning with those presently cut off from direct access to daily sustenance and livelihood.

By striving to ensure that all people enjoy access to productive land, Jesus' followers affirm that the earth is a gift that God has made graciously available to all. As Johann Arndt writes, the person who walks in the love of Christ "sees how the love of God stretches itself over all" human beings, as is testified in "the whole of nature." The greatest as well as the humblest person, he says, "lives under the same sun, in the same air, on the same earth and by the same water . . . they are mine and my neighbor's."[45] Those who

---

45. Arndt, *True Christianity*, 129.

have received the revelation of God in Jesus Christ and now participate in the holy way of inclusive love see God's universal grace manifest in the earth's gifts freely offered to all. Just as Christ's holy way of life and death is not given exclusively to an elite few, but "for me" and "for many," so, too, the gifts of the earth and their productive capacities are bestowed by God upon everyone without distinction. For the God of Jesus Christ "makes his sun rise on the evil and on the good, and sends rain on the righteous and on the unrighteous" (Matt 5:45).

An economy rooted in the ongoing severance of people from direct access to the earth as a free means of sustenance and livelihood is an economy operating contrary to God's gracious love. According to English reformer Gerrard Winstanley, founder of the Diggers or True Levellers, the enclosure of common lands is a direct manifestation of the sin of covetous self-love. Writing during the first wave of English enclosures, Winstanley locates the origins of human sin in the "selfish imaginations" and "covetousness" of those who first sought to rule over others. He writes:

> The earth, which was made to be a common treasury of relief for all, both beasts and men, was hedged in to in-closures by the teachers and rulers, and the others were made servants and slaves: And that earth that is within this Creation made a common store-house for all, is bought and sold, and kept in the hands of a few, whereby the great Creator is mightily dishonored, as if he were a respecter of persons, delighting in the comfortable livelihood of some, and rejoicing in the miserable poverty and straights of others.[46]

As Winstanley saw clearly, the enclosure of common lands by the rich, for the purposes of being able to charge the poor greater "rent, fines, and homage," is inherently bound up with violence. The sinful covetousness, which leads one brother to desire "a full possession of the Earth, and a lordly Rule over another brother," he says, culminates in the forceful insistence upon exclusive ownership, which the one must have "or else he will enslave or kill his brother."[47] As a web of relationships bound up with innumerable acts of violence against the people of the earth (*ochlos*), our modern economic life together is thus an unholy communion grounded in the exclusionary force of unmitigated self-love.

46. Winstanley, *True Levellers*, 10.
47. Winstanley, *The Law of Freedom in a Platform, or True Magistracy Restored*, 77.

In the unholy context of modern global capitalism, Jesus' followers are called to participate in God's inclusive love by creating and preserving common spaces where all people, especially the poor and excluded, can enjoy access to the food and fiber necessary to sustain life. For Winstanley and the Diggers, at the very beginnings of modern capitalism, this meant seeking out un-enclosed lands, which they might cultivate, "manure," and sow with carrots, parsnips, and beans. It also meant actively inviting the poor and dispossessed to join them in their vision to "work together and eat together" in charity and equality. Though a small venture at first—the first day saw twelve workers, though numbers quickly increased before they were violently expelled by the "country gentlemen"—the Diggers sought to "lay the foundation of making the earth a common treasury for all." In so doing, they believed that others would see in this act of faithfulness that God "is no respecter of persons, but equally loves his whole creation."[48]

In our time, one of the ways individuals and communities are participating economically in Jesus' inclusive way of life is by forming and tending community gardens. Often located in economically and socially impoverished areas, community gardens are common spaces—albeit small—where the public is provided access to land to be able to meet many of their fruit, vegetable, and fiber needs and in some cases, to raise livestock animals and fish. In the context of the United States, in particular, community gardens have been organized since at least the 1890s in a variety of forms—e.g., vacant lot, school, prison, church, civic space, hospital, rooftop, and neighborhood gardens.[49] Though models of ownership differ, and parameters are often set regarding land management and gardening techniques, most community gardens share a common vision that all people ought to enjoy free access to the basic means of life.

A community land trust is another concrete way in which to preserve land as a common fund of wealth for all and thus participate economically in the gracious nature of God's perfect love. In a community land trust, land acquired through gift or purchase by an individual or group is placed into a legal trust, which is cooperatively governed by a representative group of stakeholders in the surrounding community. The trust maintains ownership of the land for the common good, while making it available for individuals in the area to use through long-term leases. Land is thus removed from the speculative market, where it may become prohibitively expensive

48. Winstanley, *True Levellers*, 15.

49. See Lawson, *City Bountiful: A Century of Community Gardening in America.*

to local residents as property values rise or be bought up by absentee owners disconnected from the needs of the community. At the same time, however, those who lease the land and manage it according to the principles stipulated by the trust (e.g., utilizing only sustainable farming practices) own the "improvements" they make to the land (e.g., buildings, fences) as well as the economic fruits of their labor.[50] In this way, the land and its resources, which God has given for the flourishing of everyone, are preserved as a common ground of wealth and livelihood for all.

On a broader scale, those called to follow in the gracious way of Jesus' wholly inclusive love are simultaneously led to engage in efforts to bring about policy and legal changes at the national and international levels to ensure that all people have immediate access to the productive potentialities of the earth. The Diggers did not only act directly and locally to recover land commons for the poor. They also published a series of tracts to justify their actions and to plead for comprehensive social reform, addressed variously to fellow citizens, lawyers, lords of manors, ministers of the universities, the house of commons, and finally to "the powers of England, and to all the powers of the world." Winstanley's culminating literary work, *The Law of Freedom in a Platform*, sets forth a detailed proposal for a radically reconstituted English society based on the premise that a "true commonwealth freedom lies in the free enjoyment of the earth."[51] He envisioned an England in which abbey lands, crown lands, and all enclosed parks, forests, and waste lands were freed for common use so that "the poor oppressed people of the land" might "plant and manure this their own land, for the free and comfortable livelihood of themselves and posterities."[52] For Winstanley, those who claim to love Christ are called to obey the command of Christ to "do unto others, as you would have them do unto you" (Luke 6:31) by ensuring that land is made common for all. For by doing so, he affirms, there will be "food and raiment, ease and pleasure plentiful, both for you and your brethren; so that none shall beg or starve, or live in the straights of poverty."[53]

Today, men and women around the world continue to follow in the inclusive way of Jesus by working for comprehensive land reform. Throughout the twentieth century, land reform movements on nearly every continent

50. See Morehouse, ed., *Building Sustainable Communities*.

51. Winstanley, *Law of Freedom*, 66.

52. Ibid., 105.

53. Ibid., 132.

struggled for the just redistribution of concentrated lands for the benefit of the landless poor. In Latin America, in particular, both Catholic and Protestant liberation movements throughout the 70s and 80s consistently identified accessibility to productive land as the central factor in working toward a more just political economy. As a council of Peruvian bishops wrote in a pastoral letter during this time, "the urgent solution of the problem of land is previous and necessary to the creation of a climate of peace and brotherhood, without which there can be no development."[54] Amidst the unjust distribution of land and the predatory assaults by the powerful against peasants, small farmers, and Amerindians, entering into solidarity with the poor has specifically meant engaging in struggles to enable the victims of land injustice to regain access and control over the natural and productive resources of the earth.

So too, in the United States, Christians are called to participate in the inclusive nature of God's love in Jesus Christ by advocating for the just distribution of the earth and its resources. One of the founding fathers of the modern environmental movement in North America, Liberty Hyde Bailey (1858–1954), recognized the fundamental linkages between a genuinely democratic society, proper care for the land, and the universal access of all citizens to what he called the "holy earth." Precisely because the earth, as Bailey saw it, is a "gift" from God and "is not selfish" but "is open and free to all" and "invites everywhere," we should "begin to understand the awful sin of partitioning the earth by force."[55] One of the principle lessons of the earth, rather, "is of liberality for all, and never exploitation or very exclusive opportunities for the few."[56] Bailey's vision for this country was that "every person should have the right and the privilege to a personal use of some part of the earth."[57] And although he did not

54. From May, *The Poor of the Land: A Christian Case for Land Reform*, 81.

55. Bailey, *The Holy Earth*, 31, 34. "More iniquity follows the improper and greedy division of the resources and privileges of the earth than any other form of sinfulness," 11.

56. Ibid., 32.

57. Ibid., 35. Alongside the just division and distribution of the land, Bailey emphasized the importance of cultivating the necessary knowledge base and moral vision among the citizenry that they might use and enjoy the goods of the earth rightly. Much of this vision is rooted in a specifically biblical understanding of stewardship: "We are here, part in the creation. We cannot escape. We are under obligation to take part and to do our best, living with each other and with all the creatures . . . When once we set ourselves to the pleasure of our dominion, reverently and hopefully, and assume all its responsibilities, we shall have a new hold on life . . . If God created the earth, so is the

set forth precisely how the land should be divided and redistributed, he insisted that the task of accomplishing it form the basis of "the best political program," for nearly all of the problems in both city and countryside, he believed, "relate themselves in the end to the division of the land."[58] For those seeking to follow the gracious way of Jesus Christ in the context of North American society, working to accomplish Bailey's vision of land reform so that all might have access to the productive potentialities of the holy earth remains an urgent task.

It would be a mistake to assume that the only way Christians might respond to the worldwide problem of the enclosure of the commons, however, is by supporting the strengthening of national or global institutions to preserve, protect, or redistribute lands. While large-scale reforms through democratic processes will ultimately be necessary in addressing the pervasive scope of the problem, Christians need not wait for the political will and vision to develop that will be required to enact such large-scale structural reforms. In fact, as Jack Kloppenburg recognizes, "to begin the global task to which we are called, we need some particular place to begin, some particular place to stand, some particular place in which to initiate the small, reformist changes that we can only hope may some day become radically transformative."[59] Moreover, as Nobel Prize economist Elinor Ostrom has demonstrated, successful models of the governance and management of what she terms "common-pool resources" (CPR), such as farmer-managed irrigation systems, communal forests, inshore fisheries, and grazing and hunting territories, are all relatively small in scale, precisely because they operate at the level of a local community.[60] In this sense, while advocating for larger structural land reforms, Christians are simultaneously called to support initiatives in their local communities in which a collective of people

---

earth hallowed; and if it is hallowed, so must we deal with it devotedly and with care that we do not despoil it, and mindful of our relations to all beings that live on it . . . To live in sincere relations with the company of created things and with conscious regard for the support of all men now and yet to come, must be of the essence of righteousness" (11).

58. Ibid., 43.

59. Kloppenburg, "Coming into the Foodshed," 41.

60. Ostrom, *Governing the Commons.* In a smaller-scale CPR, she writes, "individuals repeatedly communicate and interact with one another in a localized physical setting. Thus, it is possible that they can learn whom to trust, what effects their actions will have on each other and on the CPR, and how to organize themselves to gain benefits and avoid harm. When individuals have lived in such situations for a substantial time and have developed shared norms and patterns of reciprocity, they possess social capital with which they can build institutional arrangements for resolving CPR dilemmas" (183–84).

—whether a group of houses, a neighborhood, a single congregation or group of faith communities, township, or an entire county—work together to acquire common property rights of farmland, pastures, woodlands, watersheds, etc. Such lands can be made available in turn to the public, with proscriptive guidelines, for growing fruits and vegetables, the sustainable harvest of timber, fishing, animal husbandry, wildlife conservation, or the simple beauty of well-cared for landscapes.[61] In so doing, by participating in the gracious nature of God's love manifest in Jesus Christ for the wellbeing of all *in a particular place*, Christians thereby prepare the ground for the possibilities of broader structural reforms to come.

Conclusion

The divine host of creation invites us to share in abundant life together through God's gracious love for all people. In Jesus Christ, God's holiness is made available to us in his wholly inclusive way of life "for you" and "for many" for the common flourishing of all in peace. In the midst of an unholy economy knit together by myopic self-love, resulting in the ongoing exclusion of many from the basic means of life, Jesus' followers are called today to participate in the divine work of reconciliation by striving to ensure that everyone has access to those goods that God has made available to all. By sharing in inclusive economic models like community gardening, land trusts, and common property ownership, as well as working for comprehensive land reform, Jesus' disciples faithfully participate in the divine holiness knitting all things together in perfect love. Holy Communion is wholly loving life together in which all are made whole. Joined together in the gracious nature of God's love, beginning with the ways we are gathered together to eat and drink, we "remember" Jesus, the "Holy One of God" whose way of life is the path that leads to peace.

---

61. For a list of relevant models, see Donahue, "The Resettling of America," in Wirzba, ed., *The Essential Agrarian Reader*, 34–51.

2

The Holy Spirit Joins
Everyone Together

THE HOLY SPIRIT OF God joins everyone together within the feast of life. As the divine presence within wholly charitable communions, the Holy Spirit weaves each participant into mutually beneficial relationships with the others. God's holiness is God's perfect love, and in the fullness of divine love, all things are made whole. In the Holy Spirit, the divine holiness in which the creation is fully alive, is present as *convivial love,* which is "poured out in our hearts" (Rom 5:5) as the vitalizing force of healthy life together. Faithful acceptance of God's invitation to participate in Holy Communion, then, includes faithfully abiding within the fellowship of the Holy Spirit, in which all things are united in symbiotic edification. "So, whether you eat or drink, or whatever you do . . . let all that you do be done in love" (1 Cor 10:31, 16:14). Holy Communion, within the charitable bonds of the Holy Spirit, is wholly harmonious life together.

But how are those called to new life in the Spirit to participate in the convivial love of God in the midst of an economy woven through with the divisive energies of self-love? Divorced from the fullness of God's love, self-love inevitably leads to fragmentation, for the self-interested individual separates existence into isolatable parts to be exploited for private gain. The modern global economy is therefore marked by a discordant social dynamic in which the exchange of commodities draws the world's people and geographies together while simultaneously fracturing long-standing, intimate relationships. Within the modern agro-economy, in particular, the commodification of every aspect of food production for financial profit has resulted in the ongoing dismantling of stable communities and complex ecosystems. In this context, abiding within the convivial love of the Holy Spirit in economic life—and thus participating more fully in the divine holiness—will involve harmoniously inter-weaving the various elements of our agro-economic life together in ways that nurture health.

The Wholly Convivial Love of God in the Holy Spirit

Understanding the divine holiness present in the Holy Spirit as the convivial (*con-* "together" + *vivere* "to live") love of God begins with an avowal of the relational nature of God's triune life. The life of God the Father/Mother, Son, and Holy Spirit is *life together*. As Jürgen Moltmann affirms, drawing on the ancient Eastern Orthodox concept of *perichoresis* (i.e., round dance), God is a communion of distinct persons who mutually indwell one another in a perfectly loving harmony. "The Father exists in the Son, the Son in the Father, and both of them in the Spirit, just as the Spirit exists in both the Father and the Son."[1] It is appropriate, and in fact necessary, to speak with the scriptures of the particular nature and work of each of the three divine persons—God the Creator, Redeemer, and Sustainer. Yet, as Moltmann says, "by virtue of their eternal love they live in one another to such an extent, and dwell in one another to such an extent, that they are one."[2] Understood in this way, we can affirm that the God of Jesus Christ and the Holy Spirit is neither three isolable persons (tritheism) nor one person revealed through three different "modes" (modalism). For God as an aggregation of divided individuals or God as a singular monad cannot be avowed, with scripture, to *be* love (1 John 4:8). Rather, the God who calls us to participate in divine holiness is a communion of three persons eternally interwoven in convivial love.

The divine holiness, of course, is most often identified with the Spirit of God. It is the Spirit of God's interpersonal life together who is called Holy, and thus also the Holy Spirit who is especially associated with the loving *togetherness* of the divine life. Within the convivial dance of God, the self-offering of the Holy Spirit is distinctly bound up within the *koinonia*—the communing, participating, uniting, sharing, partnering—that enjoins the divine persons. The ancient Christian benediction pronounces the blessings of the grace of Jesus Christ, the love of God, and "the *fellowship* of the Holy Spirit" (2 Cor 13:13). It is "the Spirit of holiness" (Rom 1:4),

1. Moltmann, *The Trinity and the Kingdom*, 175.
2. Ibid.

then, who with the Father/Mother and Son, binds the divine communion together in convivial unity.

The convivial love of God, though perfect in and of itself, is not secluded or insular, but rather is a superabundant fullness that overflows out into the creation for the sustainment of the creaturely world. The good creation *is* because, as the father of German Pietism Johann Arndt said, "God wished to flow out completely . . . in all his goodness, for God is a goodness that completely shares itself."[3] Like a cup overflowing with the festal wine of gladness, the divine holiness spills forth from the trinitarian perfection in generative love of the world. The creation is grounded in the ecstatic love of God, as Moltmann says, because God's love "leads him to go out of himself and to create something which is different from himself but which none the less corresponds to him."[4] To the extent we regard the life of any particular creature, of a specific time or space, or of created life itself as "holy," we do so, then, in recognition that our creaturely share in holiness is based entirely on the gift of God's superabundant love with and for us.

The overflow of God's holiness, or God's charitable life together, into the creation is most directly associated, again, with the person of the Holy Spirit. Though the Father/Mother, through the Son, is traditionally avowed to be the *source of* the creation, it is the Holy Spirit who is most often affirmed as God's *presence within* the creation. English Dissenter Gerard Winstanley speaks of "the Spirit of the Whole Creation" whom God "has spread forth in every form."[5] Radical Pietist Gottfried Arnold writes of "Divine Sophia," whom the Lord has drawn "out upon all his works, upon all flesh, according to its measure."[6] The divine Spirit of holiness within the creation, moreover, is present precisely as the fount of convivial bonds that are woven into the fabric of existence. Moltmann writes:

> If the Holy Spirit is "poured out" on the whole creation, then he creates the community of all created things with God and with each other, making it that fellowship of creation in which all created things communicate with one another and with God. The existence, the life, and the warp and weft of interrelationships subsist in the Spirit . . . [As such], relationships are just as primal as things themselves . . . For nothing in the world exists, lives and moves *of*

3. Arndt, *True Christianity*, 32.

4. Moltmann, *God in Creation*, 76.

5. Winstanley, *The Law of Freedom in a Platform*, 111.

6. Arnold, "The Mystery of the Divine Sophia," in Erb, ed., *Pietists*, 219.

itself. Everything exists, lives, and moves *in others*, in one another, with one another, and for one another, in the cosmic interrelations of the divine Spirit . . . The patterns and the symmetries, the movements and the rhythms, the fields and the material conglomerations of cosmic energy all come into being out of the community, and in the community, of the divine Spirit.[7]

The holy presence of God's Spirit in the creation, then, is a holiness active within the manifold bonds interlinking the whole of created life.

The convivial love of God in the Holy Spirit is the source of all *health*. As the fourteenth-century mystic John Ruusbroec affirms, the Holy Spirit is the "eternal sense of *well-being*" that abides within the triune community,[8] precisely because it is the Spirit who "takes the lead," with the Father/Mother and Son, in interweaving the Three as a peaceable, harmonious One. To avow that the divine holiness is present in the world as the power of conviviality that flows forth from God's own life together, then, is simultaneously to affirm that God's intention for created life is its healthful flourishing in and through the bonds of harmonious life together. In the Spirit, the divine holiness nurtures the *aliveness* of living and the *vitality* of life that pulsates amidst the interwoven dance of God's diverse creation. Notice here the semantic kinship that ties together the words holy, whole, hallowed, and heal. Wholeness or healthiness is what God, in and through the Holy Spirit, intends for the creation, which is why, as Moltmann writes, "we experience whole, full, healed, and redeemed life" in the presence of the Holy Spirit. "The Holy Spirit," he says, "is the unrestricted presence of God in which our life wakes up, becomes wholly and entirely living, and is endowed with the energies of life."[9] In the Spirit, we share in God's gift of holiness, which we experience as the vital flourishing of our lives in harmonious togetherness with others.

If God's intention is for the healthful flourishing of the whole of creation through the loving bonds flowing out from God in the Holy Spirit, then sin is present in the *divisive fragmentation* of that which God has knit together in perfect love. Sin is *unholy*, in that it "tears asunder" the wholeness of "what God has joined together" (Matt 19:6), and the sin of self-interested love is especially divisive. In being principally turned in upon him or herself, the self-seeking sinner breaks away and separates off from

---

7. Moltmann, *God in Creation*, 11.

8. Ruusbroec, *The Spiritual Espousals*, 110.

9. Moltmann, *The Source of Life*, 10–11.

the wholeness of God's convivial love. Whereas the life of holiness "in the Spirit" is life with and for others, the life of unholy self-love is life turned away from all others in being curved in upon the self. As Thomas à Kempis writes, "nothing is sweeter than love [of another], nothing stronger, nothing higher, nothing wider, nothing more pleasant, nothing fuller or better in heaven or death; for love is born of God, and can rest only in God," but "when a man is self-seeking he abandons God's love."[10] To "abide in love" (1 John 4:16) is to participate in the charitable life together that flows forth from God, which is why, according to Dietrich Bonhoeffer, "all who countenance that they need only to come to themselves, in order to be in God, are doomed to hideous disillusion in the experience of being, persisting, and ending-up-turned-in-upon-themselves utterly."[11] Sinful self-love divides where God unites, causing wounds in the creation that result in *sickness*. Left unattended, separated from the convivial power of God's love, sinfulness ends in death, for death is ultimately the result of wounds that cannot heal. The opposite of holiness as healthful aliveness, then, is neither immorality nor profanity but death. "The free gift of God is eternal *life*," but "the wages of sin is *death*" (Rom 6:23).

Where sinful self-love fractures the bonds of healthful life together, the holiness of God in the Holy Spirit is present in the *healing* of that which sin has divided. This is the divine gift of sanctification (from Latin *facere* "to make" and *sanctus* "holy") at work, through the Spirit, within the creation. To heal, as Moltmann says, "means making something whole that has been divided." In a world fractured by sin, then, "what is holy is that which has become whole again."[12] Though the sundered creation, if left alone, would degenerate toward death, the sanctifying grace of God in the Spirit is steadfastly at work restoring health and vitality through the spiritual energies of love. For where sinful self-love divides, the convivial love of God binds together and makes whole. "Everything depends on love," the mystic Johannes Tauler professes, for "it is love that keeps us from perishing" in self-enclosed isolation.[13] As Arndt affirms, God has created us such that we are "unable to live without love."[14] Outside the bonds of God's convivial love, life is threatened by the disintegrating pull of death, because "where

10. Thomas à Kempis, *The Imitation of Christ*, 98–99.

11. Bonhoeffer, *Act and Being*, 42.

12. Moltmann, *The Spirit of Life*, 175.

13. Tauler, *Sermons*, 133.

14. Arndt, *True Christianity*, 141.

love is, there is life," Christoph Friedrich Blumhardt says. In fact, "this *is* the Holy Spirit—the love of God for the world," he writes. "This love is what flows from the Holy Spirit, this and nothing else . . . God's Spirit *is* love."[15] And the love of God in the Holy Spirit, amidst a sickly creation wounded by sinful self-seeking, is present as the healing power of sanctification that makes us whole.

Faithfully responding to God's invitation to participate in the divine holiness, then, means abiding in the spiritual bonds of convivial love. We become holy as God is holy by "sharing in the Spirit" (Phil 2:1), who is present as the source of harmonious life together. For this reason, love for God and love of neighbor are ultimately inseparable, for when we love one another we are sharing in the convivial love of God, which is ever present to us in the Holy Spirit. And because the love of the triune God is an ecstatic love that flows out, in the Spirit, into the creation, we share in the holiness of God by going out of ourselves in loving service toward others. Whereas the sinner is turned in upon him or herself in insular self-love, those who abide within the Holy Spirit are sanctified in the fulsome love of God that draws them out into charitable relations with others. This is why Johann Christoph Blumhardt charges the self-enclosed sinner to "get out of yourself" and "do something for God's cause" by loving your neighbor.[16] We are made holy as we participate in the wholeness of God's convivial love, with and for others, in the Spirit.

In being drawn out in the Spirit into loving relationship with others, we simultaneously participate in God's charitable work of healing. Abiding "in the Spirit" nurtures health and well-being, precisely because health is a state of harmonious interrelationality. In this sense, the spiritual life is the therapeutic life, in which those made holy in the Spirit seek out places of division and fracture and work to mend what has been torn asunder through the charitable restoration of healthful relationships. To be holy as God is holy is to make whole as God makes whole, which is why those who dwell in the *koinonia* of the Holy Spirit concurrently nurture the flourishing of life in and through the bonds of convivial love.

God's invitation to participate in the restorative power of loving relationality, moreover, encompasses the full breadth and depth of life. The call to holiness is not restricted, in other words, to certain spheres or relationships, for the will of God is for our *entire* sanctification (1 Thess 5:23). This is

---

15. Christoph Blumhardt, in Blumhardt and Blumhardt, *Thy Kingdom Come*, 133–34.
16. Johann Blumhardt, in ibid., 4.

a "going on to perfection," as John Wesley described it—an ever-deepening alignment with the love of God in the Holy Spirit infusing all the relationships of life. "By perfection," he writes, "I mean the humble, gentle, patient love of God and our neighbor, ruling *all* our tempers, words, and actions."[17] Entire sanctification is the becoming holy in the whole of life, "so that in the *whole* life and walk of man," Arndt says, "pure divine holiness" might "appear and shine forth."[18] Ultimately, what entire sanctification points toward is the entire healing of creation, in which all creatures share wholly in the healthful conviviality of God in and through the Spirit of charitable life together. "Nothing else need take place," Christoph Blumhardt avows, "except that the love of God penetrate into *all* things,"[19] for within the loving communion of God is realized the holiness, or wholeness, of all creation.

To summarize: God's holiness is God's perfect love, and in the convivial bonds of the Holy Spirit, the superabundant love of God overflows out into the creation as wholly harmonious love, which nurtures health. The unholy nature of self-interested love is evident in the divisive fragmentation of that which God has knit together, which results in sickness. God's holiness makes whole, and amidst the multiple wounds caused by sin, God in the Spirit is present in the healing of creation through the re-knitting of sundered relationships. We faithfully participate in the divine holiness by abiding in the Holy Spirit, who draws us into charitable, harmonious relationships with others in every sphere of life.

The Wholly Harmonious Communion Meal

Holy Communion, in the presence of the Holy Spirit, is wholly harmonious life together. The convivial nature of God's perfect love is present in the Spirit that we might be holy as God is holy in our social, relational existence with others. Faithfully to accept God's invitation to Holy Communion is to participate in a way of life that weaves all members or participants in a particular social nexus into convivial relationships with others. This is the way of health, for wholly harmonious life together promotes wholeness and wellbeing. All this is present through the Holy Communion meal, in which the Spirit joins all together in perfect harmony and to which we are invited as participants.

17. Wesley, *A Plain Account of Christian Perfection*, 112.
18. Arndt, *True Christianity*, 29.
19. Christoph Blumhardt, in Blumhardt and Blumhardt, *Thy Kingdom Come*, 134.

During the course of his final meal with the disciples, Jesus promises that, although he will soon depart from the earth, his followers will not be left without the presence of God in their midst. Having manifest the love of God for those gathered "to the end" (John 13:1), including those who will betray him, Jesus assures his disciples that the triune God will continue to dwell with them. He makes clear that the Father and the Son share life together as one God. Though the two are not the same—for the Son who was sent must now return to the Father—nevertheless "I am in the Father," Jesus says, "and the Father is in me" (John 14:11). So, too, the Father and Son share the divine life together with the Holy Spirit, whom Jesus promises the Father will send in the Son's absence "to be with you forever" (14:16). Not only will the Holy Spirit abide with you, Jesus says, but "he will be in you," and when the Spirit flows forth from the Godhead, the disciples will know "that I am in my Father, and you in me, and I in you" (14:17, 20). The triune God, who is love, continues to be present in the Spirit, and those who abide in the Spirit are drawn into the loving conviviality of the triune God. As Jesus emphasizes throughout his farewell supper address, the Spirit of God is present with and in his followers to the extent that they continue to gather together within the divine love. To love one another as the triune God loves is to abide with others in the love of God that has been made available, in the Spirit, forever, and in doing so, our joy for living is made complete (John 15:11). In the context of his last supper with the disciples, Jesus assures them that the vitalizing love of God, who is a communion of three persons, will ever spill forth and abide with those who dwell in the convivial love of the Holy Spirit.

The meal gathering, as is clear throughout the New Testament writings, is the central nexus within which we are invited to participate with others in the charitable bonds of spiritual conviviality. The partaking of a meal with others is perhaps the most discernible realization of social connectivity.[20] For good or ill, the ties of family, friendship, work, and civil society are all formed and solidified within the context of a shared meal. Meal gatherings not only signify but substantively create the social boundaries, obligations, and relational bonds at the foundations of society. As Dennis Smith shows in his work on the banquet tradition in the ancient world, the eucharistic table fellowships of the early church were the primary social

---

20. Rarely, unless forced by external circumstance, do we share the intimacy of a meal with those with whom we have no association or no intention of entering into some kind of relationship.

spaces within which the closely bonded communities of early Christianity formed. With charitable commensality, persons of diverse social, economic, gender, and cultic identities were able to express the bonds of intimate love typically experienced only amongst familial or tribal relationships.[21] To the extent that Jew and Gentile, male and female, slave and free (Gal 3:28) became brothers and sisters in the "family of faith" (6:10), this new social formation occurred within the love feast of the Lord's Supper. Eating with others *is* communion (i.e., participating, sharing, partnering), which is why, throughout the New Testament, the question of just *how* we are gathered together to eat is addressed as a decidedly spiritual issue.

The divine holiness that abides with us within the loving fellowship of the communion meal is present, then, not in any one particular element of the meal itself, but within the charitable bonds that constitute the gathering. This is the central theological point for Paul amidst the various food controversies of the early church—e.g., whether Christians ought to eat "meat sacrificed to idols" (1 Cor 8, 10), whether to affirm those who "eat only vegetables" or those who "believe in eating anything" (Rom 14:2). In response to those who would designate certain foods per se as holy or unholy, clean or unclean, Paul responds by affirming that "nothing is unclean in itself," and in fact, if consumed rightly, "everything is clean" (14:14, 20). Above all, what matters according to Paul, is that we remain in loving relationship with one another. As such, although it may be "lawful" to eat all foods—"for the earth and its fullness are the Lord's" (1 Cor 10:26)—in certain circumstances, it may be necessary to refrain out of consideration for another. Whatever the situation, "do not seek your own advantage," he says, "but that of the other" (10:24), for the holiness of God is present not in any particular food or drink per se, but within the "righteousness and peace and joy in the Holy Spirit" (Rom 14:17). In the gathering together that occurs in the Holy Communion meal, the holiness of God is present in and through the relational ties that bind diverse elements and participants together in love.

The convivial nature of God's love that flows forth from the divine communion into harmonious creaturely gatherings, embodied uniquely within charitable meal fellowships, reveals the unholy nature of divisive table practices. To be gathered together in such a way that a "brother or sister is being injured by what you eat," as Paul says, is no longer to abide in love, and therefore, to no longer receive the divine gift of "peace and joy in the Holy

---

21. Smith, *From Symposium to Eucharist*, 282–83.

Spirit" (Rom 14:17). For sin tears asunder that which God has knit together, and what God in the Spirit knits together in Holy Communion is a vibrant nexus of wholly harmonious relationships. In Paul's letter to the Corinthian church, he makes clear that the sin of self-oriented love fractures the relational bonds of genuine community. What he describes is a form of table fellowship in which some members indulge in a feast of over-consumption while others go hungry. The Corinthian supper is a gathering together of self-consumed individuals, in other words, rather than a true *convivium* of festal participants. "When you come together as a church," it is not "for the better but for the worse," Paul thus says, because the self-interested way in which you are gathered is causing "divisions among you" (1 Cor 11:17–18). These wounds in the body, he says, are the reason why many in the assembly have become sick—and even died (11:30)—for unhealed divisions caused by sin ultimately result in death. To gather in such a way, then, "is not really to eat the Lord's Supper" (11:20), because Holy Communion is only truly shared when all of the members are united together, in and through the Holy Spirit, within a feast of loving conviviality.

In the midst of fractious forms of commensality, the Holy Spirit is at work in the drawing together of that which has been divided by sin. It is the Holy Spirit who, following Peter's vision in which he is commanded by the Lord to eat what he had considered unclean, leads him to go and share a meal with the Gentile believers. Many among the circumcised believers criticized Peter, precisely because they understood the holy life to entail separation from particular foods and isolation from certain groups of people. In response, Peter declares that "the Spirit told me to go with them [i.e., the Gentiles] and not to make a distinction between them and us" (Acts 11:12). Moreover, he says that when he entered into the Gentile man's home to share a meal with uncircumcised believers, he discovered that "the Holy Spirit fell upon them just as it had upon us" (11:15). Holiness makes whole, and in the Holy Spirit, God's charitable presence spills forth to heal the relational wounds of separation by drawing everyone together within the bonds of loving conviviality.

We are invited to abide within the wholly harmonious love of God—to be holy as God is holy—by faithfully sharing in convivial meal practices with others. When we gather together to eat in ways that draw diverse members together in genuinely loving relationships, we participate in the sanctifying love of God that is healing the sundered creation. In the Holy Spirit, our love is turned outward, and our consumption becomes an eating and drinking for the charitable fulfillment of one another. This is the way of wholeness and health, the work of God that "makes for peace and for mutual edification" (Rom 14:19). In certain situations, the holy life of love requires that we abstain from certain foods, or simply wait until all are able to join together. At other times, we are called to enjoy every good fruit of God's creation. Whatever we do, whether we eat or drink, abstain or commence, we are invited to abide within the presence of God the Holy Spirit by allowing all that we do to be done in love (1 Cor 10:31, 16:14).

Divisive Communion: Fragmentation of Bonded Communities

Proponents of modern capitalism often portray the modern market economy as if it were a near-perfect mechanism for weaving the world's people, geographies, and natural resources into a web of harmonious partnership. Through the non-coercive coordination of society's self-interested actors, the free market is purported to be able to bring about general equilibrium for society and individual well-being for its participating members. "The market system," as Charles Lindblom writes, "is the world's broadest and most detailed organizer of social cooperation . . . No other method of social cooperation matches the market system in scope and detail."[22] The reality, however, is that, while the exchange of commodities in and across markets worldwide is binding more and more people, places, and materials together, longstanding social and ecological bonds are simultaneously being torn asunder. In the modern agro-economy, in particular, the commodification of society and nature within market societies is bound up with the ongoing fracturing of bonded social and ecological communities, leading to sickness and ultimately death.

The continuous severing of the majority of the world's people over the last several hundred years from direct access to land, and thus livelihood, is closely related to the profound disruption of social and ecological communities within the modern global economy. As Berry writes, modern

22. Lindblom, *The Market System*, 41. See also Mankiw, *Principles of Macroeconomics*. "When each person specializes in producing the good for which he or she has a comparative advantage, total production in the economy rises. This increase in the size of the economic pie can be used to make everyone better off . . . [Thus] trade can benefit everyone in society because it allows people to specialize in activities in which they have a comparative advantage" (56). Similarly, trade between countries "allows countries to specialize in what they do best and to enjoy a greater variety of goods and services" (8).

industrial economies are "based squarely upon the principle of violence toward everything on which they depend," including especially "violence toward nature" and "human communities."[23] One of the central principles of our exploitative economy, he says, is to divide in order to control (*divide et impera*), a principle manifest in the dissection of existence into isolatable parts to be manipulated for financial gain. In the process, the kind of social and ecological relationships that thrive on stability, long-suffering, and fidelity—relationships gathered together in local communities, small neighborhoods, ecosystems and bioregions, even covenantal relations between marriage partners and within families—are continually torn asunder.

The "great transformation" at the heart of modern market economies, according to Karl Polanyi, took place through the detachment of the economic sphere from social and political determinations through the commodification of all aspects of nature and society.[24] Whereas in traditional societies, he says, the exchange of goods through local markets was intimately embedded within social relationships,[25] modern market societies are constituted by the overturning of this order, such that market exchange comes to determine all aspects of social life. "Instead of economy being embedded in social relations, social relations are embedded in the economic system."[26] Shiva makes a similar distinction between traditional markets and the modern market. Traditional markets, she says, are "based on direct relationships and face to face transaction," whereas the modern market replaces such encounters with the anonymous flow of monetary wealth according to such logics as efficiency, economy of scale, and profit accumulation.[27] The pivotal concept that has driven this transformation, according to Polanyi, is that of the *commodity*, which can be defined as an object produced solely for the purpose of sale through the market.[28] In a society determined wholly by the self-regulating market, all aspects of life—beginning principally with land, labor, and money—are made into commodities. The result, both Polanyi and Shiva argue, is social and

---

23. Berry, *Citizenship Papers*, 46.

24. Polanyi, *The Great Transformation*, 71.

25. Ibid., 46.

26. Ibid., 57.

27. Shiva, *Earth Democracy*, 18.

28. Polanyi, *The Great Transformation*, 72. Marx defines a commodity as an object whose worth is determined by its exchange-value rather than by its use-value. See *Capital*, part I, chap. 1.

ecological disintegration. "To allow the market mechanism to be the sole director of the fate of human beings [labor] and their natural environment [land], indeed, even of the amount and use of purchasing power [money]," Polanyi argues, inevitably "results in the demolition of society" and the defilement of landscapes.[29]

One of the predominant characteristics of market societies is individualism. The view of the human being set forth by the proponents of unfettered capitalism is *homo economicus*—the economic man.[30] John Stuart Mill, who was the first to use this term, wrote that political economy "does not treat the *whole* of man's nature as modified by the *social* state, nor of the *whole* conduct of man in *society* [my emphasis]. It is concerned with him solely as a being who desires to possess wealth, and who is capable of judging the comparative efficacy of means for obtaining that end."[31] The *homo economicus*, then, is envisaged as a rational, informed, and purely self-interested individual detached from his material-historical context and relational ties. Based on this view of human existence, modern political economies have been structured to support neither communal nor interpersonal existence but the self-oriented desires of isolated individuals.[32]

In his 1930 essay, "A Critique of the Philosophy of Progress," southern agrarian Lyle Lanier argued that the endless production and consumption of commodities in industrial societies for the satiation of individual desires, while certainly beneficial for the owners of corporate business, is

29. Ibid., 73. See also Schumacher, who points out the destabilizing effect of commoditizing the foundational elements of society. "Trade in the pre-industrial era was not a trade in essentials, but a trade in precious stones, precious metals, luxury goods, spices . . . The basic requirements of life had to be indigenously produced . . . But now [because everything is a commodity, an object produced solely for exchange via the marketplace] everything and everybody has become mobile. All structures are threatened, and all structures are *vulnerable* to an extent that they have never been before" (*Small Is Beautiful: Economics As If People Mattered*, 64–65).

30. See Daly and Cobb, *For the Common Good*, esp. chap. 8.

31. Mill, *Essays on Some Unsettled Questions of Political Economy*, 137.

32. Daly and Cobb write that "the individualism of current economic theory is manifest in the purely self-interested behavior it generally assumes. It has no real place for fairness, malevolence, and benevolence, nor for the preservation of human life or any other moral concern. The world that economic theory normally pictures is one in which individuals all seek their own good and are indifferent to the success or failure of other individuals engaged in the same activity. There is no way to conceive of a collective good—only of the possibility that there can be improvement for some without costs to others . . . It would be difficult to imagine a more consistent abstraction from the social or communal character of human existence" (*For the Common Good*, 159–60).

ultimately incompatible with genuine society. "The only reality which is ultimately worth considering," he wrote, "is that of human beings who associate together." Such "real communion" or "real association," moreover, is only possible where there are concrete opportunities "for persons to grow and to realize their potentialities through free contact with one another."[33] These are the very conditions, he said, that long existed in rural communities, in the small villages and towns founded upon a more stable population with long-standing acquaintances. With the industrialization of American society and the shift of the nation's energies "toward an endless process of increasing the production and consumption of goods,"[34] the so-called "progress"[35] promised to rural communities through the purchasing of expensive machinery and other "modern" conveniences resulted only in their ultimate dismantling. As the greater part of the population moved into urban centers and into exploitative working conditions, Lanier observes, genuine association was replaced by "casual, fleeting, formal contacts with great numbers of anonymous people."[36] Spurred by the progressivist mantra—"do not allow yourself to feel homesick; form no such powerful attachments that you will feel a pain in cutting them loose"[37]—the inevitable result of an industrial, commoditized economy, he concludes, is "personal isolation" and the "fractionation of life."[38]

33. Twelve Southerners, *I'll Take My Stand*, 147.

34. Ibid., 148.

35. In a remarkable passage at the start of the essay, Lanier writes that "progress is perhaps the most widely advertised commodity offered for general consumption in our high-powered century, a sort of universal social enzyme whose presence is essential to the ready assimilation of other commodities, material and intellectual . . . A steady barrage of propaganda issues through newspapers, magazines, radios, billboards, and other agencies for controlling public opinion, to the effect that progress must be maintained. It requires little sagacity to discover that progress usually turns out to mean business . . . General sanction of the industrial exploitation of the individual is grounded in the firm belief on the part of the generality of people that the endless production and consumption of material goods means 'prosperity,' 'a high standard of living,' 'progress,' or any one among several other catchwords" (ibid., 123).

36. Ibid., 146.

37. Quoted from Ransom's essay, "Reconstructed But Unregenerate" in ibid., 6.

38. Ibid., 148. See also Buber: "The era of advanced Capitalism has broken down the structure of society. The society which preceded it was composed of different societies: it was complex, and pluralistic in structure . . . Centralism in its new, capitalistic form succeeded where [older forms] had failed: in atomizing society. Exercising control over the machines and, with their help, over the whole society, Capitalism wants to deal only with individuals; and the modern State aids and abets it by progressively dispossessing

Nowhere in American society, in fact, has the modern economy's effect upon bonded communities been more evident than in the fracturing of rural communities following the industrialization of agriculture. As Berry asserts, the dismantling of rural life in the United States, which had been rooted in thousands of decentralized and fairly independent local food economies, began when the local community became increasingly subject to economic forces beyond itself.[39] Whereas pre-industrial forms of agriculture depend upon *on-the-farm* seed (saved from the previous year's harvest or exchanged via farmer cooperatives), energy inputs (from solar, human, and animal power) and fertilizer (via manure, leguminous crops, and rotation), industrialized agriculture is driven entirely by the infusion of capital-intensive or commoditized energy inputs (heavy machinery requiring non-renewable fossil sources, primarily petroleum) and hybrid or GMO seeds, fertilizers, and pesticides/herbicides (all purchased from agribusiness corporations like Monsanto and Cargill). One of the principal effects of the commodification of agriculture, therefore, is that the flow of wealth ultimately moves from the farm and farming communities to corporate businesses and their stockholders who are located in larger urban areas and who rarely, if ever, re-invest their capital in ways that benefit the rural communities—including their local businesses, schools, churches, etc.—on which they ultimately depend. As Berry bluntly states, the global food economy is in no way structured, "to help the communities and localities" that produce the food we eat. Rather, "it exists to siphon the wealth of those communities and places into a few bank accounts."[40] The result of this extractive, divisive economy, of course, has been the systematic decline of political, cultural, and communal vitality throughout rural America.[41]

---

groups of their autonomy. The militant organizations erected against Capitalism—Trade Unions in the economic sphere and the Party in the political—are unable in the nature of things to counteract this process of dissolution, since they have not access to the life of society itself and its foundations: production and consumption" (*Paths in Utopia*, 139).

39. Berry, *Sex, Economy, Freedom & Community*, 126.

40. Ibid., 129.

41. Berry writes: "I remember, during the fifties, the outrage with which our political leaders spoke of the forced removal of the populations of the villages in communist countries. I also remember that at the same time, in Washington, the word on farming was 'Get big or get out.' The only difference is that of the method: the force used by the communists was military; with us, it has been economic. The attitudes are equally cruel, and I believe that the results will prove equally damaging" (*Unsettling*, 41). See also: "Since World War II, the governing agricultural doctrine in government offices, universities, and corporations has been that 'there are too many people on the farm.' This

Predictably, the exportation of American agro-economic policies and practices as part of the so-called "development" of non-Western nations has had a similar effect upon bonded communities worldwide. In her first book, *The Violence of the Green Revolution*, Vandana Shiva relates contemporary social conflict in Asian societies to the implementation of the Green Revolution. Disputing the prevalent notion that the roots of communal unrest and dissolution in regions like Punjab in India are based on religion, Shiva argues that the developmentalist policies of the 40s and 50s were intentionally designed to fragment the politically subversive—because relationally bonded—communities of rural Asia.

> Rural development in general, and the Green Revolution in particular, assisted by foreign capital and planned by foreign experts, were prescribed as means for stabilizing the rural areas politically . . . This strategy was based on the idea of an agricultural revolution driven by scientific and technological innovations, since such an approach held the promise of changing the agrarian relations which had previously been politically so troublesome . . . Ecological breakdown in nature and the political breakdown of society were essential implications of a policy based on tearing apart both nature and society.[42]

Since 1950, the percentage of people engaged in farming throughout the industrial world has plummeted, in some places by over 80 percent.[43] As a result, the kinds of communities that have traditionally been most resistant

---

idea has supported, if indeed it has not caused, one of the most consequential migrations in history: millions of rural people moving from country to city in a stream that has not slackened from the war's end until now. And the strongest force behind this migration, then as now, has been economic ruin on the farm . . . The farm-to-city migration has obviously produced advantages to the corporate economy. The absent farmers have had to be replaced by machinery, petroleum, chemicals, credit, and other expensive goods and services from the agribusiness economy . . . But these short-term advantages all imply long-term disadvantages, to both country and city . . . When the 'too many' of the country arrive in the city, they are not called 'too many.' In the city they are called 'unemployed' or 'permanently unemployable.' But what will happen if the economists ever perceive that there are too many people in the cities? There appear to be only two possibilities: either they will have to recognize that their earlier diagnosis was a tragic error, or they will conclude that there are too many people in country and city both—and what further inhumanities will be justified by that diagnosis?" (Berry, *What Are People For?*, 124–25).

42. Shiva, *The Violence of the Green Revolution*, 14–15.

43. Halweil, *Where Have All the Farmers Gone?*, 60.

to capitalistic economic structures—agrarian, cooperative, subsistent—are facing global extinction.

The social ills caused by such a disruptive economy are immense. Although proponents of the globalized agro-economy maintain that farmers who are unable to compete with large agribusinesses can simply retrain for "better" jobs in more "attractive" urban areas, the loss of farm and land is often deeply traumatic. Throughout the U.S. "farm crisis" of the past several decades, thousands of family farms have foreclosed or gone bankrupt, the rural population has plummeted below the poverty line, and many small communities have ultimately collapsed. Throughout this period, the suicide rates across rural America have tripled and cases of depression and violence have spiked.[44] The spread of industrial agriculture worldwide has had an equally devastating effect on farmers in the Two-Thirds world. Vandana Shiva links the sharp rise in suicides across the Indian countryside, for example, to the industrialization of Indian agriculture over the past decade. "According to India's National Crime Bureau," she writes, "16,000 farmers in India committed suicide in 2004 alone," oftentimes by drinking the pesticides or herbicides that were supposed to increase yields/profits but which only contributed to insurmountable debts.[45] Although the word suicide typically denotes an individual action, when "viewed as the result of economic policy," she says, "this is not suicide; it is genocide."[46]

From the start, one of industrial agriculture's fundamental promises has been its claimed goal of "feeding the world's hungry," with large-scale, monocultural, and techno-chemically intensive methods offered as the only way to nourish a growing global population. The reality, however, is that developmentalist policies are a primary cause of hunger for the 800 million people who go hungry every day. From 1970 to 1990, at the height of industrial agriculture's global expansion, the number of hungry people worldwide increased by more than 11 percent in every country except China.[47] The reasons for this are varied. First, many of those facing long-term hunger or starvation around the world are victims of land enclosures who have been unable to secure one of the low paying jobs in the industrial centers. Trapped in urban slums and shantytowns, they have no access either to land on which they might grow food or income with which they

---

44. See Dosman and Cockroft, eds., *Principles of Health and Safety in Agriculture*.

45. *Earth Democracy*, 120.

46. Ibid., 123.

47. Kimbrell, ed., *Fatal Harvest Reader*, 9.

might buy it in local markets.[48] Second, hunger is increasingly prevalent among farmers and rural communities in the U.S. and around the world because of rising indebtedness and poverty. It is one of the great ironies of our current agro-economy that a high percentage of those who grow and harvest the food that is bought and sold on the global market are themselves malnourished and hungry. Third, many of the "cash crops" produced by global corporations on enclosed lands are luxury high-profit items—i.e., flowers, sugarcane, cotton, coffee, eucalyptus—that have replaced staple foods for the local population. In Africa, in particular, the food shortages, hunger, and famines that have devastated the continent in recent decades are "linked directly to the underdevelopment of Africa's food production by cash-crops leading to a decline in food production."[49] As Shiva claims, far from serving the needs of the world's poor, the industrialization and internationalization of agriculture is actually "responsible for more hungry people than both cruel wars and unusual whims of nature" combined.[50]

The modern industrial economy's fracturing of nature has been just as aggressive and destructive. From an ecological perspective, a healthy ecosystem is a natural area (i.e., a pond, a forest, grassland) within which a dynamic complex of plant, animal, and micro-organism communities interact in such a way as to sustain the diversity of life forms in an integrated whole. In one of the foundational texts of the sustainable agriculture movement, *The Soil and Health*, Sir Albert Howard describes the intricate web of interconnections constituting natural ecosystems:

> Her sowings and harvestings are *intermingled* to the last degree, not only spatially, but in succession of time, each plant seizing its indicated opportunity to catch at the nutrient elements in air, earth, or water, and then giving place to another, while some phases of all these growing things and of the animals, birds, and parasites which feed on them are going on *together* all the time. Thus the prairie, the forest, the moor, the marsh, the river, the lake, the ocean include in their several ways an *interweaving* of existences which is a dramatic lesson; in their lives, as in their decay and death, beasts and plants are absolutely *interlocked*.[51]

48. "Currently, more than half a billion rural people in the third world have become landless or do not have either sufficient land to grow their own food or money to buy that food" (Kimbrell, ed., *Fatal Harvest Reader*, 8).

49. Shiva, *Violence of the Green Revolution*, 222.

50. Barnet, *The Lean Years*, 171, quoted in Shiva, *Earth Democracy*, 33.

51. Howard, *The Soil and Health*, 62–63.

Stated simply, the life of creation is always *life together*.

One of the chief strategies of industrial agriculture, of course, has been to separate, isolate, and then manipulate certain plant varieties or animal species/traits in order to amplify food production. Driven by the logic of efficiency, economy of scale, and the profit-motive, modern agro-economic policies have replaced small, highly diversified farms, which typically incorporate a variety of plants, animals, woodsheds, waterways, and wildlife, with massive, monocrop or livestock operations that focus on a singular part of the food economy. Although generations of farmers, over the last 10,000 years, have bred almost 50,000 different plant species for human consumption, today only four species—rice, corn, wheat, and soybean—provide the majority of calories and protein consumed by the world's population.[52] These major "cash crops," moreover, are currently planted "fence-row-to-fence-row," thereby significantly reducing field margins, wetlands, shelterbelts, woodlots, and other uncultivated areas that had been the prime habitat for wildlife species.[53] Similarly, nearly all of the meat products bought and sold through the global market now originate from factory farms, which raise thousands of livestock (e.g., cattle, chickens, hogs) in highly concentrated, confined conditions entirely isolated from their natural habitats. In each case, the strategy is to dissect natural ecosystems, sequester isolatable units, discard non-profitable parts, and exploit the remainder for monetary gain—in other words, to divide and conquer (*divide et impera*), for profit.

The inevitable result of the exploitative, divisive economy governing modern existence is the progressive devastation of nature. The Green Revolution's primary strategy of increasing global food production through the use of technologies such as large-scale machinery, synthetic nitrogen fertilizers, pesticides and herbicides, which have had such a disastrous effect on the health of rural communities, contributes directly to many of today's ecological crises as well. Following World War II, the U.S. government's enormous surplus of ammonium nitrate, which had been used to make explosives, was converted into chemical fertilizers that

52. Shiva, *Stolen Harvest*, 79. As Shiva notes, there has been a tremendous loss of diversity within each of these species as well. "Traditionally, 10,000 wheat varieties were grown in China. These had been reduced to only 1,000 by the 1970s. Only 20 percent of Mexico's maize diversity survives today . . . In the Philippines, where small peasants used to cultivate thousands of traditional rice varieties, just two Green Revolution varieties occupied 98 percent of the entire rice-growing area by the mid-1980s" (80).

53. Tucker, "Wildlife Health," in Kimbrell, ed., *Fatal Harvest Reader*, 211.

could be mass produced, sold to farmers, and spread across America's farmland (and later shipped abroad). Likewise, many of the poison gases developed for the war were refashioned into pesticides and herbicides. Although they initially produced increased crop production, these "savior" technologies have also been responsible for such ecologically ruinous consequences as a 30 percent loss in the world's farmable land over the past 40 years[54] and the present release of over 25 percent of the world's CO_2 emissions, 60 percent of all methane gas emissions, and 80 percent of nitrous oxide emissions, all major contributors to global warming.[55] It is now an undisputable fact that:

> Decades of industrial agriculture have been a disaster for the environment. Its chemical poisoning has caused ecocide among countless species. And it has resulted in irreversible soil loss, reduction in soil and water quality, and the proliferation of non-native species that choke out indigenous varieties. Without question, the tilling, mowing, and harvesting operations of industrial agriculture have affected, and continue to catastrophically destroy, wildlife and soil and water quality.[56]

The promise of the global economy is that the peoples of the world and the earth's resources will be brought into a harmonious equilibrium that serves the greatest good for the greatest number through the market's coordination of self-interested individuals. What an "awakened analysis" of our context (Herzog) makes clear, however, is that the ubiquitous commodification of nature and society is causing the fragmentation, sickness, and even death of bonded human communities and ecosystems throughout the world. An economy that is dependent upon the ongoing fracture of ecosystems and human communities is one that is directly opposed to the nature of God's convivial love. As Christians join together to share in the elements of agro-industrial meals, therefore, they do so as participants in an unholy communion marked by division and death.

54. "Earth has lost a third of arable land in past 40 years, scientists say" (*Guardian*, Dec. 2, 2015, https://www.theguardian.com/environment/2015/dec/02/arable-land-soil-food-security-shortage).

55. *Earth Democracy*, 103–4.

56. Kimbrell, ed., *Fatal Harvest Reader*, 31.

Holistic Communion: Harmonious Interconnection of All Participants and Elements

If Holy Communion, within the bonds of the Spirit, is wholly harmonious life together, how are those inspired to abide in the Spirit to share in the convivial love of God in the midst of an economy woven together by the divisive, and ultimately deadly, energies of selfish gain? Specifically, in the context of an agro-economy dependent upon the fragmentation, and in some cases, death, of local communities and healthy ecosystems, how are Christians faithfully to eat and drink in the Spirit of loving relationship in ways that nurture healthful flourishing among the many human and nonhuman participants bound together in the meal? Those striving to abide within the holy bonds of the Spirit's convivial love are being called today to participate in harmonious modes of economic life together that foster the flourishing of all. In particular, this will entail the involvement of Christians in the emergence of a more harmonious food economy, in which the many elements and participants in our food system are interwoven in ways that nourish social and environmental health.

In striving to weave the various parts of our agro-economy into a web of relationships conducive to the flourishing of life, Christians affirm that God's creation is infused with the Spirit's energies of dynamic interconnectedness. Rather than fixating on atomized parts of a dissected reality, those indwelt by God's Spirit seek after the divine holiness present wherever relational bonds—whether social, economic, or ecological—are knit together in patterns of convivial charity. They affirm what Wendell Berry describes as the central ecological insight into existence, which is that "everything in the Creation is related to everything else and dependent on everything else."[57] In the Spirit, we come to know that no one part of the creation, whether human or nonhuman, ultimately exists in isolation, but rather, as Berry says, that "everything happens in concert" within "an inconceivable series of vital connections."[58] To work toward the emergence of a more harmonious agro-economy, then, in which the production, distribution, and consumption of our daily food and drink nourishes the flourishing of life, is to give concrete witness to the convivial love of God overflowing in the Spirit into the whole of creation.

57. Berry, *Unsettling*, 46.
58. Berry, *Home Economics*, 118.

The individualistic view of the human being on which modern economic life is constructed runs counter to a spiritual understanding of the interconnected nature of all life forms, including the human person. If modernity's economic man (*homo economicus*) is envisaged as a purely self-interested individual detached from the relational ties that constitute his environs, the Christian view is that of the relational person (*homo relationalis*) whose singular identity is inextricably linked to the unlimited number of relationships, both internal and external, that constitute her life. Moreover, not only are we inherently social creatures, such that "we come into being in and through relationships" with other human beings, as Cobb and Daly argue,[59] but we are simultaneously relationally interconnected with the whole multitude of living and nonliving entities that inhabit the biosphere. Who we are as human beings, as David Suzuki writes, extends beyond our fingertips and our skin. "We are connected through air, water and soil; we are animated by the same source in the sky above. We are quite literally air, water, soil, energy and other living creatures."[60] In place of the individualism of *homo economicus*, then, Christians seeking to support the emergence of a more socially and ecologically harmonious economy do so while embracing a more spiritual understanding of the human as *homo relationalis*.

In the context of an agro-economy in which the isolation of every aspect of the food system for commodity exchange has led to the ultimate fracturing of social and ecological communities, those alive in the Spirit are called to share more fully in the convivial love of God by fostering charitable relationships within our food economy. The divine invitation to entire sanctification must be answered today not only within our private, personal lives but in the sphere of our collective economic and ecological life together as well. Those "going on to perfection" (Wesley) will therefore embrace what Berry describes as "an elaborate understanding of charity,"[61] which extends the holy pursuit of love of neighbor into the myriad social and ecological relationships bound up in the everyday act of gathering together to eat.

The outcome of a harmonious food economy that is aligned with the convivial love of God present in the Holy Spirit is the health of human communities and natural ecosystems. Precisely because participation in

---

59. Daly and Cobb Jr., *For the Common Good*, 161.

60. Quoted from Wirzba, *Paradise of God*, 93.

61. Berry, *The Gift of Good Land*, 273.

the love of God is a simultaneous sharing in the divine holiness that makes us whole, we can expect the fruits of a charitable agro-economy to be the healthful flourishing of the many life forms involved in the whole process of gathering together to eat. For a food economy to be healthy overall, however, requires that we seek after ways of nurturing mutually beneficial relationships among all the various participants and elements. As Sir Albert Howard insisted at the time of the emergence of the Green Revolution, "the whole problem of health in soil, plant, animal, and man" can only be properly understood "as one great subject,"[62] since the welfare of individual persons, local communities, and entire nation-states is directly related to the health of the land. Similarly, Berry affirms that for a particular body to be healthy, it must be whole. And yet, precisely because we are not distinct from the bodies of other people, of plants and animals, and of the earth—"for all creatures are parts of a whole upon which each is dependent"[63]—it is necessarily the case that individuals cannot be whole alone. "Only conviviality is healing," he says, which is why "we must come with all the other creatures to the feast of Creation."[64]

One of the ways in which an increasing number of farmers are beginning to participate more fully in the healthful energies of conviviality is by incorporating synergistic agricultural methods into their food production systems. Instead of relying as heavily on external commodity inputs, monocrop planting techniques, and the sequestering of plant and animal units, synergistic farming introduces a multitude of species into an environment in ways that allow all of the diverse components to influence and enhance each other through numerous complex interactions. Joel Salatin's Polyface Farm in Virginia's Shenandoah Valley is an exemplary model of a farm system that weaves the various parts of an individual agro-economy into an interconnected whole. Salatin has developed a rotational grazing production system that incorporates over 40 varieties of plants and numerous animal species. Michael Pollen describes Salatin's livestock barn, for example, where during the winter months his cattle consume hay cut from an adjacent pasture, while producing fifty pounds of manure. Rather than cleaning out the barn, however, Salatin simply covers the manure with field straw and corn, which over time forms a deep bedding. In the spring, as the cows head to pasture, he brings a few dozen hogs into the barn, who are

62. Howard, *The Soil and Health*, 145.

63. Berry, *The Gift of Good Land*, 273.

64. Berry, *Unsettling*, 103–4.

perfectly happy to snort through the compost in search of the corn. The result is a "rich, cakey" compost ready to be spread on his pastures, which will then fertilize the grasses that will again feed the cows come winter. Through these multiple symbiotic relationships, and because the animals are allowed to live in their natural environs, the livestock are healthy, the need for costly antibiotics are eliminated, and the problem of waste becomes the solution to depleted soils. Conviviality is healing.

Permaculture is another way of producing food in close alignment with the Spirit's healing energies of charitable interconnectivity. Developed by Australians Bill Mollison and David Holmgren in the 1970s, permaculture (i.e., permanent agriculture) is an agro-ecological and agro-economic design system oriented toward the healthful flourishing of all life forms through the harmonious integration of landscapes and people. As Mollison writes, permaculture is an ecological approach toward "working with, rather than against nature; of protracted and thoughtful observation rather than protracted and thoughtless labor; and of looking at plants and animals in all their functions, rather than treating elements as a single-product system."[65] In the process of designing any particular location for human settlement, such as a rural homestead, a city block, or a watershed, the permaculture designer begins by identifying, through patient, attentive observation, all of the living and non-living components that are or will be present—i.e., plant, animal, and human inhabitants; buildings, roads, and paths; land and water features; soil types and conditions; climatic aspects of sun, wind, and rainfall. Next, the designer compiles a comprehensive list of the products and activities, intrinsic qualities, and needs of the most significant and representative elements. Having done so, she then creates and progressively implements a site design in which the needs of the various elements are provided by the yields of other elements through the intentional arrangement of each in relative location to all the others. The result is a dense web of mutually beneficial interconnections that mimics a natural ecosystem. As Toby Hemenway writes:

> A natural landscape is patterned in ways that harvest the energy (sun, wind, heat) and matter (water and nutrients) that flow through it, casting a living net that collects these resources and shuttles them into myriad cycles that transform them into more life. Nearly everything that enters a natural landscape is captured and used, absorbed and reincarnated into vibrant biodiversity.

65. Mollison, *Introduction to Permaculture*, 1.

> Anything produced in that landscape, from by-products . . . to "wastes" . . . is recycled, swallowed up again, and reincorporated into new living tissue . . . It is this interconnectedness—this linking of one species' "outputs" to another's "inputs"—that we seek to re-create in the ecological garden [and farm, neighborhood, bioregion, etc.].[66]

By shifting emphasis away from increasing the yields of a singular crop for commodity exchange, which is motivated by the myopic, fractious energies of self-interested love, and toward a broader focus on nurturing convivial relationships among a complex diversity of natural and agricultural participants, those adopting a permacultural approach share in the healing energies of God's convivial love present with us in the Holy Spirit.

Not only farmers and gardeners, those who produce our "daily bread" and "common cup," but a growing number of consumers as well are beginning to participate more deeply in the divine holiness by purchasing consumptive goods that have been produced in a socially and ecologically healthy manner. As Frederick Kirschenmann argues, people are increasingly focused upon "*relationships* as part of their purchasing experience."[67] Through the purchase of Fair Trade products, for example, the consumer is not only satiating his own desires in enjoying good coffees, teas, or chocolates, but is simultaneously seeking after the good of others by supporting living wages, just working environments, and the economic and social development of local communities. Similarly, many of those who choose to pay more for fruits, vegetables, meats, and other products from farmers who practice ecologically sound methods do so not only to promote the health of their own bodies but the overall health of the land within which the particular farm is embedded. Whereas the self-interested consumer, the *homo economicus*, makes purchasing decisions based solely on what is best for him or herself, the charitable consumer, the *homo relationalis*, seeks after the flourishing of every participant involved in the entire agro-economic process. In so doing, she is joining together with others in the holy and spiritual bonds of convivial love.

66. Hemenway, *Gaia's Garden*, 36.

67. Kirschenmann, "The Future of Agrarianism: Where Are We Now?," 10.

Conclusion

The Spirit of the triune God invites us to join in abundant life together through the bonds of convivial love. In the Holy Spirit, God's holiness is present with us within wholly harmonious relationships that lead to the healthful flourishing of all. In the midst of an unholy economy held together by the divisive energies of myopic self-love, resulting in the ongoing fragmentation of bonded communities, those made alive in the Holy Spirit are called today to participate in the divine work of healing by striving to interconnect the various participants and elements in our economy in ways that foster social and ecological health. By joining together in harmonious models of agro-economic life together like biodynamic farming, permaculture, and Fair Trade, Christians faithfully participate in the divine holiness drawing all things together in perfect love. Holy Communion is wholly charitable life together in which all are made whole. Joined together in the convivial nature of God's love, including especially in the ways we gather together to eat and drink, we abide in fellowship of the Holy Spirit and thereby share in the *aliveness* of living and the *vitality* of life that pulsates within the interwoven dance of God's diverse creation.

3

The Father/Mother
Nourishes Every Body

GOD THE FATHER/MOTHER NOURISHES every body in the feast of life. As the divine source of creation, the Father/Mother gives Jesus Christ and the Holy Spirit for the sustaining of our creaturely existence. God's holiness is God's perfect love, and in the fullness of divine love, all things are made whole. From the Father/Mother, God's holiness is offered to us as *enfleshed love*, which we consume in the bread and cup as the nourishment of our earthly life together. Faithful acceptance of God's summons to participate in Holy Communion, then, includes faithfully worshipping the Creator by tending to the bodily well-being of God's creation. "Present your bodies as a living sacrifice, holy and acceptable to God, which is your spiritual worship" (Rom 12:1). Holy Communion, in devotion to the Father/Mother, is wholly integrated life together.

But how are those committed to sustaining the vitality of our creaturely existence to participate in the enfleshed love of God within an economy grounded in the illusory abstractions of self-love? Disconnected from God's perfect love, self-oriented love inevitably results in falsehood, for the self-consumed individual loses sight of the whole of reality in pursuing monetary gain as the primary form of wealth. The modern global economy is thus marked by an unsustainable social dynamic in which financial wealth is amassed at the expense of the earth and its creatures. Within the modern agro-economy, in particular, the abstraction of monetary gain from ecological realities has resulted in the ongoing desecration of the earth's soil, water, and air, the depletion of its non-renewable resources, and physical harm to its many living creatures. In this context, worshipping the Father/

Mother in economic life—and thus participating more fully in the divine holiness—means finding ways of integrating all of our economic activities into the limits and needs of our creaturely life together on earth.

The Wholly Enfleshed Love from God the Father/Mother

To affirm that God the Father/Mother sent Jesus Christ as the revelation of divine love for us and the Holy Spirit as the presence of divine love with us is to affirm that God's holiness is given to us in the enfleshed form of our creaturely existence. The *"Abba"* to whom Jesus prayed is not an absentee parent, whose love remains detached from the realities of His children's lives. Rather, the Father/Mother offers Her love to us in corporeal form, so that we who are Her creatures can receive and be sustained by it. "Embodiment," as Friedrich Oetinger declared, "is the end of all God's works."[1] In Jesus Christ and the Holy Spirit, we see that the movement of God the Father/Mother's love is *from* the Creator *to* the creation. For the One whose name is holy (Matt 6:9) is a Divine Parent whose love is oriented toward the terrestrial flourishing of His sons and daughters *as* creatures.

As the source of all that is, seen and unseen, God the Father/Mother sent Jesus Christ to be the incarnation (*in*, "into" + *carn-*, "flesh") of divine holiness for our sake. Though "no one has ever seen God" the Father/Mother (John 4:12), God's life has come to us in Jesus Christ "in the flesh" (4:2). Jesus is the embodiment of divine love, which "we have seen with our eyes" and "looked at and touched with our hands" (1:1). Jesus "acts as God in the creation, among men," as Johann Christoph Blumhardt writes. He is "the glory of God on earth" in the whole of his corporeal life with us. "From him shines forth the Father of creation."[2] It is the heresy of Docetism, as Bonhoeffer observed in his christology lectures, that regards Christ's humanity in the flesh as an insignificant aspect of God's salvific work. The Docetist views Christ's bodily life simply as a means by which God has conveyed divine truth to us "as a supra-historical, absolute idea." From this perspective, "the form God chooses" to reveal Godself "is unimportant compared with the core" of God's disembodied, ideal nature.[3] By insisting on the salvific importance of Jesus' corporeal humanity, Bonhoeffer said,

---

1. Oetinger, *Biblisches und emblematisches Wörterbuch*, quoted in Herzog, *European Pietism Reviewed*, 107.

2. Johann Blumhardt, in Blumhardt and Blumhardt, *Thy Kingdom Come*, 11.

3. Bonhoeffer, *Christ the Center*, 76.

the early church rejected the notion that God is fundamentally disinterested in our creaturely existence. Though human eyes have never seen the One who sent Jesus, we can affirm that the holiness springing forth from the Father/Mother is lovingly manifest for us in the flesh.

So, too, the Father/Mother sends the Holy Spirit to dwell with us bodily within the creation. "The Spirit must embody itself," Johann Christoph Blumhardt writes. "It must enter into our earthly life." For "God is active Spirit only when he gets something of our material underfoot."[4] The scriptures, particularly in the Old Testament, provide an account of the Holy Spirit as the enlivening presence of God within all created flesh. In the second chapter of Genesis, we read that "the Lord God formed man of dust from the ground, and breathed into his nostrils the breath of life; and man became a living being (2:7). Job declares that "the spirit of God has made me, and the breath of the Almighty gives me life" (33:4). Not only human beings, but all creatures abide in and through the outpouring of God's presence with us in the Spirit. "The earth is full of your creatures," the Psalmist avows. "When you send forth your spirit, they are created," and "when you take away their breath, they die and return to their dust" (104:24, 29–30). The Holy Spirit who abides as God with us, as Moltmann affirms, is the "giver of life" (Nicene Creed) or the "fountain of life" (Calvin) in whom the whole of creation "lives and moves and has its being" (Acts 17:28). In sending the Spirit, "God the Creator takes up his dwelling in his creation and makes it his home,"[5] he writes. Although the love of the Father/Mother originates from Her abode in the heavens, Her holiness inhabits the created realm through the Spirit as the power of life in every creature.

Our Heavenly Parent who sends the Son and the Holy Spirit as the enfleshment of divine love with and for us is the Hallowed Creator who has knit the human being together as a unity of body and soul. To affirm, with the second chapter in Genesis, that God fashioned humankind (*adam*) out of the dust of the ground (*adamah*) is to affirm that the fleshly body belongs to humanity's essence. In this sense, notions of the human being, religious or otherwise, that attempt to abstract the core of human nature from earthly corporeity are foreign to a biblical anthropology. As Bonhoeffer writes in his commentary on Genesis 2:7, "the body is not the prison, the shell, the exterior, of a human being." In just the same way that "Christ is wholly his body," so, too, "a human being is a human body." For "the body is the form

---

4. Johann Blumhardt, in Blumhardt and Blumhardt, *Thy Kingdom Come,* 18.

5. Moltmann, *God in Creation,* 96.

in which the spirit exists" just as "the spirit is the form in which the body exists."[6] We human beings are lovingly created by our Holy Father/Mother as unified creatures, as enfleshed spirits or enlivened flesh.

The Creator whose holiness is revealed in the body of Jesus and present in the enlivening Spirit has simultaneously fashioned humankind in terrestrial unity with the whole of nature and every living being. To claim that human existence is bodily existence means that it is also inherently natural existence. "In their bodily nature," Bonhoeffer affirms, "human beings are related to the earth and to other bodies; they are there for others and are dependent upon others."[7] Human beings are not separable from the natural world. We are bound to the earth community in our essential being, such that we share, as Moltmann says, "in a common destiny with the whole world and all earthly creatures."[8] To re-phrase Martin Luther King, Jr., whatever affects one part of the earthly creation directly, human or non-human, affects all indirectly. For in and through our bodies, "we are caught up in an inescapable network of mutuality."[9] The Holy Father/Mother who lovingly fashioned all things created humankind as an indissoluble thread in the garment of nature.

The enfleshed love of God that originates from the Father/Mother, then, is wholly oriented toward the sustainment of life on *earth*. God's love is for us in Jesus Christ and with us in the Spirit for the sake of our terrestrial flourishing. The holy way of Christ, who incarnates God's gracious love, is the way that leads to "peace on earth" among humankind (Luke 2:14). Likewise, the convivial love of God present in the Holy Spirit weaves creatures together for the sake of an earthly health and well-being. As Johann Christoph Blumhardt writes, the work of God is not, as most think, oriented toward heaven.

> It is the heavenly coming to reality upon earth . . . It is earthly because it is a concern that the situation on earth become good and righteous, and that God's name be hallowed on earth, that his kingdom come on earth and his will be done right here on earth. The earth is to manifest eternal life.[10]

---

6. Bonhoeffer, *Creation and Fall*, 76–78.

7. Ibid., 79.

8. Moltmann, *God in Creation*, 68.

9. King Jr., "Letter from Birmingham City Jail," 290.

10. Johann Blumhardt, in Blumhardt and Blumhardt, *Thy Kingdom Come*, 3.

The divine love sent from the Father/Mother is not a love that seeks to rescue us from the finite limitations of earthly existence for an otherworldly, ethereal paradise. Rather, the Creator's holiness is enfleshed in Jesus Christ and the Spirit for the sustaining of the earth itself and the flourishing of all its creatures.

If the holiness of God the Father/Mother is given to us in the form of enfleshed love, then sin is operative in the *false abstraction* of certain goods from the inherent unity of God's earthly creation. Where God's perfect love is made incarnate in and for the body, insular self-love disregards corporeal limits and needs for the sake of private gain. The sin of abstraction originates most often in the self-oriented individual's greed for a generalized "more" that distorts his perspective of the unitive nature of himself, human and non-human others, and the natural world. Driven by a lust for more wealth, more possessions, more experiences, more accolades, more power, and more knowledge, the concupiscent sinner sees only what she perceives to be valuable in her frenzy of constant accumulation. The sin of abstraction is unholy, because it fails to see the wholeness of things as they truly are. False abstraction, therefore, necessarily entails a *transgression* against the love of God enfleshed in and for the creation. Instead of respecting the limits and needs of embodied existence, the self-oriented sinner violates the created integrity of other bodies, human or otherwise, by valuing only those aspects in them that might serve the fulfillment of her own aims. Whereas the Father/Mother's fulsome love provides life and sustainment for the creatures of the earth, sinful self-love extracts life and vitality from the flesh of creation.

The unholy sin of false abstraction is involved in religious beliefs and practices that violate the enfleshed nature of the Father/Mother's love in and for Her creation. In particular, forms of religiosity that denigrate bodily, finite, earthly existence in the pursuit of an ethereal, unlimited, otherworldly realm are in direct conflict with God's love enfleshed in Jesus Christ and the Holy Spirit. As the young Karl Barth, who was greatly influenced by the Blumhardts on this matter, wrote: "Perhaps nowhere else has Christianity fallen further from the spirit of her Lord and Master than precisely in this estimation of the relation between spirit and matter, inner and outer, heaven and earth." Redemption, he says, is not a matter of our ascending to heaven, but rather God coming to us "in matter and on earth."[11] Most

---

11. Barth, "Jesus Christ And The Movement For Social Justice," in Green, ed., *Karl Barth: Theologian of Freedom*, 104–5.

often, the motivation driving the religious pursuit of otherworldliness is not actually a pure love for God but a self-interested desire to flee from the constraints of earthly life for something "more." Like Adam and Eve's ambition to be "like God" (Gen 3:4) and the intent of mortals to build a tower reaching into the heavens (Gen 11:4), religious pursuits for a disembodied paradise in heaven transgress the Father/Mother's will for our creaturely flourishing on earth.

In response to the transgressive sin of false abstraction, the holiness of God the Father/Mother operates in the *embodiment* of truth revealed in Jesus Christ and present in the Holy Spirit. Jesus Christ, anointed by the Spirit of life, manifests God's perfect love in the form of a wholly human and worldly life. He is the true human being. His fully human life is "the way, the truth, and the life" (John 14:6). God became human in Jesus Christ, not so that we might become disincarnate but, rather, that we might become truly human and truly worldly like him. "Whoever looks at Jesus Christ," as Bonhoeffer says, "sees in fact God and the world in one. From then on they can no longer see God without the world, or the world without God."[12] As the One who is Emmanuel, Jesus reveals that God's response to humanity's illusory state of sinful abstraction—religious or otherwise—is the embodiment of holiness in a fully human, perfectly loving, entirely earthly life.

Both the transgressive sin of false abstraction and the enfleshed nature of God's unyielding love are manifest in the crucifixion and resurrection of Jesus Christ. Each of the powers complicit in the death of Jesus on the cross—the political, religious, and public—are guilty of transgressing Christ's body in pursuit of goods abstracted from the overall integrity of God's earthly creation. The chief priests and scribes who hand Jesus over to be flogged are devoted principally to upholding theological purity and religious tradition. The collective mass of individuals who refuse to receive Jesus from Pilate are concerned primarily with the preservation of their personal security. And the imperial authorities who execute Jesus are committed almost exclusively to the maintenance of social control. Taken together, these three powers humiliate, torture, and ultimately sacrifice the body of Jesus, along with the bodies of countless others, for the sake of partial interests.

In response to the unholy transgression against Jesus' body, the Father/Mother sends the Spirit of Life to resurrect Jesus in the flesh. What

---

12. Bonhoeffer, *Ethics*, 82.

had been despised and rejected—the body of Christ—is now raised up to newness of life through the love of the Father/Mother. The scriptural accounts of Jesus' post-resurrection appearances are clear that Jesus was not simply present to his disciples in a kind of ephemeral, disembodied form. Likewise, the resurrection is not just a symbol of the ongoing "spirit of Jesus" among his followers. In the resurrection, Jesus' whole, bodily person is raised up from the dead. This proves that God's perfect love, even amidst the transgressive sin of false abstraction, is unceasingly enfleshed in and for the body.

Faithfully responding to God's invitation to participate in divine holiness, then, means worshipping the Father/Mother by nurturing the bodily well-being of created existence. The movement of the Father/Mother's love is from the Creator toward the earthly creation, which means we properly "worship the Father in spirit and in truth" (John 4:23–24) by tending to the flourishing of the earth and all God's creatures. True spiritual piety, as Johann Christoph Blumhardt writes, must "present itself as true for the body, as right for the body, as freeing the body for God." Otherwise, he says, we remain only "pious cripples" trapped in a false religiosity. Instead, "we must learn to be genuine creations of God through which life can stream out in all directions, as is the intention for all creation."[13] Precisely because the love from God the Father/Mother is lavished upon us in bodily form, we are called to share in the holiness of God *as* earthly creatures in harmony with the whole of nature.

The summons of God to be holy, then, is a call to become more deeply and fully human. We participate in the divine holiness, which is sent from God the Father/Mother in Jesus Christ and the Holy Spirit, not by seeking to escape our earthly nature for a bodiless, otherworldly, or interior existence. Rather, the holy life is the wholly unitive life, in which, as Ruusbroec describes, "body and soul, heart and senses, and all the exterior and interior powers" are enveloped "in the unity of love."[14] Jesus Christ, who is the true human being, calls us to be conformed to his likeness and image, which means that God's will for us is to grow into the fullness of being human. "Human beings are not transformed into an alien form, the form of God," as Bonhoeffer writes. "Human beings become human because God became human."[15] Likewise, the summons to abide within the holiness present in

---

13. Johann Blumhardt, in Blumhardt and Blumhardt, *Thy Kingdom Come*, 19–20.

14. Ruusbroec, *The Spiritual Espousals*, 79.

15. Bonhoeffer, *Ethics*, 96.

the Spirit is an invitation that calls us, not away from our creaturely lives here on earth, but into a more awakened, dynamic state of earthly existence. As Moltmann writes:

> The gift and the presence of the Holy Spirit is the greatest and most wonderful thing which we can experience—we ourselves, the human community, all living things and this earth . . . Where the Holy Spirit is present, God is present in a special way, and we experience God through our lives, which become wholly living from within. We experience whole, full, healed, and redeemed life, experience it with all our senses. We feel and taste, we touch and see our life in God and God in our life.[16]

Faithful worship of the Father/Mother means tending to the earthly well-being of God's good creation. We honor the Holy Parent by embodying the divine love in our human lives with and for other creatures. Modes of worship or spiritual practices, which draw us away from "the things of this earth," are therefore false pieties, for they work against the love of God revealed in Jesus Christ and present in the Spirit. This is why the Christian, as Bonhoeffer says, is not a *homo religiosus*. We are not called to the religious life, but to life itself. In the face of the unholy sin of abstraction, which transgresses the limits placed by the Creator upon creaturely existence, true devotion to the Mother/Father is lived out in an entire life of faith rather than isolated acts of religiosity. For "the "religious act," as Bonhoeffer says, "is always something partial," whereas "'faith' is something whole, involving the whole of one's life."[17] When Jesus pronounces his body to be the true temple (John 2:20–21), he declares himself, the whole of his corporeal life, to be true religion. Because the holy temple of God is Jesus' body—his fully human and worldly life given to and for us—we faithfully worship the Father/Mother by affirming and caring for the earthly nature of creaturely existence.

To summarize: God's holiness is God's perfect love, and in Jesus Christ and the Holy Spirit, the eternal love of the Father/Mother is given to us in the flesh for the sustainment and flourishing of life on earth. The unholy nature of self-interested love is at work in the abstraction of particular goods from their inherent unity within the whole of creation, which entails a transgression against God and others. God's holiness makes whole, and in response to the transgressive sin of false abstraction, the holiness of

---

16. Moltmann, *The Source of Life*, 10.

17. Bonhoeffer, *Letters and Papers*, 362.

God the Father/Mother is operative in the embodiment of truth revealed in Jesus Christ and present in the Holy Spirit. We participate faithfully in the divine holiness as we worship the Father/Mother by affirming our corporeity and nurturing the well-being of God's good earth.

The Wholly Integrated Communion Meal

Holy Communion, in worship and praise of the Creator, is wholly integrated life together. The enfleshed love of God the Father/Mother is offered to us that we might bodily participate in the divine holiness in our relational lives with all other living entities. To accept faithfully God's invitation to Holy Communion is to share in a way of life that respects the unitive nature of created existence. This is the way that leads to the flourishing of the earth and its manifold creatures. All of this is given to us in the Holy Communion meal, in which the Father/Mother provides the life-giving elements of bread and wine to all who are invited.

The enfleshed love of God the Father/Mother nourishes our bodies in the meal elements of bread and wine. In Jesus Christ, through the Spirit, our Holy Parent offers us the perfection of divine love in a form that we can see and touch and taste. In the final meal Jesus shares with his disciples before he gives his body over to be crucified, he breaks a loaf of bread and says, "This is my *body*." And while lifting a cup of wine, the last he will share until he returns at the resurrection of all things, Jesus says, "This is my *blood*." The holiness of God is not a concept of divine love or a philosophy of abundant life. The Father/Mother does not offer Her love to us as if we were disembodied spirits. Jesus Christ is bread and wine. His body is the "true food" and his blood is the "true drink" (John 6) sent by the Father/Mother so that those who feast upon the divine love might be made fully alive in the flesh. In this sense, although the divine holiness "comes down from heaven" from the Father/Mother, it is a love enfleshed in the body and blood of Jesus' fully human life.

The nourishment that is given in Jesus Christ is the incarnate work of God on earth. "My food," Jesus says, "is to do the will of him who sent me to perfect his work" (John 4:34). As the enfleshment of God's holiness, Jesus' love is expressed in the totality of his life for us—as a vulnerable child in the manger, a young Jewish boy growing in wisdom and in years, a friend of the poor with no place to lay his head, a pastoral healer tending to the bodies of the sick and diseased, a prophet proclaiming God's reign amidst competing powers, a tortured body hanging on a Roman cross, and a resurrected Lord seen and touched by his disciples. His work is accomplished in the body and for the body for the sake of our earthly flourishing. This is the food sent from God the Father/Mother, which "gives life to the world" (John 6).

By offering himself to us as bread and wine, Jesus embodies true worship of God the Father/Mother. His body, given over for the bodily health of others—in his life and ministry, sacrificial death, and resurrection—is the offering most pleasing to our Heavenly Parent. Jesus is the high priest, "holy, blameless, and undefiled" (Heb 7:26) who has entered into the Holy of Holies and put an end to abstract religiosity "through the power of an indestructible life" (7:15). There is no longer any need for ritual sacrifices of piety cut off from everyday life. The time for bodily regulations, religious ordinances, and holy sites set apart from the ordinariness of human existence has come to an end. The "new and living way" (10:19) of the flesh and blood of Christ, "who through the eternal Spirit offered himself without blemish" in perfect devotion to the Father/Mother (9:14), has burst open the Holy of Holies so that all of life is now the proper sanctuary of reverence and praise. Through the Holy Spirit, the ancient "lampstand, table, and bread of Presence" have become the daily bread of Jesus' body and the blood of his life given over for others in true worship of the Father/Mother.

As the author and perfecter of true holiness, Jesus renounces all forms of piety abstracted from a living worship of God the Father/Mother in the whole of everyday existence. Many of Jesus' harshest judgments are leveled at the religious authorities as they fixate upon a singular element of a religious practice—the ritual washing of hands before the meal, for example, or the cleansing of foods purchased at the market—while missing the more important call of God to tend to the flourishing of earthly life. When the Pharisees and scribes point out to Jesus that his disciples are breaking the tradition by eating with "defiled hands," Jesus quotes from the prophet Isaiah: "This people honors me with their lips, but their hearts are far from me; in vain do they worship me" (Mark 7:7). And when his disciples are criticized for plucking grain on the Sabbath to nourish their bodies, Jesus responds that religious practice—i.e., the Sabbath—ought to serve human life, rather than human life serving religious practice (Mark 2:27). "I desire mercy and not sacrifice" (Matt 12:7). True holiness is not related to the perceived purity of any particular food, to the presence of specific ritual actions surrounding a meal practice, or to the observance of fasting or feasting on prescribed "holy" days. What matters to the Father/Mother above all else, Jesus says, are the "weightier matters of the law" regarding human interaction and social wellbeing, like "justice and mercy and faith" (Matt 23:23). To be consumed with such weighty expressions of love, which promote the flourishing of our earthly life together, is to feed upon the divine holiness sent from the Father/Mother in Jesus Christ. Whereas religious practices cut off from the fullness of God's perfect love provide a food that cannot satisfy.

We worship faithfully the Father/Mother by consuming and re-membering the enfleshed love of God as we give ourselves for the flourishing of all creatures. In response to God's offering us the divine holiness in the flesh, we eat the body of Jesus, which is given for our sake that we might be made whole, and we drink his blood, which is spilled for all in obedient devotion to the Father/Mother (Phil 2:8). In doing so, the enfleshed love of God nourishes us such that we become what we have consumed. For "those who eat my flesh and drink my blood," Jesus says, "abide in me, and I in them" (John 6:56). In and through the Spirit, our lives become life-giving food, so that we re-member Jesus by giving ourselves as sustenance for other creatures in faithful worship of God the Father/Mother. To love the Lord our God in this way, as we love our neighbors as ourselves, Jesus says, "is much more important than all whole burnt-offerings and sacrifices" (Mark 12:33). We honor the Father/Mother, according to Paul, by presenting our *bodies* "as a living sacrifice" (Rom 12:1). Feeding upon the sacrifice of Christ's body and blood given for us, we become living food in the Spirit for the earthly sustenance of others. This is the worship that is "holy and acceptable to God" (12:1).

Disembodied Communion: Detachment of Financial Wealth from Earthly Existence

Those who champion modern global capitalism point out that the economic coordination of individual interest through free markets is the single most powerful generator of wealth in human history. As Charles Schultze, a former chair of the president's Council of Economic Advisers, has said, "harnessing the 'base' motive of material self-interest to promote the common good is perhaps the most important social invention mankind has achieved."[18] Over the last several hundred years, the standard of living has indeed risen sharply wherever the profit-motive of individual actors

18. Quoted in McKibben, *Deep Economy,* 10.

has powered the production, distribution, and consumption of goods and services within a given society. At the same time, however, the perpetual growth of financial wealth in the modern global economy is based in the ongoing destruction of the real wealth of biospheric well-being. In the modern agro-economy, in particular, the abstraction of monetary gain from ecological realities has resulted in the ongoing desecration of soil, water, and air, the depletion of non-renewable resources, and physical harm to its manifold living creatures. To participate in the modern global economy, therefore, is to share in an unholy communion grounded in the transgressive power of unmitigated self-love.

The economic processes involved in the severance of people from the land and the fragmentation of human and ecological communities in the modern global economy are implicated as well in the detachment of financial accumulation from the realities of creaturely existence. By making the maximization of monetary profit the chief aim of economic life together—at the direct expense of other goods, including especially the concrete needs of human bodies and the body of the earth—capitalist economies attempt to function as if the constraints and responsibilities of corporeal, earthly life are nonexistent. This fundamental tendency of modern political economy[19] represents a profoundly unrealistic idealism, which, if left unrestrained by the requirements and contributions of embodied existence, ultimately results in the parasitic ravaging of the physical world.

The key component necessary to the operation of capitalist economies—the commodity concept—is based in a fundamental and determinative abstraction. A commodity is an object that is assigned value based upon the amount of money it garners in a market transaction. This is its "exchange-value," as Marx described. In a capitalist economy, neither the "use-value" of an object, determined by its practical usefulness within society, nor its inherent worth, is significant. As eco-socialist Joel Kovel writes, "use-value is essentially concrete; it is a *qualitative* function, composed of sensuous distinctions with other aspects of the world."[20] In other words, the useful or practical value of a particular entity is intrinsically tied to its material, corporeal, or natural constitution embedded within a particular human or ecological context. The exchange-value of a commodity, on the

---

19. "This pulling-away of the natural ground from the foundations of every industry . . . is the tendency of capital" (Marx, *Grundrisse*, quoted in Kloppenberg, *First The Seed*, 19).

20. Kovel, *The Enemy of Nature*, 135.

other hand, is determined entirely by money, which is simply a numerable medium that replaces, or is abstracted from, the tangible objects it represents.[21] Because the sole aim of all parties within a capitalistic economy is to increase their respective monetary wealth, quantity necessarily triumphs over quality in a market society. As such, since "all that is retained as the mark of exchangeability is quantity," as Kovel says, "the sensuous and concrete" are thereby "eliminated by definition and *a priori*."[22]

Precisely because the ascendancy of quantity over quality results in the abstraction of value within a market society, all goods are ultimately collapsed into a non-differentiated mass of saleable products. In his influential essay, "The Role of Economics," agrarian economist E. F. Schumacher writes that "there are fundamental and vital differences between various categories of 'goods,' which cannot be disregarded without losing touch with reality."[23] The logic of market-exchange, however, does not allow for these very real distinctions, he says. Once commoditized, all goods are simply assigned a price tag by the market, thereby creating the perception that their significance and meaning to human life and the natural world are of equal value. As a result, the incessant production and consumption of *any* kind of commoditized product becomes the central and defining activity around which participants in a market society orient themselves. In their "Statement of Principles," the Vanderbilt Agrarians observe that consumption itself, however, is no true end. The industrial economy "never proposes a specific goal," they write; rather, "it initiates the infinite series."[24] Consequently, although "we have more time in which to consume, and many more products to be consumed," we nevertheless "pay the penalty in satiety and aimlessness."[25] In other words, the disregard of tangible distinc-

21. Korten describes the difference in this way: "Real wealth consists of those things that have actual utilitarian or artistic value: food, land, energy, knowledge, technology, forests, beauty, and much else . . . Money by contrast has no intrinsic utilitarian or artistic value. It is only a number on a piece of paper or an electronic trace in a computer file. It is an accounting chit that has value only because by social convention people are willing to accept it in exchange for things of real value" (*The Great Turning*, 68).

22. Ibid., 135–36. This is the sense in which Marx describes the character of a commodity as being "mystical" or "mysterious," because although "there is a physical relation between physical things . . . it is different with commodities. There, the existence of the things *qua* commodities . . . have no connection with their physical properties and with the material relations arising therefrom" (*Capital*, 43).

23. Schumacher, *Small Is Beautiful*, 47.

24. Twelve Southerners, *I'll Take My Stand*, xlviii.

25. Ibid., xlvi.

tions in a capitalist economy in lieu of increasing production/consumption at all costs results in a pervasive societal nihilism regarding the corporeal-material quality of everyday life.[26]

In her book, *Food Politics*, nutritionist Marion Nestle details the detrimental impact of the contemporary food industry[27] on human health. Although scientific nutritionists have consistently concluded that a healthy diet is based primarily on organic fruits, vegetables, and whole grains, the American population is increasingly confused about what and how to eat. The cause of this confusion, Nestle says, is the amount of public disinformation spread by food companies that would "have people believe that there is no such thing as a 'good' food (except when it is theirs); that there is no such thing as a 'bad' food (except when it is not theirs)" and that "all foods (especially theirs) can be incorporated into healthful diets."[28] The result of a commoditized food system, in other words, is the relativization of the nutritional *quality* of food choices. Moreover, despite the clear nutritional evidence linking a significant number of chronic diseases with over-eating, the percentage of the American public that is overweight—now over half—continues to grow. According to Nestle, the reason is clear: driven by the logic of profit accumulation by way of increasing the *quantity* of produc-

---

26. Economist Julie A. Nelson notes that because most economists view their "science" as entirely "objective" and "value-free," they intentionally avoid any criteria that might be seen as "subjective." Distinguishing between various goods, in other words, is viewed as a task that has no place in the structuring of economic life together. In a free market, they argue, "value judgments" are left to the sphere of private opinion or taste. As such, "concerns about the environment, the healthiness of consumption patterns, or the justness of the distribution of income have all been set aside, because these are concerns about which people sometimes disagree. Also set aside have been questions about the effects of corporate power, media advertising, histories of colonialism, problems of misinformation and dishonesty, and many other factors a thoughtful person might consider to be important in judging the performance of an economic system" (*Economics for Humans*, 23).

27. Nestle uses the term "food industry" to refer to "companies that produce, process, manufacture, sell, and serve foods, beverages, and dietary supplements. In a larger sense, the term encompasses the entire collection of enterprises involved in the production and consumption of food and beverages: producers and processors of food crops and animals (agribusiness); companies that make and sell fertilizer, pesticides, seeds, and feed; those that provide machinery, labor, real estate, and financial services to farmers; and others that transport, store, distribute, export, process, and market foods after they leave the farm. It also includes the food service sector—food carts, vending machines, restaurants, bars, fast-food outlets, schools, hospitals, prisons, and workplaces—and associate suppliers of equipment and serving materials" (*Food Politics*, 11).

28. Ibid., 21.

tion/consumption, the food industry intentionally promotes an environment in which people are pressured to over-eat. "Many of the nutritional
problems of Americans—not the least of them obesity—can be traced to
the food industry's imperative to encourage people to *eat more* in order to
generate sales and increase income in a highly competitive marketplace."[29]

One of the core fallacies of modern economic abstraction is the denial
of the primacy of land/nature in capitalistic production, which thereby "ig-
nores man's dependence on the natural world."[30] Rather than viewing the
soil, air, water, and the whole of living nature as fundamentally different
than a manufactured product to be bought and sold through the marketplace, the methodological presuppositions of capitalism treat the processes
and elements of nature as, at best, one potential commodity among others.
The problem, as Schumacher says, is that the natural world is not simply
one among a list of possible goods but rather the "essential precondition of
all human activity."[31] Daly and Cobb trace this methodological "fallacy of
misplaced concreteness," in part, to John Locke's view that economic value
is calculable only in relation to the amount and quality of human labor
expended on the land, a view that is based in the supposition that land/
nature does not play an active, contributing role in the determination of
economic value.[32] As Vandana Shiva writes, the view that nature is a passive
participant in production, however, is clearly naïve:

> Natural resources are produced and reproduced through a
> complex network of ecological processes. Nature is the world's
> dominant producer . . . the production of humus by forests, the
> regeneration of water resources, the natural evolution of genetic
> products, the creation of fertile soil from eroding rock . . . Human
> production, human creativity shrinks to insignificance in com-
> parison with nature.[33]

By continuing to ignore nature's productive capacities and by commoditizing its self-renewing resources—so that the resources of water and
soil become "private property" or "raw materials" that are valued only by
their market price—modern economics operates as if it were free from the
physical world. In fact, although economics is often criticized for being

29. Ibid., 4.
30. Schumacher, *Small is Beautiful*, 41.
31. Ibid., 48.
32. Daly and Cobb Jr., *For the Common Good*, 109–10.
33. Shiva, *Earth Democracy*, 16.

too materialistic, "in a deeper, philosophical sense, it is much more allied to idealism," Daly and Cobb argue, because "it neglects the land, and that means in general the physical basis of human existence."[34]

The treatment of the soil within modern, industrial agriculture is a prime example of the modern economy's idealistic—and profoundly dangerous—naiveté concerning the natural world. Looked at from an ecological perspective, the soil, as Wes Jackson says, is the "placenta" providing nourishment for all of earth's life forms.[35] The health of soil is so fundamentally important, according to Sir Albert Howard, that the vitality of plants, animals, humans, and entire civilizations depend upon it. In the pursuit of higher production yields, and therefore higher financial profits, however, modern agriculture has, until only quite recently, completely ignored the detrimental effects of soil compaction due to heavy machinery, soil loss from tillage, and soil ruination due to the use of chemicals and over-irrigation (salinization). The resulting worldwide destruction of soil fertility "on a colossal scale," Howard says, reveals just how unrealistic and ultimately impractical it is to allow the profit-motive to so wholly determine agricultural practices.

> Is profit to be the master? Is it to direct and tyrannize over the aims of the farmer? Is it to distort those aims and make them injure the farmers' way of living? Is it to be pushed even further and to make him forgetful of the conditions laid down for the cultivation of the earth's surface, so that he actually comes to defy those great natural laws which are the very foundation and origin of all that he attempts? If this is so, then the profit principle has outrun its usefulness: it has been dragged from its allotted niche in the world's economy, set on a high bar, and worshipped as a golden calf.[36]

One of the principal ways that the quite tangible human and ecological costs of an abstract economy are hidden is through the "externalization of costs," or what Berry calls the "false accounting" of a money-oriented economy. In our present economy, the success of businesses and corporations is due in large part to their ability to externalize, or pass along, as many of their production costs as possible. In other words, while owners of production extract innumerable goods from the commons and privatize them through various forms of enclosure, they simultaneously are allowed

---

34. *For the Common Good*, 105.

35. Jackson, *New Roots for Agriculture*, 10.

36. *Soil and Health*, 60.

to unload the massive human and ecological costs of production onto the public. Within the agricultural sector, for example, based on the logic of efficiency and economy of scale, a hog confinement operator stands to benefit economically by producing as many animal units within as compact a farm factory as possible. Unless limited by state regulations, he will not be financially responsible for the loss of neighboring farmers who are unable to compete, for the contamination of groundwater and streams, or the air pollution drifting off his operation, to say nothing of the suffering experienced by the confined hogs. The *true* costs of production include all such "externalities," but because producers are not always required to include them in their bottom lines, many of the worst social and ecological effects of the global economy remain hidden from the final market price.[37]

A related fallacy tied to modern economic abstraction, as both Schumacher and Daly have pointed out, is the idealistic belief in limitless economic growth. Proponents of unfettered capitalism continue to argue that there is no limit to the global economy's capacity to expand, both by extending the number of those "enjoying" first-world consumptive lifestyles and by continually "improving" standards of living with newer and "better" commodity goods. But "it does not require more than a simple act of insight," Schumacher asserts, "to realize that infinite growth of material consumption in a finite world is an impossibility."[38] The absolute dependence of modern, industrial societies on nonrenewable resources—coal, oil, and natural gas in particular—represents, perhaps, the most obvious limit to economic growth.[39] However, precisely because the market is unable to distinguish between different categories of goods—in this case, between

37. Food activist Frances Moore Lappé quotes French organic farmer Jean-Yves Griot, who responds to the common complaint that local, organic foods are often more expensive than the industrially produced, highly processed foods found at the grocery store. "Consumers don't realize we pay for our food not just once, but many times. We pay at the store, yes. But we pay again in taxes going to subsidies for the biggest producers, who don't need them. We pay a third time in the costs of pollution we endure from large farms destroying our soil, water, and air. Then we pay again in social services for those squeezed out by factory farms. And we pay again in the costs of urban crowding and sprawl. So, sure, you can say the price tag of our network's food is often a little higher—producing sustainably costs more in labor, for instance—but conventional foods are not really less expensive. It's just that their costs are hidden" (*Hope's Edge*, 222).

38. Schumacher, *Small Is Beautiful*, 114.

39. "Since the whole economy is based today on very large use of nonrenewable energy, especially oil, and since supplies of oil will be giving out within forty years, one of the most critical issues of land use is energy policy in this narrow and direct sense" (Daly and Cobb Jr., *For the Common Good*, 261).

renewable or nonrenewable resources—the economic fantasy of infinite growth continues to spur the unsustainable spread of lifestyles dependent upon industrial production around the globe. Ultimately, the industrial model of social and economic organization "does not fit into this world," Schumacher says, "because it contains within itself no limiting principle, while the environment in which it is placed is strictly limited."[40]

Modern industrial agriculture, of course, relies utterly on the steady supply of fossil fuels, in particular, natural gas and oil. Whereas traditional forms of agriculture were powered by solar energy, the farming methods initiated by the Green Revolution—including the heavy application of fertilizers, pesticides and herbicides to increase crop yields, and the use of large machinery to power massive monocrop farm operations and transport agricultural inputs and outputs—are all dependent on these two nonrenewable resources. As energy scholar Richard Heinberg says, the global food economy is "a method of using soil to turn petroleum and gas into food."[41] Every calorie of industrially produced food today, he points out, requires approximately ten calories of fossil-fuel inputs, and nearly 350 gallons of petroleum is needed to feed just one person in the United States each year.[42] As the era of cheap, readily accessible fossil-fuels comes to an end, the profoundly tangible and immediate question of how the global population is going to eat will be anything but an abstract concern.

The promise of the global economy is that the worldwide market coordination of self-interested actors will bring about the ongoing expansion of economic growth for the benefit all who participate in the logic of market exchange. The reality that an "awakened analysis" of our context (Herzog) discloses, however, is that the growth of financial wealth in the modern global economy is based in the ongoing destruction of the real wealth of the earth and her many creatures. From the perspective of an affirmation of God's holiness, an economy rooted in the abstraction of monetary wealth from corporeal-material realities stands against the nature of God's

---

40. Ibid., 27. Schumacher was quite prescient about the global political implications of the worldwide peak of oil supply. As he wrote in 1973, "the oil crisis will come, not when all the world's oil is exhausted, but when world oil supplies cease to expand. If this point is reached . . . when industrialization will have spread right across the globe and the underdeveloped countries have had their appetite for a higher standard of living thoroughly whetted . . . what else could be the result but an intense struggle for oil supplies, even a violent struggle" (121).

41. Heinberg, "Fifty Million Farmers."

42. Ibid., 7.

enfleshed love. Whenever Christians join together to share in the elements of agro-industrial meals, therefore, they do so as participants in an unholy communion marked by falsity and transgression.

Holistic Communion: Integration of Economic Activities into Earthly Realities

If Holy Communion, in faithful devotion to the Father/Mother, is wholly integrated life together, how are worshippers to participate in the enfleshed love of God in the midst of an economy based upon the transgressive abstractions of self-love? In particular, in an agro-economy in which the bodily health of the earth and her manifold creatures are sacrificed at the altar of financial accumulation, how are Christians faithfully to consume the body and blood of Jesus, which the Father/Mother has provided that we might, through the Holy Spirit, embody what we have received? Those striving to worship the Father/Mother are being called today to participate in integrated modes of economic life together that promote the earthly flourishing of the world God so loves. Specifically, this will mean the involvement of Christians in the emergence of a more integrated food economy, in which the production and consumption of our "daily bread" and "common cup" is grounded in the limits and needs of creaturely existence on earth.

By working to integrate all of our economic activities into the ecological realities of life on earth, Christians embrace the bodily-material nature of creaturely existence and the terrestrial unity that exists within every part of God's creation. Whether we acknowledge it or not, the human economy is only a sub-economy within what Wendell Berry calls "the Great Economy."[43] The Great Economy encompasses the whole of God's created world, of which human beings are but a part. From the Great Economy, we receive a near infinite fund of goods necessary for the sustenance of life—e.g., healthy soil filled with micro-organisms, minerals, earthworms, insects, and decaying plant material; fresh water stored in lakes, rivers, and aquifers; plants bearing fruits, nuts, grains, medicines, flowers, and more; weather systems regulating temperatures and distributing and recycling moisture. Not only does nature nourish and sustain human life, but as creatures formed from the "dust of the earth" (Gen 2), human beings are themselves an inextricable part of the fabric of nature. "You and I don't end at our fingertips or skin," as David Suzuki has written. "We are connected

43. Berry, "Two Economies," 54–75.

through air, water and soil . . . We are quite literally air, water, soil, energy, and other living creatures."[44] In this sense, the aim of achieving greater harmony between our human economy and the Great Economy is not only the health of nature but the flourishing of human life as well. In the midst of an industrial economy based upon a parasitic ravaging of the natural world, the participation of Christians in sustaining, integrated modes of economic life is a participation in the incarnate holiness of God the Father/Mother.

Recognizing that we human beings are only one part of the broader and more complex economy of creation entails affirming our true status as finite creatures fashioned by the Father/Mother. According to Bonhoeffer, this is one of the key themes of the second creation narrative in Genesis. God's placement of the Tree of Life in the middle of the garden, he says, reflects the natural orientation of human beings toward the Creator at the center of all creation. By placing the source of life at the center of human existence and simultaneously establishing it as a boundary not to be transgressed, God offered humanity the freedom to live as creatures. To be a creature is to have one's life originate from outside oneself and to live within the limits of finitude. Only God is properly capable of existing at the center as the infinite and limitless source of life. Humanity's fall from paradise begins with the refusal to be a limited creature and the desire to be "like God" (Gen 3:5) at the center of reality. By transgressing the boundary, which God had given as a gift, humanity places itself in the middle of creation, with no boundaries to limit desires or behavior. The rebellion of humanity thereby leads to the destruction of our creaturehood, for we are not fashioned to live from out of our own finite resources. "And in all this," Bonhoeffer recognized, "it is not merely a moral lapse but the destruction of creation by the creature," for "the extent of the fall is such that it affects the whole created world."[45] The salvation of human beings, then, along with that of creation, entails our being placed back into our natural state as finite creatures oriented toward a source of life that flows from outside ourselves. God the Father/Mother saves us from our transgressive choice to be "like God" by giving us Jesus Christ in the flesh, who is the true center and source of our lives and the whole of creation.

By situating our economic activities within the limits and requirements of earthly existence, we thereby acknowledge our creaturely finitude, accept that humanity is not at the center of creation, and affirm that the

44. Quoted in Wirzba, *The Paradise of God*, 93.
45. Bonhoeffer, *Creation and Fall*, 120.

Great Economy—i.e., the Tree of Life—is the focal source through which God offers life for all. Those who begin with the recognition that our human economy exists within the bio-physical framework of a closed ecosystem will therefore strive toward what Herman Daly calls a "steady-state" economy. In such an economy, the total input of material resources and energy into an economy and the total output of waste materials and heat do not exceed the regenerative and absorptive capacities of the biosphere. A truly sustainable economy, as Daly says, requires mechanisms that internalize rather than externalize the full costs of production, distribution, and consumptive use to ensure we do not extract more from the earth's "natural capital"—the primary source of all wealth—than we put back.[46] The paradox is that as we respect the regenerative needs of the earth's biosphere and place appropriate limits upon our economy activities, we allow the Great Economy to serve as the perpetual source of everything humans need for the flourishing of our earthly lives. "By understanding accurately his proper place in Creation," as Berry says, "man may be made whole."[47]

An economy driven by self-centered love rather than the perfect love of God is based in a fundamental distortion of reality. As Schumacher observed, greed obstructs "the power of seeing things as they really are, of seeing things in their roundness and wholeness."[48] This is why abstraction represents the death of authentic religious life, as Southern Agrarian writer Alan Tate claimed. A truly religious perspective, he wrote, is concerned with the "whole horse," that is, with the entirety of any particular created being or object within its natural environs. By contrast, the modern economic perspective sees only "half of the horse," in particular those aspects that can be quantified, measured, and put to work for financially profitable ends. Such "half-religionists," as Tate calls the purveyors of the modern economic mindset, simply ignore whatever does not fit into their narrow worldview, including the destructive consequences of their myopia. The truly religious mind, he says, "wants the whole horse, and it will be satisfied with nothing less."[49] Whereas "the Devil's work is abstraction—not the love of material things, but the love of their quantities,"[50] as Berry says, the holy

---

46. See Daley, "Economics in a Full World."

47. Berry, *Unsettling of America*, 98.

48. Schumacher, *Small Is Beautiful*, 29.

49. Twelve Southerners, *I'll Take My Stand*, 157.

50. Berry, *Gift of Good Land*, 278.

work of God the Father/Mother is the incarnation of love in the whole of reality for the flourishing of creaturely life on earth.

Those rooted in a vision of the perfect love of God the Father/Mother will seek to participate in modes of production and consumption that affirm the significance of the whole plant rather than whatever parts might be divided up and sold for profit; the whole community of organisms that constitute healthy soil rather than just the inorganic chemical fertilizers that can be applied to boost short term production gains; the whole living agroecosystem of soil, air, waterways, wildlife habitat, plants, and livestock instead of whatever external inputs are required to produce a financially profitable growing season; the whole farmer in the fullness of his or her familial, social, spiritual, intellectual, and vocational person rather than only those work hours that contribute to the bottom line; and the whole countryside of fields, forests, streams, farmland, rural communities, and native cultural histories rather than simply general characteristics of the land that might be calculated to determine the comparative advantage of producing a single monocrop throughout an agro-region.

A sustaining, integrated economy aligned with the enfleshed nature of divine love is therefore centered on the concrete use-value of real goods and services rather than the abstract exchange-value of commoditized products. While the exchange-value of a product is determined by whatever monetary return it might achieve in the market, use-value is determined by a product's socially recognizable usefulness in fostering human and environmental well-being. Use-value is material, concrete, and sensuous; exchange-value is abstract, immaterial, and discarnate. In this sense, economic activity oriented toward the nurture of earthly life is focused primarily upon the sustainable production and equitable distribution of material goods and services necessary for creaturely well-being: food, clothing, shelter, medicine, as well as tangible opportunities for fellowship, creativity, and the development of diverse human capabilities. In an economy in which the value of a product is determined solely by the financial amount gained through market exchange, goods and services, that have no use-value but are unnecessary or even detrimental to human flourishing are valued often much higher than these human goods. In such an economy, for example, it is possible for an abstract financial instrument like a grain hedge fund or derivative, which does not nourish human life, to attain greater value in the agricultural marketplace than the farmer's labor or the grain itself. The result is an unholy misuse of individual and social energies toward ends that cannot satisfy, because they controvert the bodily-material nature of human existence and the incarnate nature of God's holiness.

It is not an accident that sustainable agriculture constitutes the vibrant center of emerging economic alternatives to the abstract modern economy. Organic, whole foods that are produced in ways that nourish the farmland, the farmer, and the consumer are real goods that foster creaturely well-being. The use-value of a chemical-free apple is tangibly evident in its natural beauty, tastefulness, and nutritional sustenance. The real wealth of organically rich soil, bio-diverse farmland mixed with wildlife habitat, and strong rural communities is visibly apparent. Moreover, the enjoyment of selecting locally grown fruits, vegetables, herbs, meats, and flowers at an outdoor farmer's market, while intermingling with town residents, children, and civic leaders, is palpable. Supporting the emergence of sustainable agriculture as an alternative to the abstractive modern agroeconomy is therefore a crucial way for Christians to participate in the enfleshed nature of God's love in and for the world.

In an integrated economy centered on the sustainable production and consumption of goods for the sake of human well-being, qualitative value is as important an indicator of economic health as quantitative value. When economic well-being is determined solely by the total amount of goods and services produced and consumed, distinctions concerning the quality of those goods and services are leveled. In an economy oriented toward the sustenance of the earth and all its creatures, however, the key question is no longer simply "how can we produce, market, and sell the greatest number of commodities for the highest possible financial return?" Instead, questions related to the qualitative properties of products and the manner in which they were produced become equally significant. Is this product healthy for human bodies? Can this product be produced and distributed in harmony with nature? Is this product well made, such that it will not be hastily thrown away before necessary? Is it biodegradable? Can the workers involved in the production, distribution, and sale of this product do their work without suffering harm? What are the impacts of certain goods or services upon the local communities and bioregions in which they are produced and sold? Making the transition toward a more integrated, sustainable economy does not necessarily require eliminating markets, the exchange of goods, or the use of currencies. Rather, the driving aim of economic life shifts from an exclusive focus upon increasing short-term, abstract financial value to a more holistic promotion of such qualitative goods as neighborly communities, meaningful work with others, the humane treatment of other creatures, clean water, well-crafted, beautiful products, and healthy children. Bodily-material goods such as these are tangible manifestations of the enfleshed love of God in Jesus Christ and the Holy Spirit.

The distinction that Christians are called upon to make in their economic lives, then, is not between materialism and spirituality, but between true and false forms of materialism. Clerical and denominational pronouncements that warn against the dangers of "rampant materialism," as if materiality itself were a spiritual threat, therefore, only serve to conceal the problem of an abstract economy that feeds upon the destruction of the earth and her manifold creatures. What are needed are forms of Christian materialism that can be used, as Bonhoeffer says, "against the worldly in the name of a better worldliness."[51] The reality, however, is that most Christians are not earthly enough, as Berry argues.

> Apparently because our age is so manifestly unconcerned for the life of the spirit, many people conclude that it places an undue value on material things. But that cannot be so, for people who valued material things would take care of them and would care for the sources of them. We could argue that an age that properly valued and cared for material things would be an age properly spiritual . . . The so-called materialism of our own time is, by contrast, at once indifferent to spiritual concerns and insatiably destructive of the material world.[52]

Berry points to holiness-communitarian traditions like the Amish as models of Christianity that practice the "right kind of materialism." As a dissident sect forced from their native homeland, often upon unwanted lands with poor soil, the Amish have used farming practices like crop rotation, diversification, the use of manure, and the planting of nitrogen-rich legumes, all of which have led to improved soil structure and health, enhanced water-holding capacity, and increased fertility. Their love for God and one another is thereby enfleshed in the materiality of the world through their care for the land and production of life-serving goods for human wellbeing.

The enfleshment of love in the materiality of the world is true worship of God the Father/Mother. Specifically in our economic lives, we honor the One who nourishes our bodies in Jesus Christ and the Holy Spirit by

51. Bonhoeffer, *Ethics,* 60.

52. Berry, "Preserving Wildness," 144–45.

presenting our daily lives as concrete offerings of love—in the way we work, in the goods we produce, and in the products and services we consume. Religion in this sense, as Berry says, is thus less something "to be celebrated in rituals than practiced in the world."[53] Those involved in the sustainable production and provisioning of healthy, whole foods offer perhaps the most direct model of worshipful lives given over for the sustenance for others and the nourishment of the earth. Their daily actions of soil care, water conservation, skilled animal husbandry, and the harvesting of fruits, vegetables, herbs, and grains are a clear remembrance of the body and blood of Jesus, given by the Father/Mother for the sustainment of our earthly wellbeing.

Conclusion

The Father/Mother invites us to the feast of abundant life together in which the divine love is enfleshed as health-giving food for every body. In Jesus Christ and the Holy Spirit, the holiness of God our Parent is given to us as wholly incarnate nourishment for our earthly well-being. In the midst of an unholy economy rooted in the abstract and transgressive orientation of self-centered love, those who seek to worship the Father/Mother in spirit and truth are called today to participate in the divine work of embodying truth by integrating all of our economic activities into the rhythms and limits of creaturely existence. By engaging in the production, distribution, and consumption of real goods and services that foster the flourishing of the earth and her many creatures, Christians faithfully participate in the divine holiness gathering all things together in perfect love. Holy Communion is wholly integrated life together in which all are made whole. Held together in the enfleshed nature of God's love, including especially the ways we prepare and provide food for one another, we present our bodies as living sacrifices that are holy and acceptable to God our Father/Mother.

---

53. Berry, "Christianity and the Survival of Creation," 102.

4

The Triune God Arranges Guests as Companions

GOD THE FATHER/MOTHER, SON, and Holy Spirit arranges the dinner guests as companions around the feast of life. As a divine fellowship of co-equal persons, the triune God gathers together a community of servants, each one assisting another for the sake of the common good. God's holiness is God's perfect love, and in the fullness of divine love, all things are made whole. Within the fellowship of local assemblies, the holiness of the Father/Mother, Son, and Holy Spirit is shared as *mutual love*, through which members are empowered to upbuild a more neighborly life together. Faithful acceptance of God's invitation to participate in Holy Communion, then, includes faithfully conforming ourselves to the Holy Trinity by loving our neighbors as ourselves with mutual affection. "Each of us must please our neighbor for the good purpose of building up the neighbor" (Rom 15:2). Holy Communion, patterned after the triune God, is wholly cooperative life together.

But how are members of local congregations to participate in the mutual love of God in the midst of an economy shaped by the oppressive compulsions of self-oriented love? Disjoined from the depth and breadth of God's love, self-love inevitably results in injustice and oppression, for the selfish individual is inherently motivated to supercede his neighbors in amassing more power, wealth, and status. Modern economic life is thus marked by an imbalanced social dynamic in which the ongoing centralization of corporate and state power in the name of "modernization," "efficiency," and "economies of scale" undermines local, egalitarian forms of governance. Within the modern food economy, in particular, the consolidation of control by fewer and fewer transnational agribusiness corporations over the means and methods of production and the processes of distribution has resulted in the erosion of local, public, and democratic food economies. In this context, conforming to the mutual love of the triune God in economic life—and thus participating more fully in the divine holiness—will include building up local food economies in which monetary and political power is justly shared in cooperative, neighborly communities.

The Wholly Mutual Love of the Triune God

The holiness of God revealed in Jesus Christ as grace, present in the Holy Spirit as conviviality, and given from the Father/Mother in the flesh is shared among the triune persons in mutual love. Although each of the three persons engages in the holy work of perfect love in distinctive ways, there is no hierarchy within the divine fellowship ranking the different operations of love accomplished by the Father/Mother, Son, and Holy Spirit. The inclusive love manifest in Jesus Christ as the way that leads to peace is no more and no less important than the harmonizing love of the Holy Spirit that nurtures bonds of relational health. Similarly, the incarnate love sent from the Father/Mother for the flourishing of the earthly creation is neither a lesser nor a greater demonstration of the perfect love of God than the charitable works of the other two persons. For in God, as Moltmann writes, "there is no one-sided relationship of superiority and subordination, command and obedience, master and servant." Rather, "in the triune God is the mutuality and the reciprocity of love."[1] God the Father/Mother, Son and Holy Spirit is a holy fellowship of partners engaged in different yet co-equal works of love.

Not only are the distinct operations of God's love commensurate but also each of the divine persons participates in the holy work of the other two in mutually supportive ways. Bound up within the gracious love of Jesus Christ for all people is the love of the Father/Mother who sent the Son to enflesh divine holiness for our sake in the power of the Holy Spirit. The Son, whose earthly ministry is infused with the convivial energies of the Holy Spirit, departs to allow the Father to send the Spirit of life. The love of the Father/Mother is enfleshed, of course, through the participation of Jesus Christ and the Holy Spirit in their being sent for and with us. The operations of love distinctive to each of the divine persons are not isolatable,

---

1. Moltmann, *God in Creation*, 16–17.

therefore, as if the divine persons worked in private seclusion from one another. Rather, the triune God is a cooperative of mutual servanthood. The Father/Mother and Son assist with the convivial love of the Holy Spirit; the Son and the Holy Spirit support the enfleshed love of the Father/Mother; and the Holy Spirit and the Father/Mother aid in the gracious love of the Son. "What we are looking at here," as Moltmann says, "are the threefold relationships of the Son, the Father and the Spirit, and the reciprocal trinitarian efficacies in God, which are multiple in kind."[2] The holiness of the God who *is* love is shared in the mutuality of the divine life together.

Because God does not withhold any aspect of the divine holiness from us, the mutual love of God shared in the triune fellowship is therefore also present within God's works of holiness in the world. The Father/Mother, Son, and Holy Spirit, in their distinct operations of love, simultaneously work together to upbuild communities of mutuality. Wherever God is active in the world, members of the creation are gathered together in assemblies resembling the cooperative, mutual love of the triune God. In other words, God's holiness is not operative in the world apart from the formation of assembled communities marked by mutual self-giving.

In Jesus Christ, the holiness of God's mutual love is operative in his gracious inclusion of those cut off from the bonds of fellowship into a congregational life together with others. In between the time of his ascension and his return in the coming kingdom of God, Jesus Christ reveals the gracious way of inclusive love in and as the church community. As Bonhoeffer affirms, "the New Testament knows a form of revelation, 'Christ existing as church-community.'"[3] As particular churches receive and participate faithfully in the justifying grace of Jesus Christ, congregational life is the social sphere in which the ongoing revelation of Jesus Christ as the way that makes for peace takes place. This is why "to be in Christ," as Bonhoeffer says, "is synonymous with to be in the church-community."[4] The divine ministry of reconciliation, which is Christ's ministry for us and for all, does not happen in an asocial manner. Reconciliation happens as the excluded are graciously welcomed into the life of "Christ existing as 'church-community.'" In this way, the mutual love of the triune God is intrinsically operative in the gracious love of Jesus Christ *pro me* and for all people.

2. Moltmann, *The Spirit of Life*, 71.

3. Bonhoeffer, *Sanctorum Communio*, 141.

4. Ibid., 140.

Similarly, the presence of the convivial love of the Holy Spirit in the world is inevitably marked by the assembling of diverse others into communities of cooperation and mutuality. "The church is present," as Moltmann says, "wherever the manifestation of the Spirit (1 Cor 12:7) takes place."[5] We experience the spiritual flourishing of our lives, not in isolation from community, but in harmonious life together with others. In community, those who have been divided from one another are sanctified and made whole. The therapeutic love of the Holy Spirit is operative, moreover, not only between human beings but among the whole of creation as well. "The church participates in the uniting of men with one another, in the uniting of society with nature and in the uniting of creation with God," Moltmann writes. "Wherever unions like this take place, however fragmentary and fragile they may be, there is the church."[6] The bonds of convivial *koinonia* within which the Spirit is present in the world thus congregate human and non-human creatures into assemblies resembling the mutual love of the triune God.

The enfleshed love of the Father/Mother, who sends Jesus Christ and the Holy Spirit for the sake of our earthly flourishing, is also given to us in the form of ecclesial life together. The church is the *body* of Christ. "Christ is for us," as Bonhoeffer says, "not only in his word and his attitude toward us, but in his bodily life," and following the ascension, "the body of Christ is his church-community."[7] The Father/Mother lovingly sustains our creaturely lives on earth by giving us a concrete community within which we receive gracious acceptance and belonging. The holiness of God our Heavenly Parent is not unavailable, unreachable for us. "It is there, at hand, accessible, existing"[8] in the real presence of visible, tangible communities of Jesus Christ. Likewise, the Holy Spirit is active in and between the *members* of the church body. The church is a community made up of real human beings who are woven together by the convivial love of the Spirit. Within the holy fellowship of the Spirit, as Moltmann says, "the *congregatio sanctorum* is the 'assembly,' the 'congregation,' 'Christian people,' who live in mutual concern for one another and mutual self-giving."[9] Through the holy operations of Jesus Christ and the Holy Spirit enfleshed in communities of

---

5. Moltmann, *The Church in the Power of the Spirit*, 65.

6. Ibid.

7. Bonhoeffer, *Discipleship*, 217.

8. Bonhoeffer, *Act and Being*, 103.

9. Moltmann, *Church in the Power of the Holy Spirit*, 314.

mutual charity, the Father/Mother's love is given for the sake of our earthly flourishing.

The mutual love of the Father/Mother, Son and Holy Spirit is present-ed to us, then, in the immediate form of our *neighbor*. We are welcomed into the social body of gracious congregations by particular brothers and sisters. We are incorporated into the spiritual fellowship of particular communities as individual members share their lives with and for us. Our physical lives are nurtured through countless acts of material kindness and love offered to us by others. The church formed from the mutual love of the triune God is therefore not a general social reality. We do not receive the gracious, convivial, and enfleshed love of God through remote encounters with the institution of the church or an idea of ecclesial existence. We are included, connected, and sustained by the specific neighbors we encounter in a particular local community existing in a concrete time and place. As Bonhoeffer writes:

> Who is God? Not in the first place an abstract belief in God . . . That is not a genuine experience of God, but a partial extension of the world. Encounter with Jesus Christ. The experience that a transformation of all human life is given in the fact that "Jesus is there only for others." His "being there for others" is the experi-ence of his transcendence . . . Faith is participation in this being of Jesus. Our relation to God is not a "religious" relationship to the highest, the most powerful, and best Being imaginable . . . but our relation to God is a new life in "existence for others," through par-ticipation in the being of Jesus. The transcendental is not infinite and unattainable tasks, but the neighbor who is within reach in any given situation. God in human form.[10]

We encounter the holiness of the triune God, whose love is shared through an eternal mutuality of self-giving, in direct encounters with the neighbors in our midst.

If the mutual love of the Father/Mother, Son, and Holy Spirit is shared with us in the form of cooperative fellowship with our neighbors, then sin is active in the *unjust hoarding* of resources by an individual or group. Hoard-ing is unholy for it destroys genuine community. The self-oriented sinner focuses not upon the upbuilding of his neighbor but on his own aggran-dizement. Neighborly regard cannot last in the face of an unjust distribu-tion of resources, for those with greater power inevitably assume a stance of

10. Bonhoeffer, *Letters & Papers*, 381.

inherent, deserved superiority, thereby breeding resentment and jealousy among the less powerful. Even more, the unjust hoarding of resources, resulting in an unbalanced accumulation of power, allows for the *oppression* of the powerless by the powerful. Hoarded power inherently leads to *power over* another. The other becomes someone to be used, coerced, and exploited for one's own purposes. She is no longer a fellow neighbor, someone I am given to serve, but a faceless means toward self-centered ends. In this state, the oppressor has set himself outside the sphere of the mutual love of God. As Jacob Boehme describes, the soul so cut off from the charitable will of God is filled with a lust "to be mighty, great and dominant, to subjugate all things to itself, and to rule with control." Such a one despises humility and equality and is overtaken by such a possessiveness that "the noble love of the soul [is] brought low."[11] Whereas the holiness of the triune God fosters reciprocal relationships of giving and receiving, the unholy compulsions of the self-oriented sinner are oriented only toward what he can coerce from another for the upbuilding of himself.

Wherever the sin of unjust hoarding and the resulting dynamics of oppression are present, the holiness of the triune God *uplifts the lowly* and *brings down the mighty*. Precisely because God's intention for everyone is to share in the mutual love of the triune fellowship, the divine holiness actively re-establishes co-equal bonds of neighborly esteem in the midst of situations of injustice and oppression. Those possessed by the drive to hoard resources unjustly and wield power over others experience the love of the triune God as a condemnation upon the unholy accumulation of goods. The word of God that "the first shall be last" (Matt 20:16) is received as an unwelcome threat of judgment. The oppressed experience the mutual love of God as empowerment to claim equal status with others and to enjoy a just sharing of resources and governance. Here, the divine word that "the last shall be first" (20:16) is received as a great promise of liberation and justice. Ultimately, however, the charitable purposes of God are not simply to reverse roles such that the oppressor becomes oppressed and the oppressed becomes oppressor. The true aim of divine holiness is to upbuild not cycles of domination and retribution but communities of reciprocal respect and mutual service.

Faithfully responding to God's invitation to "be holy as I am holy," therefore, means conforming to the triune God by joining with and being for our neighbors in the upbuilding of concrete communities of mutual

---

11. Boehme, *The Way to Christ*, 229.

service. "Life in God means gathering," as Eberhard Arnold affirms. The will of God is that we be knit together in an "organic unity composed of many members who are committed to one another and support one another."[12] In the Spirit, we participate in the mutual love of God by intentionally assembling *with* our neighbors to share in a life of reciprocal service. "We must perceive one another in the Holy Spirit," as Christoph Friedrich Blumhardt says, "so that we can serve one another even as we let ourselves be served." For just as God asks us to serve others as often as possible, he says, "just so, at another point, he asks you to let yourself be served—even by a person you may consider beneath you" in order that you "might learn to regard the other person as higher than yourself."[13] So, too, we follow in the gracious way of Jesus Christ by being *for* one another in communities of mutual support. A Christian comes into being and abides within Christ's holy church, Bonhoeffer says, as "one person bears the other in active love, intercession, and forgiveness of sins." This "being-for-each-other" is constitutive of Christ's church existing as "the community of love."[14] We participate in the enfleshed love given from the Father/Mother, moreover, as we assemble "with-each-other" and "for-each-other" in concrete, bodily ways. We are called to gather with one another in the mutual love of God not in abstraction but in the flesh, just as we are called to be for one another with our physical bodies, our material possessions, and throughout the entirety of our earthly lives. As we enter into the work of upbuilding fellowships that so resemble the mutual love of the Father/Mother, Son, and Holy Spirit, we are joining in the divine holiness working to make all things whole.

Similarly, by working to ensure that power and honor is shared equally in our congregational life together, we more closely conform ourselves to the reciprocal love of the triune God. In the community of Jesus Christ, given to us by the Father/Mother, *all* members are graced by the Holy Spirit with particular gifts for the upbuilding of the whole body. For "to each is given the manifestation of the Spirit for the common good" (1 Cor 12:7). No one member is of greater or lesser importance to the spiritual wellbeing of the community. In fact, "the members of the body that seem to be weaker are [just as] indispensable" (12:22) as the more prominent members, for "God has so arranged the body" (12:24) that "members may have the same care for one another" (12:25). There is no act of Christic love for one's

---

12. Arnold in Yoder, *God's Revolution*, 111, 113.

13. Christoph Blumhardt, in Blumhardt and Blumhardt, *Thy Kingdom Come*, 54.

14. Bonhoeffer, *Sanctorum Communio*, 191.

neighbor that could be ranked below that of another's. There is no form of charitable gathering in the Spirit with a brother or sister that is more crucial to upbuilding of the body than any other. Not only a select few, but "every Christian," as Philip Jacob Spener insists, "is bound not only to offer himself and what he has" but also to engage in the study of scripture, to teach others, and "to chastise, exhort, convert, and edify" other members of the church community. The church "is too weak without the help of the universal priesthood," he writes, since one person "is incapable of doing all that is necessary for the edification of the many."[15] As each member actively receives the power of priesthood and offers love, guidance, and edification for her neighbors, the fellowship of the church is built up more and more into conformity with the triune God.

In situations of oppression caused by the sinful hoarding of resources, we participate in the mutual love of God by empowering those who are oppressed and admonishing those who have accumulated an unjust balance of power. We join in the holiness of God at work in the world by entering into situations of oppression and by joining in solidarity with the poor and marginalized in their struggles for a more just and equal distribution of power and resources. "God needs to have one of his children in every hell," as Christoph Friedrich Blumhardt writes, in every place of powerlessness and abandonment, "because it is only through them that he can enter that hell in order to bring it to an end."[16] To the oppressors, those who wield their hoarded power over others as masters and lords, we pronounce the holy word of God as we unmask the dishonest means they have used to accumulate power and wealth and as we call them to give up their power over others for the sake of a more egalitarian, fraternal society. Though "the form of this admonition will have to vary depending on the individual sinner," as Bonhoeffer says, it is "with gentleness that the defiant must be disciplined" for the goal is always that of "leading the sinner to repentance and reconciliation."[17] For in the end, we strive, through the power of God's holiness, to uplift the lowly and to bring down the mighty for the upbuilding of neighborly relationships of mutual service.

To summarize: God's holiness is God's perfect love, and in the operations of the Father/Mother, Son, and Holy Spirit, the perfect love of the triune God is shared as wholly reciprocal and egalitarian love, which is

15. Spener, *Pia Desideria*, 94.

16. Christoph Blumhardt, in Blumhardt and Blumhardt, *Thy Kingdom Come*, 169.

17. Bonhoeffer, *Discipleship*, 289.

directed toward the upbuilding of the neighbor. The unholy nature of self-consumed love is manifest in the unjust hoarding of power and resources by an elite few, which inevitably leads to oppression. God's holiness makes whole, and in situations of injustice and oppression, the persons of the triune God work to uplift the lowly and bring down the mighty so that all might equally share in a just use of power and resources. We faithfully participate in the divine holiness by conforming to the Holy Trinity through concrete expressions of love, support, and admonishment shared with and for one another.

The Wholly Cooperative Communion Meal

Holy Communion, in conformity to the triune God, is wholly cooperative life together. The mutual nature of divine love is shared by the triune God that we might be holy as God is holy in our assembled existence with others. Faithfully to accept God's invitation to Holy Communion is to participate in a congregational way of life that shares power and resources equitably. This is the way that directs us to serve the neighbor in our immediate midst, for egalitarian life together depends upon concrete acts of edification offered with and for another. All this is shared with us in the Holy Communion meal, within which the triune God arranges us as co-equal companions and to which we are invited as participants.

In his farewell address, delivered during his final meal with the disciples, Jesus describes the cooperative work of divine love he shares in with the Father/Mother and Holy Spirit. Jesus emphasizes that he has been sent by the Father to share the love of God in and for the world. Although Jesus fulfills the particular work he is given to do, he affirms that he does not act alone, "because the Father is with me" (John 16:32). In fact, Jesus makes clear that even the act of communication is not entirely his own, for "I do not speak on my own," he says, "but the Father who dwells in me does his works" (14:10). Jesus thus gives glory to the Father by accomplishing the enfleshment of divine love, just as the Father glorifies the Son in his accomplishment (17:4–5). Moreover, in his departure from this world, Jesus acts in concert with the Father/Mother and Spirit, for his return to the Father/Mother allows for the sending of the Holy Spirit to be our ever-present Advocate and guide (16:7). The Spirit, likewise, does not work alone, for "he will not speak on his own," Jesus says, "but will speak whatever he hears" (16:13) in reminding us of all that Jesus has revealed to us about the nature of divine love. The mutual work of the Father/Mother, Son, and Holy Spirit is thus shared with us as a living reality. "The glory that you have given me," Jesus says to the Father/Mother, "I have given them, so that they may be one, as we are one" and may know that "you . . . have loved them even as you have loved me." (17:22–23). In the context of sharing his final meal with the disciples, Jesus shares with them a tangible depiction of the cooperative nature of God's love.

The meal gathering is one of the primary spheres in which social rankings are established. Both in terms of who is invited to share in particular meals and the arrangement of seating assignments, table fellowships embody the similarities and differences of status that exist within a society. The social context in which Jesus' ministry took place was no different. A typical banquet meal in the ancient world would have begun with the host creating a guest list and sending invitations prior to the evening gathering. As guests arrived, a servant would lead them to the dining room where additional servants removed their shoes, washed their feet, and offered a basin of water for hand washing. The host would have been responsible for assigning the seating arrangements for guests upon their arrival, with the highest position at the table given to the guest of honor and the other diners placed to his right according to their rank in society. Those who sat in the most prominent seats, in fact, often enjoyed finer and more copious amounts of food. According to Dennis Smith, the meal banquet thus served not only to mirror but also to establish social rankings in society at large. "Individuals were to be judged as to their relative status according to their age, political office, or some other similar distinction," he writes. "Such distinctions and honors were considered essential to the makeup of cultured society, and the banquet normally functioned within society to buttress its view of status."[18] Throughout his ministry, Jesus places great emphasis upon the roles and arrangements we establish at our meal gatherings, precisely because where someone is seated at the meal table, if she is seated at all, demonstrates clearly how much power and honor a society deems she is worthy to receive.

In his instructions concerning seating arrangements and table roles, Jesus reveals that the holiness of God's mutual love is shared in humble service to others. In the context of a dispute among the disciples about who deserves to sit next to Lord Jesus, the guest of honor in the coming messianic banquet, James and John disclose their sinful understanding of

18. Smith, *From Symposium to Eucharist*, 57.

greatness as the attainment of power and status over others. In his response, Jesus overturns the expected social hierarchies performed around the meal table. Not only are the disciples instructed, as they are elsewhere, that "when you are invited by anyone to a wedding feast" to not "sit down in a place of honor" but rather to "go and sit in the lowest place" (Luke 14:8–10); even more, they are told that "whoever wishes to be first among you must be a slave (*diakonos*) of all" (Mark 10:44). Since *diakonos* is a technical term for table service, Jesus reveals here that true greatness involves taking upon oneself the role of the table servant—the one who greets guests with warm welcome, walks them to the dining room, washes their feet, and serves the meal. "For who is greater, the one who reclines at table, or the one who serves? Is it not the one who reclines at table? But I am among you as one who serves" (Luke 22:27). Here, Jesus provides a concrete description— concurrent with the gracious nature of the incarnate love he shares with the disciples—of just how one is to "love your neighbor as yourself" (Mark 12:31). The call to discipleship, to life in the Spirit, to true worship of the Father/Mother, is an invitation to assume the holy role of serving others in conformity to the mutual love of the triune God.

Jesus conversely admonishes those who wield accumulated power by assuming seats of elevated status over others. He warns his disciples to "beware of the yeast"—that is the table practices—of the religious elites and rulers of imperial power (Mark 8:15). It is these who "like to walk around in long robes, and love to be greeted with respect in the market-places, and to have the best seats in the [assemblies] and places of honor at banquets" (Luke 20:46). Jesus unmasks the inherent connection between the dynamics of unequal power and the oppression of the weak, for it is those who strive to be exalted over others, he says, who are responsible for the devouring of what rightfully belongs to another (20:47). Nowhere is the relationship of centralized power to exploitation and violence more evident than in Herod's birthday feast. As Rome's proxy king of Palestine, Herod's coercive reign was marked by the rebuilding of the Temple in dedication to Augustus, which both solidified his status among the wealthy priestly class and drove the majority of the exploited population—who owed tribute to Rome, taxes to Herod, and tithes to the Temple—deep into poverty.[19] On the occasion of his birthday, Herod seized the opportunity to silence one of the more vocal critics of his abusive reign by presenting John the Baptist's head on a platter to the banquet participants (Matt 14:1–11). By assur-

---

19. See Horsley, *Jesus and Empire*, 31–34.

ing his listeners that those who so "lord it over" others (Luke 22:25) will "receive the greater condemnation" (20:47)—for "all who exalt themselves will be humbled" (Matt 23:12)—Jesus admonishes all who assume seats of hoarded power that they are operating far outside the holy realm of God's mutual love.

We are invited to live our common life in conformity with the co-operative love of the triune God by mutually serving one another in our meal practices together. In the context of the last supper he shares with his disciples, Jesus acts the part of table *host*, procuring a furnished room and arranging food preparations (Luke 22:8–13), and because he is their Teacher, Lord, and Master, the disciples also accord Jesus the highest status of *honored guest*. What the disciples do not expect, however, is for Jesus to assume the lowliest role of *table servant*. In so doing, he incarnates the holy logic of the first becoming last and the last becoming first, not because God desires the perpetuation of inequality, but because mutual service is the only way to replace master/servant relationships with the co-equal nature of true friendship (John 15:15). After he finishes washing the feet of each of the disciples, Jesus then says: "I have set you an example, that you also should do as I have done to you" (John 13:15). This is the recognizable sign of authentic Christian community, that Jesus' followers "have love for one another" (13:35). By conforming the communal life we share with our neighbors to the mutual love of the triune God, we participate in the divine holiness at work in the world.

Following Jesus' departure, his followers are called to abide in the Spirit by sharing in the cooperative love of God in the particulars of their daily life together. As Paul recognized, we share in the ongoing enfleshment of Christ by giving our lives over to one another, in small and large gestures of charity, for the upbuilding of the whole. Amidst questions of how to share life with those who hold divergent dietary beliefs, Paul affirms that although it is technically "lawful" either to eat or to abstain, we are to walk in the love that edifies by not seeking our own advantage, "but that of others" (1 Cor 10:24). As we do so, he says, we participate faithfully in the holy meal we received from the Lord. Is not the cup we bless and the bread we break "a sharing in the body of Christ?" he asks. For "we who are many are one body" (10:16–17). Because we are members one of another, we are to do "nothing from selfish ambition or conceit, but in humility regard others as better than" ourselves (Phil 2:3), and thus "through love become servants to one another" (Gal 5:13). It is precisely this aim of congregational mutuality that leads Paul to collect financial resources from the wealthy to share with the poor "in order that there may be a fair balance" of resources (2 Cor 8:14). For as we share our lives with and for one another, including our material and financial possessions, we share in the mutual love of the triune God given for us, through the Spirit, in the one body and cup.

Unjust Communion: Centralization of Power Among Elite Few

One of the recurring claims made by proponents of modern capitalism is that the global market economy operates with no central direction or organization. The modern market system, they argue, "is a method of social coordination by *mutual* adjustment among participants rather than by a central coordinator."[20] While it is certainly true that the global economy is constituted by a worldwide network of partnerships, it is also the case that the ongoing consolidation of corporate and state power is centralizing economic and political control among fewer and fewer actors. Mutual self-interest is undoubtedly a very potent driver of social coordination, generating an impressive level and efficiency of co-action among diverse individuals and organizations. Separated from the neighborly oriented nature of God's mutual love, however, self-oriented love inevitably leads to an unjust and oppressive imbalance of power, as the most effective—because most self-interested—actors overtake all others in accumulating greater levels of power for themselves.

A global economy held together by self-love is therefore marked not only by multiple forms of violent exclusion, divisive fragmentation, and false abstraction but also by the ongoing usurpation of local-public-collective power by transnational-private-corporate rule. What Naomi Klein means by "corporatism,"[21] Michael Nollert by the "emergence of transnational economic elites,"[22] John Perkins by "corpocracy,"[23] and Hardt-Negri by "empire" or "biopower,"[24] Wendell Berry describes as "the centralization of our economy" and "the gathering of the productive property and power into fewer and fewer hands." The result of such an unjust hoarding

20. Lindblom, *The Market System*, 23. See also Sowell, *Basic Economics*, esp. chap. 4.
21. See Klein, *No Logo*.
22. See Nollert, "Transnational Corporate Ties."
23. See Perkins, *Confessions of an Economic Hit Man*.
24. See Hardt and Negri, *Empire*.

of resources, Berry says, is the "consequent destruction, everywhere, of the local economies of household, neighborhood, and community."[25]

At the heart of concerns about "centralized power" is a denunciation of the modern corporation.[26] Economist and anti-corporatist author, David C. Korten—whose early work in rural development and village organization in Southeast Asia led him to contest the profit-driven policies of global developmentalism[27]—argues that modern corporations have become "*the dominant governance institutions on the planet.*"[28] Korten traces the rise corporate power to fifteenth- and sixteenth-century England and Holland, where large landowners who had amassed considerable agricultural wealth from the enclosure of common lands were looking to invest their capital in new ventures for profit. Unlike the business form of partnerships they replaced, in which small groups of people who knew each other ran businesses they co-owned, the new corporate form of the joint-stock company allowed for the sale of stock to strangers by corporate managers.[29] This new form, Korten writes, combined two ideas:

25. Berry, *What Are People For?*, 128.

26. The most basic definition of a corporation is an institution that is composed of a board of directors, a set of executive officers, and a fluctuating set of shareholders to whom the directors and officers are legally accountable. The overriding mission of corporations is to maximize financial returns on behalf of stockholders.

27. See Korten, *Community Organization and Rural Development*. In his anti-globalization manifesto, *When Corporations Rule the World*, Korten describes his transformation: "As a young man, I wanted to help eliminate world poverty and to that end spent thirty years of my life as a development worker in Africa, Latin America, and Asia . . . To those who look no further [than certain outward signs of progress—i.e., modern airports, shopping malls, gated communities], it seems that development has been a stunning success . . . But behind the façade billions face an ever more desperate struggle for survival. By the hundreds of millions they are being displaced from the lands on which they once made a modest living, to make way for dams, agricultural estates, forestry plantations, resorts, golf courses, and myriad other development projects . . . Often the most evident beneficiary is a global corporation" (5). In a more recent book, *The Great Turning*, Korten identifies "friend and colleague" Vandana Shiva's agrarian vision for the rebuilding of local, sustainable food economies as a primary source of inspiration for his ongoing work (357).

28. Korten, *The Post-Corporate World*, 60.

29. Adam Smith, the so-called "father" of modern political economy, revered the former while warning against the latter business form. Patricia Werhane, in *Adam Smith and His Legacy for Modern Capitalism*, writes that "Smith [had a] genuine fear of institutions, as shown in his critique of the system of mercantilism, of monopolies, and of political or economic institutions that favor some individuals over others. Smith questions the existence of 'joint-stock companies' (corporations), except in exceptional

the sale of shares in public markets and the protection of owners from personal liability for the corporation's obligations. These two features made it possible to amass virtually unlimited financial capital within a single firm, assured the continuity of the firm beyond the death of its founders, and absolved owners of personal liability for the firm's losses or misdeeds.[30]

According to Korten, one of the principle reasons that joint-stock, limited liability companies were originally sanctioned, particularly in England, was because the ruling classes were able to use the corporate form to counteract incipient attempts of egalitarian, democratic governance. By the beginning of the seventeenth century, with the English parliament's newly gained power to supervise the collection and disbursement of taxes, the monarchical class found that "by issuing corporate charters that bestowed monopoly rights and other privileges on favored investors [i.e., those with direct financial linkages to the Crown], they could establish an orderly and permanent source of income through fees and taxes that circumvented parliamentary oversight."[31] Having access to enormous sums of financial capital through private investors, English corporations were quickly able to overwhelm the more egalitarian labor guilds that had previously controlled the means of production. Not only were limited-liability, joint-stock companies beneficial to the ruling classes domestically, however, but they also were central to the Crown's colonization of foreign territories. Chartered corporations such as the British East India Company in India and China and the Massachusetts and Hudson Bay Companies in North America functioned as ruling proxies in the expansion and administration of the British Empire and the extraction of wealth by exploiting native peoples and natural resources worldwide.

The history of the United States, Korten writes, is in large part shaped by the rise of corporate rule. The first colonial settlements in America, he observes, were essentially corporate estates authorized by the Crown to generate financial profits along the coast. Following multiple rebellions and the revolution of the colonists against the monarchy and its chartered corporations, however, there were periods in the early years of the American

---

circumstances, because the institutionalization of management power separated from ownership creates institutional management power cut loose from responsibility. Smith's fear is that such institutions might become personified, so that one would regard them as real entities and hence treat them as incapable of being dismantled" (125).

30. Korten, *The Great Turning*, 131.

31. Ibid., 130.

republic when the reach of corporations was held in check through the strict oversight of individual states over corporate practice, jurisdiction, longevity, and even profits. In many areas of the country, Korten writes, "family farms and businesses were the mainstay of the economy," as were "neighborhood shops, cooperatives, and worker-owned businesses."[32] Massive profits generated during the Civil War, however, allowed corporate interests to progressively gain control over both legislative and judicial bodies and thereby steadily erode public restraints on the reach of corporate power.

A key turning point was the 1886 Supreme Court case, *Santa Clara County v. Southern Pacific Railroad*, which ultimately led to the extension of constitutional rights for individual persons to private corporations. Korten writes:

> Thus corporations came to claim the full rights enjoyed by individual citizens while being exempted from many of the responsibilities and liabilities of citizenship . . . The subsequent claim by corporations that they have the same right as any individual to influence the government in their own interest pits the individual citizen against the vast financial and communications resources

32. Korten, *When Corporations Rule*, 63. This is the period in which Jefferson's decentralized "agrarian ideal"—shrouded by the internal contradictions of chattel slavery—of local production, active citizen engagement in local decision-making, and the centrality of self-sufficient farming/husbandry was most realized in American history. In the well-known passage from his *Notes on the State of Virginia*, Jefferson writes: "The political economists of Europe have established it as a principle that every state should endeavor to manufacture for itself: and this principle, like many others, we transfer to America . . . In Europe the lands are either cultivated, or locked up against the cultivator [i.e., enclosure]. Manufacture must therefore be resorted to of necessity not of choice [i.e., through the loss of direct access to the means of production], to support the surplus of their people. But we have an immensity of land courting the industry of the husbandman . . . Those who labor in the earth are the chosen people of God, if ever he had a chosen people, whose breasts he has made his peculiar deposit for substantial and genuine virtue . . . Corruption of morals in the mass of cultivators is a phenomenon of which no age nor nation has furnished an example. It is the mark set on those, who not looking up to heaven, to their own soil and industry, as does the husbandman, for their subsistence, depend for it on the casualties and caprice of customers [i.e., the capitalist class, the owners of industry] . . . Generally speaking, the proportion which the aggregate of the other classes of citizens bears in any state to that of its husbandmen, is the proportion of its unsound to its healthy parts, and is a good-enough barometer whereby to measure its degree of corruption" (170–71). Well aware of the threats that corporations posed to this vision, Jefferson later wrote: "I hope we shall crush in its birth the aristocracy of our monied corporations which dare already to challenge our government to a trial of strength, and bid defiance to the laws of our country" (quoted in Goodwyn, *The Populist Moment*, xxviv).

of the corporation and mocks the constitutional intent that all citizens have an equal voice in the political debates surrounding important issues.[33]

As a result, corporations have subsequently argued for, and successfully achieved, First Amendment free-speech protection against various attempts to restrict the reach of corporate influence in the public sphere, including food-related efforts, for example, to limit billboards for fast food restaurants, to ban the advertising of soft drinks in schools, and to restrict financial contributions of agribusiness corporations to political campaigns. The corporate food industry has used Fourth Amendment protections against unreasonable search and seizure to limit environmental, health, and safety inspectors from investigating industrial farm malpractices. Because corporations like Monsanto or Cargill are granted limited liability status, their individual corporate managers, board members, and stockholders are rarely held responsible for any of their social and ecological crimes.[34] In other words, as a legal "person," the modern limited-liability, joint-stock corporation in America has gained tremendous power to shape contemporary social and political life, at the same time that restrictions against the gross abuse of such power have been minimized.

As with British imperialism, the imperial expansion of U.S. power, Korten argues, has been driven by private corporations seeking to extract wealth from foreign countries through coerced property enclosures, the commodification of cheap goods, and the exploitation of land and labor. Pointing to the Monroe Doctrine (1832), the annexation of Haiti (1893), the Spanish-American War (1898), and countless military interventions in places like Argentina, Japan, Nicaragua, Cuba, Panama, Haiti, and Honduras, Korten states that the reasons for American expansionism have almost always been "related to the investments of one or more U.S. corporations."[35] The goal in each case has been remarkably consistent, Korten says—"to expropriate agricultural lands and resources to produce goods for export

33. Ibid., 66.

34. Henson, "The End of Agribusiness," in Kimbrell, ed., *Fatal Harvest Reader*, 228–29. As Henson writes, "If a real person steals a motorcycle for his/her third felony ('third strike'), California mandates a sentence of 25 years to life in prison. But if, for example, UNOCAL Corporation, based in California, is convicted for the 15th time for breaking the law (as it has been), it suffers a very small fine and goes on with business as usual" (229).

35. *Empire to Earth Community*, 192.

back to the United States."[36] For over two centuries, massive corporate plantations, especially in Latin America, have been replacing small, subsistence farms and cooperative societies in order to produce monoculture cash crops for consumption in the U.S., including such food commodities as sugar cane (i.e., Domino Sugar), cocoa (i.e., The Hershey Company), bananas (i.e., Chiquita Banana), pineapples (i.e., United Fruit Company), and coffee (i.e., Folger Coffee Company).[37]

The developmentalist policies of the past fifty to sixty years, and the global institutions created to implement them, represent yet another expansion of corporate control over the global economy for the financial benefit of the few. Following World War II, Korten says, U.S. foreign policy initiatives were aimed at the creation of an integrated global economy dominated

36. Ibid., 193. Sir Albert Howard, writing in the 1940s, observed that the point is not "that every national agriculture must be completely self-contained: this would be a great pity." The point is that "the tide has been all one way," which is "only robbery on a vast scale." This "draining away of natural fertility from tropical and subtropical regions," he wrote, "is a point on which the peoples of these regions may later come to put a colossal question to the conscience of the so-called civilized countries: Why has the stored-up wealth of our lands been taken away to distant parts of the world which offer us no means of replacing it?" (*Soil and Health*, 68).

37. To give just one example, César J. Ayala, in his book, *American Sugar Kingdom: The Plantation Economy of the Spanish Caribbean*, writes about the imperial take-over of the Spanish Caribbean for U.S. sugar interests: "In the Spanish-American War of 1898 the United States seized Cuba and Puerto Rico. In 1905 it seized the customs of the Dominican Republic, and it occupied that country from 1916 to 1924. Cuba became an independent state in 1902, under the tutelage of the United States and under the shadow of the Platt Amendment. Puerto Rico became a formal colony . . . Thus the United States became an imperial power controlling the economic life of the three nations, and the Spanish Caribbean as a whole became a sphere for U.S. direct investment, a colonial region dominated by the decisions of U.S. capitalists. Although U.S. capital flowed into all economic sectors, sugar production became the primary locus of investment . . . The persistence of underdevelopment in the Caribbean in our century is not the product of the survival of precapitalist relations of production . . . To the contrary, the development of a free labor market, the introduction of the latest technological advances in the sugar mills, and fast-paced economic integration to the U.S. economy are to be blamed for the persistence of poverty and underdevelopment" (13). It is worth noting that the Vanderbilt Agrarians understood the "colonization" of the Southern United States by the industrial North in similar fashion. Industrialism, John Crowe Ransom wrote, must be "represented to the Southern people as—what it undoubtedly is for the most part—a foreign invasion of Southern soil, which is capable of doing more devastation than was wrought when Sherman marched to the sea . . . not failing to point out the human catastrophe which occurs when a Southern village or rural community becomes the cheap labor of a miserable factory system" (Twelve Southerners, *I'll Take My Stand*, 23).

by U.S. corporate interests.[38] In place of colonial methods of direct military occupation, "the United States pioneered the use of foreign aid, investment, and trade to dominate the cultures, economies, and government of client states through less overtly violent means, but with the threat of military intervention always in the background."[39] According to Korten, the primary agenda of the Bretton Woods institutions—the World Bank, the International Monetary Fund (IMF), and the General Agreement on Tariffs and Trade (GATT), which was later replaced by the World Trade Organization (WTO)—has been precisely this: to integrate foreign markets into a global economy that can be controlled by centralized corporate interests.

In particular, the developmentalist policies of the Green Revolution, which the U.S. government claimed would bring economic prosperity and self-sufficiency to foreign nations, have only left "developing" countries indebted to the U.S. controlled global lending institutions. The developmentalist argument was that, by taking on massive loans from the IMF and World Bank during the 50s and 60s, impoverished countries could "modernize" their economies by increasing agricultural production through heavy machinery, large irrigation projects and dams, chemical fertilization, and high-yielding varieties of seeds. The beneficiaries of such loans, Shiva points out, were not the debtor nations, however, but the well-connected agribusiness and construction corporations that ultimately received the billions of loan dollars to implement the Green Revolution strategies. By the 1970s, with "developing" nations facing insurmountable debts, while plunging further into poverty, the Bretton Woods institutions offered structural adjustment programs (SAPs), whereby indebted nations received new loans in exchange for liberalizing their economies—i.e., eliminating all barriers to free trade (e.g., tariffs, quotas, labor or environmental regulations), by privatizing all sectors of society, and by inviting capital investments from transnational corporations into their societies. As a result, transnational

38. Korten refers to a top-secret U.S. State Department Policy Planning Study 23, written by George Kennen in 1948: "We have about 50% of the world's wealth, but only 6.3% of its population . . . In this situation we cannot fail to be the object of envy and resentment. Our real task in the coming period is to devise a pattern of relationships which will permit us to maintain this position of disparity . . . To do so, we will have to dispense with all sentimentality and day-dreaming; and our intention will have to be concentrated everywhere on our immediate national objectives . . . We should cease to talk about vague . . . unreal objectives such as human rights, the raising of living standards, and democratization. The day is not far off when we are going to have to deal in straight power concepts" (*Empire to Earth Community*, 195).

39. Ibid., 196.

corporations, many based in the U.S., have been able rapidly to increase their ownership of foreign assets, including agricultural land, food processing plants, and distribution centers. With the implementation of the WTO's *Agreement on Agriculture*, negotiated in the 1986–1995 Uruguay Round, further impediments to the "free trade" of worldwide food commodities were lifted. As Shiva writes:

> The WTO's Agreement on Agriculture, which paved the way for the Imposition of cash crops [in developing countries], should be called the Cargill Agreement [because] it was former Cargill vice president Dan Amstutz who drafted the original text of the agreement during the Uruguay Round. WTO's rules are not just about trade. They determine how food is produced, who controls food production. The primary aim of Cargill, and hence the Agreement on Agriculture, is to open Southern markets and convert peasant agriculture to corporate agriculture . . . Converting self-sufficient food economies into food-dependent economies is the Cargill vision and the WTO strategy.[40]

At the same time that transnational corporations have gained tremendous power over the structures of the global political economy, corporate mergers and acquisitions have rapidly centralized power in almost every economic sector, including agriculture. Beginning in the 1970s, petrochemical and pharmaceutical firms with agrichemical interests began rapidly purchasing seed companies and crop-specific research operations through "an astonishing wave of mergers and acquisitions" that "swept virtually every American seed [and plant-research] company of any size or significance into the corporate folds of the world's industrial elite."[41] Since then,

---

40. Shiva, *Earth Democracy*, 35. At the time, Colombian Ambassador Fernando Jaramillio spoke against the authoritarian structure of the global lending and trade institutions: "The Bretton Woods Institutions continue to be made the center of gravity for the principal economic decisions that affect the developing countries. We have all been witnesses to the conditionalities of the World Bank and the IMF. We all know the nature of the decision-making system in such institutions; their undemocratic character, their lack of transparency, their dogmatic principles, their lack of pluralism in the debate of ideas, and their impotence to influence the policies of the industrialized countries. This also seems to be applicable to the new World Trade Organization. The terms of its creation suggest that this organization will be dominated by the industrialized countries and that its fate will be to align itself with the World Bank and IMF. We could announce in advance the birth of a New Institutional Trinity which would have as its specific function to control and dominate the economic relations that commit the developing world" (quoted in Shiva, *Biopiracy*, 112–13).

41. *First the Seed*, 16.

nearly every area of the food production system has seen both horizontal (i.e., across particular industries) and vertical (i.e., between various industries) integration. Today, for example, corporations like Monsanto and Dupont (seeds and biochemical inputs), Potash and Mosaic (fertilizer), John Deere and AGCO (farm equipment), Archer Daniels Midland and Cargill (grain trading), and Tyson, IBP, and Smithfield (meat and poultry) are now monopoly buyers and sellers of a significant percentage of the agriculturally related products around the world. In recent years, moreover, the food retail sector has consolidated as well. Bill Heffernan, rural sociologist at the University of Missouri, predicts that fewer than six transnational food retailers will soon dominate the entire global food sector.[42] Ultimately, he says, "the same firms are involved in all stages of the food system through ownership, or through the development of a variety of strategic alliances with other firms to maintain control from gene to the retail shelf." Although the network of relationships between the food conglomerates are complex, he concludes, "usually only three to four firms emerge as dominant firms in each cluster."[43] As Korten writes:

> Two grain companies—Cargill and ConAgra—control 50 percent of U.S. grain exports. Three companies—Iowa Beef Processors (IBP), Cargill, and ConAgra—slaughter nearly 80 percent of U.S. beef. One company—Campbell's—controls nearly 70 percent of the U.S soup market. Four companies—Kellogg, General Mills, Philip Morris, and Quaker Oats—control nearly 85 percent of the U.S. cold cereal market. Four companies—ConAgra, ADM Milling, Cargill, and Pillsbury—mill nearly 60 percent of U.S. flour.[44]

While proponents of the current global economy maintain that open markets and global trade are "free" from the inefficiencies and potential corruptibility of a paternalistic government, the reality is that the contemporary

42. Hendrickson et al., "Consolidation in Food Retailing and Dairy."

43. Hendrickson and Heffernan, "The Global Food System." One of the primary business objectives that drive these massive consolidated firms to develop integrated "supply chains" is to be able to control every aspect of food production and sale and thus gain a larger share of the consumer's food dollars. As a result, nearly every aspect of any particular farm operation is determined, not by the needs of the local community or the health of the land, but by corporate managers and shareholders seeking to increase their financial profits. Because those who ultimately determine how food is produced seldom live anywhere near the farm operation itself, they rarely see or live with the human and ecological consequences of their decisions.

44. Korten, *When Corporations Rule*, 208.

worldwide economy is clearly dependent upon the active role of strong, centralized states. There is nothing "natural," Polanyi argues, about *laissez-faire* economies. In fact, "the road to the free market was opened and kept open," he says, "by an enormous increase in continuous, centrally organized and controlled interventionism" by the state.[45] From large subsidies, deregulations, and tax breaks that directly assist transnational corporations, to huge military spending that protects national "interests" abroad, to the passage of "health and safety" laws that almost always work against the small producer in favor of larger operations, the public-policy orientation of the world's capitalistic nation-states has consistently aided the rise of corporate profits and control. Within agriculture, for example, over the past fifty to sixty years, farm subsidies legislated through a series of farm bills have intentionally supported the mass production of certain cash-crop commodities—i.e., corn, soybeans, cotton—which are heavily reliant upon massive machine, chemical, and seed companies. Challenging the popular notion that the U.S. "subsidizes agriculture," Wendell Berry writes that "what we have actually been doing [via our farm policy] is using the farmers to launder money for the agribusiness corporations, which have controlled both their supplies and their markets," with the result being that "the farmers have failed by the millions, and the agribusiness corporations have prospered."[46] Similarly, within the global market, whether through "gunboat diplomacy," protective subsidies and tariffs, biased agreements, or the dumping of commodities on foreign markets, dominant trading nations are continually manipulating the conditions of "free trade" in order to increase the competitive advantages of their respective corporate interests.[47]

Many critics of the corporatized global economy go so far as to say that the inevitable result of state-supported, monopolistic capitalism is a kind of "totalitarian" or "fascist" rule. In their 1930 *Statement of Principles*, the Twelve Southern Agrarians wrote that the "Industrialists" are the true Soviets or Communists, who "would have the government set up an economic super-organization, which in turn would become the government. We therefore look upon the Communist menace as a menace indeed, but not as a Red one."[48] Korten points out, in fact, that during the 30s and 40s

45. Polanyi, *The Great Transformation*, 140.

46. Berry, *Home Economics*, 170.

47. As Martin Khor has said, the reality of the globalized economy, from the perspective of those controlling trade laws, is "liberalization if it benefits us, protectionism if it benefits us, what counts is our self-interest" (quoted in Shiva, *Biopiracy*, 111).

48. Twelve Southerners, *I'll Take My Stand*, xlv.

many of America's prominent corporate leaders, including Henry Ford and James Watson (president of IBM), expressed explicit support of German and Italian fascism and were involved in efforts to build a "Soviet America."[49] Berry writes that the "glamour of bigness," or what Schumacher called the "idolatry of giantism,"[50] that shapes U.S. economic policy is intrinsically totalitarian since "it establishes an inevitable tendency toward the one that will be the biggest of all."[51] More concretely, José Bové, French farmer and spokesperson for *La Via Campesina*, an international peasant movement, presently speaks of the global food economy with the descriptors of "food totalitarianism" or "food fascism."[52] In 1999, Bové, who is a French sheep farmer, drove his tractor into a McDonald's in Millau, France, to protest what he called the "culinary imperialism" of the fast-food franchise and what it symbolizes—the destruction of local/regional food traditions, the "McDonaldization" of global culture, and the imposition by WTO agreements of genetically modified foods and hormone-treated meats on the world's population.[53] Bové insists that the United States is the most "com-

---

49. Korten, *Empire to Earth Community*, 213. In his book, *IBM and the Holocaust*, Black writes that "IBM, primarily through its German subsidiary, made Hitler's program of Jewish destruction a technological mission the company pursued with chilling success. IMB Germany, using its own staff and equipment, designed, executed, and supplied the indispensable technologic assistance Hitler's Third Reich needed to accomplish what had never been done before—the automation of human destruction. More than 2,000 such multi-machine sets were dispatched through German-dominated Europe. Card sorting operations were established in every major concentration camp. People were moved from place to place, systematically worked to death, and their remains catalogued with icy automation" (quoted in *Babylon and Beyond*, 44).

50. Schumacher, *Small Is Beautiful*, 62.

51. Berry, *Unsettling*, 41. Polanyi argues that fascism is, in fact, the inevitable outcome when the inherent tensions between democratic institutions oriented toward labor and industrial capitalists focused on profits reach an *impasse*. "The fascist solution of the *impasse* reached by liberal capitalism can be described as a reform of market economy achieved at the price of the extirpation of all democratic institutions, both in the industrial and in the political realm. The economic system which was in peril of disruption would thus be revitalized, while the people themselves were subjected to a re-education designed to denaturalize the individual and make him unable to function as the responsible unit of the body politic. This re-education, comprising the tenets of a political religion that denied the idea of the brotherhood of man in all its forms, was achieved through an act of mass conversion enforced against recalcitrants by scientific methods of torture" (*The Great Transformation*, 237).

52. Shiva also speaks of "food fascism" or "food dictatorship" (*Earth Democracy*, 152).

53. Bové was sentenced to three months imprisonment for his act of protest. Daley, "French Farmer Is Sentenced to Jail for Attack on McDonald's."

munist" country in modern history, in that every aspect of life, including especially how we eat, is being dictated by a politico-economic leviathan controlled by an elite few.[54]

According to the promise of global capitalism, the world's people are invited to share in a worldwide egalitarian community governed by the mutual interests of every market actor rather than by the dictates of a central state or set of dominant coordinators. What an "awakened analysis" of our context (Herzog) suggests, however, is that the ongoing consolidation of corporate and state power is centralizing power and control among fewer and fewer global elites. Seen in the light of God's holiness, an economy resulting in the amassment of the world's financial resources and political power by fewer and fewer actors is operating counter to the co-equal nature of God's mutual love. To the extent that the meals Christians share in are made up of elements of the agro-industrial process, therefore, Christians are participants in an unholy communion marked by injustice and oppression.

Holistic Communion: Cooperative Power Shared in Local Communities and Bio-Regions

If Holy Communion, in conformity with the triune God, is wholly cooperative life together, how are those drawn to share in the mutual love of the Father/Mother, Son, and Holy Spirit to do so in the midst of a centralized global economy ruled by the unjust and oppressive powers of self-interest? In particular, in a food economy in which fewer and fewer transnational agribusiness corporations have overtaken nearly every aspect of food production and distribution, how are Christians faithfully to assemble as neighborly members of one another in meal fellowships of mutual service? Those seeking to gather in conformity to the mutual, co-equal fellowship of the triune God are being called today to participate in cooperative modes of economic life together that promote the egalitarian sharing of power in local, neighborly communities. In particular, this will include the involvement of Christian communities in the emergence of a more cooperative food economy, in which decentralized food cooperatives, embedded in small-scale communities and bioregions, share control over the production and distribution of our daily bread and common cup.

54. See Bové and Dufour, *The World Is Not for Sale.*

By working to build up a more decentralized food economy, in which power is shared in local communities, Christians affirm that the purpose of economic life is to support the flourishing of neighborly mutuality in societies resembling the co-equal love of God. Because genuine community with others is rooted not in distant sentiment but in concrete relationships sustained over time within particular locales, an economic system conducive to neighborly fellowship is one properly scaled to foster long-term, intimate human interaction. The bonds of true community can only thrive, as Martin Buber says, "where people have the real things of their common life in common; where they can experience, discuss and administer them together."[55] I can only upbuild a particular neighbor, and he me, if we share a common life lived in close proximity to one another. For while it is true that all human beings are our brothers and sisters, as Schumacher says, "it is also true that in our active personal relationships we can, in fact, be brothers [and sisters] to only a few of them."[56] In the economic production and distribution of goods and services, as in all human activity, there is therefore a certain scale appropriate to fostering genuine neighborly fellowship. While it may be possible to bolster greater economic efficiency by increasing the size of a particular operation, any potential gains for an elite few simultaneously require sacrificing "the convenience, humanity, and manageability of smallness"[57] for the many. By working toward the emergence of a more decentralized food economy, based in the health of local communities, Christians affirm that the love of the triune God is shared in social bodies small enough to nurture neighborly familiarity and mutual service.

An economy based in the unjust centralization of power and resources among an elite few operates outside the realm of God's mutual love. Those who seek to be conformed with the divine fellowship of co-equal persons are therefore called to criticize the unjust systems and admonish its primary beneficiaries for the sake of a more just and fraternal society. As many of the medieval lay communitarian movements argued, the unequal amassment of lands and wealth by the nobility, propertied class, *and* Papal Church—often one and the same—constituted an affront to the gospel

---

55. Buber, *Paths in Utopia*, 15.

56. Schumacher, *Small Is Beautiful*, 61.

57. Ibid., 61. In his *Letters and Papers from Prison*, Bonhoeffer poses a similar juxtaposition. "Are we moving towards an age of colossal organizations and collective institutions, or will the desire of innumerable people for small, manageable, personal relationships be satisfied?" (299).

principle of brotherly charity. Grassroots communities like the Brothers and Sisters of the Modern Devotion, Beghards/Beguines, Lollards, and Bohemian Brethren all leveled critiques against a "corrupt" and "profit-seeking" class of kings, lords, and bishops by emphasizing the egalitarian nature of God's universal love. Christ "went out to all in common in his love," John Ruusbroec affirms, and he intended that the "external goods of the holy Church" be used "for all in common" and that all who live and serve in the Church would "give themselves to all in common." But today, he says, "the situation is just the opposite," as the popes, bishops, and priests "have turned completely to worldly concerns" and are so "greedy and rapacious" that they strive to draw all things to themselves.[58] As Geert Grote, founder of the *Devotio Moderna*, asserts, "the love of God cannot dwell" in those who "unjustly and against God" possess "goods of other people" or goods they "produce, prepare, or preserve in an underhanded way" to their benefit but "without the people's concurrence." Were they truly to examine their covetous hearts, he says, "they would discover that their lives actually stand outside of love."[59] In fact, it is the unholy work of the Devil, as the author of *Theologia Germanica* claims, who "puffeth up" an individual to think that "I am above all other men" such that it is "just and reasonable that I should be the lord and commander of all creatures, and that all creatures, and especially all men, should serve me and be subject unto me."[60] For those seeking to be conformed to the egalitarian nature of divine love, any economic system that allows for the concentration of wealth and power among an elite few—whether political or religious rulers—must be rejected as an unholy social order working against the perfect love of God. In our time, this will include criticizing the global structures of modern capitalism as unjust and oppressive, as well as admonishing global elites who wield control over the world's economic systems and political processes for their own private gain.

In the context of an unjust centralization of financial and political power, Christians are called to uplift the lowly for the sake of a more fraternal society by assembling with neighbors for cooperative action. As the author of "To the Assembly of the Peasantry" writes at the time of the sixteenth-century peasant revolt in Germany, "a territory or community

58. Ruusbroec, *The Spiritual Espousals,* 107–8.

59. Grote, "A Sermon Addressed to the Laity," in Van Engen, ed., *Devotio Moderna,* 93–94.

60. *The Theologia Germanica of Martin Luther,* 72.

has the power to depose its pernicious lords" because God's power is given "to build up and not to destroy" brotherly unity. In the face of "lords who issue selfish commands" and "who appropriate for themselves" the land and all its fruits, the faithful response of Christ's followers is to "assemble now!" in "all fidelity and love" for "the sake of the common peace of the land."[61] Such grassroots calls issued by lay commoners to "come together" and to "hold general assemblies" are coupled with the affirmation that the love of God, who is "no respecter of persons," is the "same for all" whether one is a "shepherd, pope, emperor, or bath-house keeper."[62] By gathering together in "brotherly charity," Christians are thereby empowered by the egalitarian love of God to ennoble the weak in seeking a more just sharing of power and wealth in society.

Most of the lay communitarian movements of the medieval and early modern period embodied their belief in the co-equality of humanity in the light of God's love by sharing in cooperative economic endeavors. The Brothers and Sisters of the Modern Devotion, for example, lived together in "gatherings" or "congregations," usually within a common house, where they worked side-by-side copying Bibles and assorted religious texts for sale or supplying textiles and laces.[63] The Waldenses, Apostolicans, Beghards/ Beguines, and Lollards all sought to reestablish the apostolic simplicity of early Christianity by sharing earnings from their common livelihood as weavers.[64] In the democratic and highly industrious agricultural villages of the Moravian Fraternities, various operations of farming, brewing, baking, milling, child-rearing, housekeeping, cloth- and cutlery-making were co-operatively interwoven, so that "everything was carried on upon a whole-sale basis, and the individual artisans worked into each other's hands."[65] The proposal of Quaker John Bellers that England's poor gather together in self-sufficient "Colleges of Industry" to pool efforts in common agricultural and manufacturing work[66] served as a primary inspiration for several of the founders of the modern cooperative movement, including Robert Owen,

---

61. Annonymous, "To the Assembly of the Peasantry," in Baylor, ed., *The Radical Reformation*, 118–19, 122.

62. Ibid., 105.

63. Introduction, Van Engen, ed., *Devotio Moderna*, 7–35.

64. See Kautsky, *Communism in Central Europe in the Time of the Reformation*, 55.

65. Ibid., 209.

66. See Bellers, *Proposals for Raising a College of Industry of All Useful Trades and Husbandry.*

Pierre-Joseph Proudhon, and Peter Kropotkin. Owen's vision of upbuilding economic cooperatives based primarily in agriculture and sustained by the principles of "united labor," "equal privileges," "mutual and common interests," and the "appropriate participation of all members in one another"[67] is fundamentally rooted in the egalitarian practices of medieval Christianity's lay communities.

In our time, one way those seeking to follow a similar pattern of communal conformity to the mutual love of God might be assembled in cooperative work-together is by upbuilding what Korten calls "local-living economies." In a local-living economy, economic activity is focused primarily upon the locally sufficient production of goods and services for bioregional consumption, with only the surplus being used for external trade. Whatever cannot be produced locally is sourced from community-oriented companies and small farms located in other economic bioregions. By keeping wealth circulating within a local region, political and economic power is thus allowed to concentrate in democratically governed townships, neighborhoods, or any variety of small collectivist organizations. As David Korten argues, a local-living economy serves the primary purpose of economic activity, which is to "allocate human and material resources justly and sustainably to meet the self-defined needs of people and community." He writes:

> When enterprises are locally rooted, human-scale, owned by stakeholders, and held accountable to the rule of law by democratically elected governments, there is a natural incentive for all concerned to take human and community needs and interests into account. When income and ownership are equitably distributed, justice is served and political democracy is strong. When needs are met locally by locally owned enterprises, people have greater control over their lives, money is recycled in the community rather than leaking off into the global financial casino, jobs are more secure, economies are more stable, and there are the means and the incentives to protect the environment and to build the relationships of mutual trust and responsibility that are the foundation of community.[68]

---

67. Buber, *Paths in Utopia*, 21–22.

68. David Korten, *Business Alliance for Local Living Economies* website.

By participating in the emergence of such economies, Christians affirm that the divine love is shared with us that we might participate in neighborly communities of mutual upbuilding.

A local-living economy resembling the divine fellowship of co-equal persons is constituted by a diverse collective of small, local companies committed to a set of cooperative, egalitarian business practices. One of the key foundations of such companies is the sharing of ownership and workplace governance among employees. In a cooperative employee ownership structure, those who create the products and subsequent wealth of a business enjoy an equal share of the generated wealth, thereby preventing an unequal balance of power and wealth between ownership and labor, managers and staff. Employees also participate democratically in the many decisions of the workplace, so that even though there are a variety of different roles and tasks to accomplish, each of the members is able to affect both the daily operations and overall direction of the workplace. Companies that are committed not only to financial profit but also community development and ecological sustainability also seek out opportunities to contribute to the people, institutions, and landscapes of which they are a part. Through concrete acts of service to the surrounding community, local bonds of support for the company's success are strengthened, creating a climate conducive for business success. As John Abrams, cofounder of an employee-owned company writes, "we give to the community, the community gives back, we reciprocate in turn, and onward it goes."[69] In the present context of the unjust and undemocratic control of corporations over more and more aspects of our daily lives, Christians seeking to participate in the mutual love of the triune God within their economic lives are being called to upbuild and maintain local companies committed to egalitarian and community-oriented business practices.

Because the love of the divine fellowship of co-equal persons is shared with us most directly in an egalitarian meal gathering, there is no better place for Christians to begin participating in the emergence of local-living economies than with the upbuilding of their local food economies. Around the world, movements for the local control of food production and distribution constitute one of the most visible and accessible alternatives to the centralizing and oppressive structures of global capitalism. In a thriving local food economy, small, independent farming operations partner together to provide consumers with healthy, whole foods at farmer's markets

---

69. Abrams, *Companies We Keep*, 175.

or cooperative grocery stores. Or, consumers partner directly with producers through models like community supported agriculture (CSA), in which local buyers purchase "shares" in a farming operation in exchange for a weekly delivery of assorted fruits, vegetables, herbs and other farm goods. As a result, neighborly bonds between those who grow and those who enjoy the fruits of the earth are strengthened, consumers are able to influence the kind and quality of the food they eat, money circulates throughout a local community for the benefit of all, and everyone participates in the health and prosperity of their bioregion. The opportunity to support, through one's labor, purchasing decisions, or financial investment, the emergence of such "food democracies" in place of the "food fascism" presently controlling our food systems is an opportunity to participate in the upbuilding of our neighbors in conformity to the mutual love of God.

Conclusion

The triune God invites us to enjoy the feast of abundant life together by assembling with others in bonds of mutual service. In the Father/Mother, Son, and Holy Spirit, the divine holiness is shared with us in the fellowship of local assemblies, through which members serve one another in reciprocal works of neighborly charity. In the midst of an unholy economy marked by the unjust and oppressive force of self-love, those seeking to be conformed to the divine fellowship of co-equal persons are called today to participate in the divine work of uplifting the lowly and bringing down the mighty by building up local economies in which monetary and political power is justly shared in cooperative, neighborly communities. By supporting egalitarian economic models committed to employee ownership, democratic governance, and community involvement, Christians participate faithfully in the divine holiness, assembling all things together in perfect love. Holy Communion is wholly cooperative life together in which all are made whole. As we sit down together as equals around the feast of God's mutual love, including while we grow, prepare and serve the food we enjoy, we share in the triune work of upbuilding our neighbors through the holy bonds of reciprocal love.

5

The Lord God Grants
Permission to Begin

THE LORD GOD GRANTS permission for the feast of life to begin. As the divine King of heaven and earth, the God of glory has blessed the commencement of the royal banquet. God's holiness is God's perfect love, and in the fullness of divine love, all things are made whole. Already in this present age, the reign of God's eternal holiness breaks forth as *creative love*, which frees us to partake in fruitful ventures of a new life together. Faithful acceptance of God's call to participate in Holy Communion, then, includes faithfully obeying the Savior in claiming our freedom to live as earthly citizens of God's heavenly kingdom. "New wine must be put into fresh wineskins" (Luke 5:38). Holy Communion, in honor of the Lord of lords, is wholly liberated life together.

But how are those striving to be loyal to the divine kingdom to participate in the creative love of God in the midst of an economy ruled by the colonizing powers of self-love? Separated from the fullness of divine love, self-love inevitably leads to bondage, for the self-oriented individual seeks to draw everything and everyone within the grasp of his or her control. The modern global economy is thus marked by a colonizing social dynamic in which the worldwide spread of free markets makes possible the ongoing expansion of corporate dominion over more and more spheres of life. Within the modern food economy, in particular, the penetration of market logic into nearly every aspect of agricultural production has resulted in corpocratic ownership over the structures and organic processes of plant and animal life, including the seed. In this context, obeying the Lord God in economic life—and thus participating more fully in the divine holiness—requires withdrawing from the industrial food system while directly engaging in alternative, widely available means of growing and sharing food.

The Wholly Creative Love of the Lord God

The holiness of the One revealed for us in Jesus Christ, immanent with us in the Spirit, and sent in the flesh for our earthly sake from the Father/Mother is also transcendent above and outside of us in the eternal kingdom. As the Alpha and Omega, the beginning and end of all things, the triune God who *is* love reigns as King of heaven and earth in "glory, majesty, power, and authority, before all time and now and forever" (Jude 1:25). As Thomas Müntzer insisted, only the God of Jesus Christ and the Holy Spirit—and no one else—is properly worthy to be addressed with such titles as "the most illustrious, first-born prince and all-powerful lord . . . the gracious king of all kings, the brave duke of all believers."[1] God alone is holy (Rev 15:4). God's holiness is therefore not bound by history, for the God of love reigns from a transcendent kingdom set apart from the dominions, powers, and thrones of this present age.

Unbound by the dynamics of history, the holy activities of the Lord God in history are entirely creative. Because God is free from the unholy power of sin leading to death, which weighs upon human history and subjects the creation to futility (Rom 8:19–22), God's love is not restrained by anything present, past, or yet to come. As King of kings and Lord of lords, God is not forced to cooperate as an unwilling participant in the dictates of historical realities. The transcendent nature of God's holiness does not mean, however, that God's love is distant or cut off from the world. The kingdom of God is not far from us. The love of God radiates freely from the divine realm and operates freely in history, such that the divine love is unrestrained in being fully with and for us. As a result, the activities of God's sovereign love in the world are marked by surprise, overturned expectations, and the eruption of novelty. God's freedom from the world allows the divine holiness to be at work with the world to create, seemingly out of nothing in the world, that which no one could have foreseen. Moreover, wherever the Lord God is active in the world, the divine holiness that radiates from the eternal kingdom frees up recipients from the expectations

---

1. Müntzer, "A Highly Provoked Defense," in Baylor, ed., *The Radical Reformation*, 74–75.

and requirements of the present age to enjoy the creativity of God's love. The transcendent operations of holiness revealed in Jesus Christ, present in the Spirit, and given from the Father/Mother are utterly creative and liberating works of divine love.

In Jesus Christ, the sovereign holiness of God's love is revealed in the creative nature of his gracious life and ministry. As the One in whom "the whole fullness of deity dwells bodily," who is "the head of every ruler and authority" (Col 2:9–10), and who lives his earthly life "without sin" (Heb 4:15), Jesus is not restricted by the political, religious, or moral realities of his time. In his person and his proclamation, he announces that God is not bound to cooperate in the expectations of the present age. Rather, "the time is fulfilled," he announces, "and the kingdom of God has come near" (Mark 1:14). Jesus is anointed in the Spirit to bring the good news that God's sovereign love breaks into history to release captives, to give sight to the blind, to free the oppressed, and to begin the time of jubilee (Luke 4:18–19). "The gospel of the kingdom of God is the gospel of the liberation of the people," as Moltmann says. "The lordship of Christ is at the same time the kingdom of the liberty of God's children."[2] Unhampered by religious prohibitions to work on the Sabbath, Jesus heals a woman bent over for most of her life by saying, "woman, you are set free from your ailment" (Luke 13:12). In spite of the social pressures to avoid associating with tax collectors, Jesus stays at the house of a chief tax collector, who surprises everyone by returning his wealth to those he previously defrauded (Luke 19:1–10). Following his arrest, sentencing, and beating by Roman authorities, and while hanging on the imperial cross of execution, the King of kings utters no words of malice or revenge but prays to the Father that his executioners be released from the debt of their wrongdoing (Luke 23:34). Because the Lord Jesus is free from the dictates of the world, he reveals throughout his gracious ministry the surprising creativity of God's sovereign love.

Similarly, the transcendent holiness of God present in the Holy Spirit is a creative love that moves in mysterious ways. The Spirit is "the Lord, the giver of life" (Nicene Creed) who, flowing forth from the divine kingdom and not the realm of history, fashions bonds of unity between unexpected groups of people. As sovereign, the divine love present in the Spirit "blows where it chooses," and although one can identify the holy marks of the Spirit's activity, it is not possible to grasp "where it comes from or where it goes" (John 3:8). Unconstrained by the world's constructed boundaries,

2. Moltmann, *The Way of Jesus Christ*, 96.

the Holy Spirit pours Her vitalizing power of convivial love upon young and old, slave and free, men and women, and on all the nations of the earth (Acts 2:5–21). Those who have been prohibited to join together because of historical customs, political loyalties, or socio-religious mores are thereby freed to unite in unexpected bonds of fellowship. "The Lord is the Spirit," Paul writes, "and where the Spirit of the Lord is, there is freedom" (2 Cor 3:17). For those indwelt by the power of the Holy Spirit that flows forth from the realm of God, even the codified law itself—religious, political, or otherwise—is no barrier to the free expression of spiritual vitality. "The fruit of the Spirit is love, joy, peace, patience, kindness, generosity, faithfulness, gentleness, and self-control." And "there is no law against such things" (Gal 5:22–23). As the sovereign Lord of life, the Holy Spirit is present in the world freeing people to live fruitful lives in the eternally creative harmonies of love.

The holiness of God the Father/Mother given in and for the flesh is also a creative love that confounds the limits of human understanding and expectation. As Lord God Almighty, the maker of heaven and earth, the Father/Mother is not beholden to the understood laws of the universe or the perceived realities of any given situation. "For my thoughts are not your thoughts," says the Lord, "nor are your ways my ways" (Isa 55:8). In the ultimate act of creativity, following the imperial execution of Jesus, the sovereign love of the Father/Mother sends the Spirit of life from the eternal kingdom to resurrect Jesus from the dead. Far outside the realm of lived experience, opposite the universal knowledge of what happens to corpses of the deceased, the almighty love of the Creator is shown—in and through the body of Jesus—to be stronger than death. Because the Father/Mother does not need to obey the decrees of an imperial power or the statutes of human reason, the enfleshed love of God freely overcomes the sting of death in the creative resurrection of Jesus' body.

The creative love of the Lord God is the holy wellspring of all that is *new*. The inbreaking of divine holiness into the world from the realm of eternal glory is the source of new life, fresh possibilities, unexpected interconnections, and novel perspectives. Through the charitable power of God, sent from the Father/Mother, present in the Spirit of life, and incarnate in Jesus Christ, "there is a new creation: everything old has passed away; see, everything has become new!" (2 Cor 5:17). A world that would otherwise be bound to an eternal perpetuation of that which has always been is continuously opened up by the creativity of God's sovereign love.

"A new reality appears, a reality that is opposed to the world's history," as Christoph Friedrich Blumhardt affirms. "It is the rulership of God. God's kingdom is the revelation of the divine life here on earth, the birth of new hearts, new minds, new feelings, new possibilities. This is God's kingdom."[3] The newness of God is not simply novelty for the sake of innovation alone, however. God's inbreaking newness arises out of the creativity of divine love in a world bound by the powers of sin and death. The God who is creative frees the creation, then, not for the banality of yet another form of sinful self-expression, but for the truly ecstatic newness of perfect love.

The holy creativity of God Almighty generates people and spaces that are set apart from that which is old and dying in the world for the sake of the eventual newness of the whole creation. Just as God's realm is separate from the world, so too "God's holiness consists in establishing a divine dwelling place," as Bonhoeffer says, "God's realm of holiness in the midst of the world."[4] Because the kingdom of God does not now overwhelm the world all at once, but enters into our reality through less expansive beginnings, the set-apart dwelling places of God's holiness often seem quite small and insignificant. The creative love of God showering forth from the eternal kingdom and breaking into our world is like the yeast that causes a loaf to rise (Matt 13:33), the salt that flavors a meal (Luke 14:34), the first fruits of a harvest (2 Thess 2:13), or the tiniest of seeds that will grow into a tree (Mark 4:30–32). To the "honor of his Father" in heaven, Johann Christoph Blumhardt says, and in the power of the Holy Spirit, Jesus "through his advent" has "put a seed into the earth." In so doing, he says, "God is now creating a new reality on earth, a reality to come first among" a few who are set apart "but finally over all creation."[5] Those people and spaces in which the creativity of God is doing a new thing are set apart, therefore, not as a means of judgment over against the world, but as the beginnings of a sovereign love that will eventually, by God's holiness, grow up into the fullness of an entirely new creation.

If the holiness of God's kingdom breaks into the world as creative love, then sin is evident in the *imperial conquest* of expanding spheres of existence by those consumed with self-gain. The sin of conquest is unholy in that it seeks to occupy and gain ownership over that which the Lord God has already claimed to be free. Never satisfied with what he already

---

3. Christoph Blumhardt, *Action in Waiting*, 18–20.

4. Bonhoeffer, *Discipleship*, 254.

5. Johann Blumhardt, in Blumhardt and Blumhardt, *Thy Kingdom Come*, 3.

possesses, the sinner seeks continually new realms to overtake. This "lust for possessiveness," as Jacob Boehme describes, wishes "to draw to it and to possess everything." No longer trusting in God's providence, those driven by self-love are led by their "desire and possessiveness to the creatures and to the earth," as well as to fellow human beings and their property. That they have lost "proper love for God" is evident, he says, in their susceptibility to the Devil's cunning—which they believe to be their own subtle reasoning—that although "you are now dominant, mighty, high and noble," it is necessary that you "become greater, richer, and still more dominant."[6] The unholy sin of imperial conquest is thus intrinsically related to the *bondage* of whoever or whatever one has conquered. Whereas God's sovereign holiness opens up the world to enjoy the divine love, sinful self-love captures and enslaves the creation in service to its unquenchable desire for more.

In situations of bondage caused by imperial conquest, the holiness of the Lord God breaks into the world to *redeem* those held in captivity by sin. Unrestrained by any legal or political strictures that have been codified to protect colonizing self-interests, the sovereign love of God is free to release those imprisoned by the unholy powers of sinful self-love. Not only does the Almighty redeem those trapped in bondage by the sin of others, but the love of God also liberates those enslaved by their own unquenchable lust for possessiveness. In the gracious love of Jesus Christ, manifest throughout his life and even amidst his wrongful execution on the cross, God breaks into the world that "he might redeem us from every lawless deed" (Titus 2:14) and thereby "set us free from the present evil age" (Gal 1:4). For the righteous holiness of God in Christ is disclosed "apart from the law" of this world, as Paul affirms, "through the redemption that is in Christ Jesus" (Rom 3:21, 23). So, too, through the convivial love of the Holy Spirit, the Lord God liberates those held captive by the unholy powers of the present age, for "the Spirit of life . . . has made [us] free from the law of sin and death" (Rom 8:2). In the resurrection of Jesus from the dead, the Father/Mother makes clear that the divine love enters into the world to liberate not only hearts and minds from sin's colonizing reach but earthly bodies as well. Wherever the sin of imperial conquest leads to bondage, the divine holiness breaks through every internal and external manifestation of slavery to bring about the full redemption of all who are enslaved.

Faithfully responding to God's invitation to participate in the divine holiness, then, means obeying the Lord God in claiming our freedom to live

---

6. Boehme, *The Way to Christ*, 229–30.

as earthly citizens of the divine kingdom of love. Having been set free by the transcendent King of kings and Lord of lords, we accept the liberty we are given to "obey God rather than any human authority" (Acts 5:29). For we know that "our citizenship is in heaven," (Phil 3:21) and that the inbreaking of God's sovereign love into this world authorizes us to "stand firm" and "not submit again to a yoke of slavery" (Gal 5:1). To be holy as God is holy does not entail the freedom to submit to the cravings of sinful self-love, therefore, which only leads to the bondage of the self and others. Rather, "having been set free from sin," we are called to obey our eternal Lord by becoming "slaves of righteousness" (Rom 6:18). Because God's righteousness is God's perfect love, the holy life is marked by the freedom to love as God loves without restraint, regardless of the prohibitions of any worldly authority, and in spite of any legal ramifications. "For the one who loves another has fulfilled the law" (Rom 13:10). In the confidence that nothing in all of creation could ever "separate us from the love of God" (8:39), we are emboldened, as Bonhoeffer suggests, "to obedient and responsible action . . . in exclusive allegiance of God."[7] As we accept the freedom we are given to share in God's love, we participate in the sovereign holiness of Almighty God breaking into the world.

Obedience to the Lord God's creative love also means participating in the new world that the divine holiness is generating in the midst of the old. The sanctified life is one that is clothed "with the new self" according to the image of God "in true righteousness and holiness" (Eph 4:23–24). As a result, faithful allegiance to the kingdom of God in the midst of the present age requires an acceptance that one will be set apart from the sinfulness of the world. We are called to be non-participants in the realm of unholy self-love, which as Tauler says, "means that we must turn away and withdraw from all that is not God pure and simple."[8] The new life that God's sovereign creativity is opening up in this age is very much a worldly reality, however. "The 'unworldliness' of the Christian life," as Bonhoeffer says, is one that takes place entirely "in the midst of this world."[9] As we participate in the newness that God's love opens up for us, we do so as people set apart from the powers of sin but as earthly citizens of the heavenly kingdom.

In situations where the unholy sin of imperial conquest leads to captivity, the holy citizens of God's eternal kingdom actively seek creative

---

7. Bonhoeffer, *Letters and Papers*, 5.

8. Tauler, *Sermons*, 80.

9. Bonhoeffer, *Discipleship*, 245.

social alternatives that will liberate the enslaved. Precisely because those who have been liberated by God's sovereign love "can never consent to any restrictions" in their "service of love and compassion toward other human beings,"[10] as Bonhoeffer says, they are free to engage directly in imaginative and emancipatory action for the sake of a new social reality. Christian freedom "is the creative passion for the possible," as Moltmann says, manifest in the implementation of "new, unguessed-at possibilities" in the world.[11] The primary aim of those striving first for God's kingdom is not to be set apart as holier than all others, therefore, but to be set apart as living signs and useful instruments toward what God intends for the whole of creation. "We must learn to be genuine creations of God through which life can stream out in all directions,"[12] Johann Christoph Blumhardt writes. Wherever there is bondage in the world, those striving to be holy as God is holy seek to embody the emancipated life as a witness that simultaneously flows outward in actions that serve to liberate others from slavery as well.

To summarize: God's holiness is God's perfect love, and in the creative love of our Lord and Savior, the sovereign love of God breaks into the world to open up the present age for the arrival of a new reality. The unholy nature of selfish love is evident in the imperial conquest of more and more spheres of life for private possession, which leads to bondage. God's holiness makes whole, and in situations of captivity, the holiness of Almighty God erupts into the world to redeem those enslaved by sin. We participate faithfully in the divine holiness by obeying the Lord God, who frees us to engage directly in creative and emancipatory alternatives for the sake of the whole of creation.

The Wholly Liberated Communion Meal

Holy Communion, in obedience to the King of kings, is wholly liberated life together. The creative nature of God's sovereign love is active in the world that we might participate in the divine holiness in our social existence with and for others. Faithfully to accept God's invitation to Holy Communion is to engage in a relational way of life that is freed up for creative and liberative actions of love in the world. This is the beginning of a new realm in the midst of the present age, which God will bring to fruition for the sake of

10. Ibid., 236.

11. Moltmann, *Spirit of Life,* 119.

12. Johann Blumhardt, in Blumhardt and Blumhardt, *Thy Kingdom Come,* 19–20.

the eventual newness of the entire world. All this is given to us in the Holy Communion meal, in which the Lord God gives us permission to begin the royal banquet of love and to which we are invited as participants.

The primary social event used throughout the scriptural narratives to depict the sovereign kingdom of God is the joyous banquet feast. The prophet Isaiah declares that on the day of salvation, when the Lord God breaks into history to redeem the creation from sin and death, the Lord of hosts makes "for all peoples a feast of rich food, a feast of well-aged wines, of rich food filled with marrow, of well-aged wines strained clear" (Isa 25:6–9). The kingdom of God's glory is not a regimented, solemn, or controlled dominion but a "festal gathering" (Heb 12:22) marked by holy revelry, spontaneous eruptions of dancing, and a liberated spirit of joyful gladness reigning among all the celebrants. Meal celebrations, of course, are central to the inbreaking of God's realm in Jesus Christ. Unlike John the Baptist, whose ministry is marked by social withdrawal, moral austerity, and fasting, Jesus is publicly known as one who continually, openly shares in banquet fellowship with others, to the point that his enemies denounce him as "a glutton and a drunkard" (Matt 11:19). Jesus' festive and disruptive meal practices are the enfleshment of his proclamation that "the kingdom of God has come near" (Mark 1:15). For the sovereign realm of God enters into this world in the form of a jovial banquet feast that we might truly "taste and see that the Lord is good" (Ps 34:8).

In the kingdom feast that breaks into the world in and through Jesus, the Lord God's creativity fashions something entirely new in the midst of this present age. The first of Jesus' many signs and wonders takes place at a wedding banquet. With the old wine dried up and the evening festivities beginning to taper off, the sovereign glory of God is revealed as Jesus provides the equivalent of over six hundred bottles of the finest wine to a party that will now erupt with music, laughter and dancing late into the night. Unrestrained by social custom or a realistic appraisal of the situation, Jesus completely overturns expectations not only by turning water into wine but by saving the choicest wine till the last (John 2:1–11). The sovereign love of God that spills into this world as new wine creates an awakened perspective of present realities and a new understanding of the future that "with God all things are possible" (Matt 19:26). It also occasions the transformation of surrounding structures, because the new wine of divine holiness necessarily bursts open the old wineskins of this present age. As a result, "new wine must be put into fresh wineskins" (Luke 3:38). God's creative love breaks into our world to bring about the beginnings of an entirely new creation.

God's holy banquet feast erupts into the world as a liberating alternative to the unholy meal practices of an age bound by colonizing self-love. Meal gatherings are intimately connected to the dynamics of ideology and power in a society, such that one does not share in a given meal without at the same time participating, both symbolically and substantively, in a broader socio-political realm. Nowhere are these connections more evident than in the cultic sacrificial system of the Greco-Roman empire. As Andrew McGowan explains, the religious practice of sacrifice in antiquity was closely tied to a complex socio-political cultic system that established the cosmic order of power relations and hierarchies embedded in society. The cultic system was inextricably tied to the political order, not only because offering sacrifices was limited to free-born males, but also because of its direct link to the Emperor who signified in his very person "an earthly embodiment of the benevolent despotism of the universe."[13] Meat and wine were the central food and drink elements involved in the sacrifice, connecting any occasion in which meat or wine was consumed to the broader socio-religious and political structures upholding the empire, not only at the temple but also at club meetings, association gatherings, or even daily meals. As such, "acceptance or rejection of the cuisine of sacrifice was not merely a symbolic enactment of social conflict but constituted conflict itself," McGowan says. "To eat or not eat was not merely a question of signaling allegiance, but of acting that allegiance out in the most important and obvious way."[14] The participation of Jesus' followers in an alternative meal practice, which both represented and manifested the universal reign of Almighty God, constituted just such a conflict.

The Lord God's invitation to join the kingdom feast liberates its participants to withdraw their commensal fellowship with the imperial orders of this present age. The unholy dynamics of imperial conquest, as John's book of Revelation describes, include expansionistic wars (6:3), unjust market manipulations that benefit the wealthy (6:5–6), coerced participation in economic trade (13:16–17), the accumulation of riches at the expense of human life (18:13), and the extermination of anyone who refuses compliance (13:7). All of this is epitomized by the red table wine with which the kings of the earth and the great imperial city of Rome become "drunk with

---

13. McGowan, *Ascetic Eucharists,* 62.

14. Ibid., 226.

the blood of the saints" (17:2, 6). Those who are held captive under an imperial power, John proclaims, are given freedom from the Lord God the Almighty to refuse the wine of unholy conquest and to "come out" from any participation in its sins (18:4). The sovereign love of the One "who was and is and is to come" (1:8) breaks into the world to create a people set apart from the unholy powers of this present age.

The freedom for non-compliance, which sets those obedient to God apart from the world, is a freedom granted not for the sake of attaining meal purity per se, however, but for the sake of loving fellowship. Amidst controversies over whether Christians are allowed to eat food sacrificed through the imperial cultic system to other rulers and deities, Paul asserts that although there are indeed many gods and many lords in the world, "for us there is one God, the Father . . . and one Lord, Jesus Christ" (1 Cor 8:5–6). As such, those who claim God's ultimate sovereignty cannot drink the Lord's cup and partake of the Lord's table while also sharing fellowship with demonic powers antithetical to God's reign (10:20–21). The criteria by which we demonstrate our allegiance to the God of Jesus Christ is not related to whether we eat or abstain from foods sacrificed to idols, however, but whether or not we use the freedom God gives us to love our fellow table guests. By participating in the sovereign love of God, regardless of whether we eat or drink, we will join in a holy meal fellowship that gives glory to God (10:31).

The festal reign of God's liberating love empowers participants of the Lord's Supper to engage directly in creative actions toward a new social reality. When teaching his followers how to pray, Jesus tells them to ask their Holy Father in heaven to "give us this day our daily bread" (Matt 6:11). Later, while passing through cornfields on the Sabbath, Jesus instructs his disciples to pluck the grains of corn directly from the fields. When confronted by the authorities, who remind him that it is illegal to dishonor God's holiness by working on the Sabbath, Jesus declares that the merciful love of God desires that those who are hungry be fed. Any law contradicting God's mercy, he says, is an illegitimate law. Unrestricted by the expectations and dictates of the present age, those who join in the feast of God's kingdom are free to engage in creative acts of love.

The Lord God invites us to participate in the holy realm of creative and emancipatory love, then, by celebrating the joyous banquet feast of God's kingdom in and for the world. In the last supper that he enjoys with his disciples before his arrest and crucifixion, Jesus informs his disciples that he "will never again drink of the fruit of the vine until that day when [he] will drink it new in the kingdom of God" (Mark 13:25). In almost all of his post-resurrection manifestations to the disciples, Jesus shares the newness of his raised and exalted body in the midst of a meal—as the twelve are sitting at the table (Mark 16:14–15); in the breaking of bread in Emmaus (Luke 24:30–35); in Jerusalem with a piece of broiled fish (Luke 24:36–43); and over breakfast next to the sea of Galilee (John 21:12–13). Jesus thereby communicates that the eternal kingdom in which he reigns with the Father/Mother and Holy Spirit continues to be alive in the world in and through the Lord's feast. "I confer on you," Jesus says, "a kingdom, so that you may eat and drink at my table in my kingdom" (Luke 22:28–30). Peter is instructed to "feed my sheep" (John 21:17) as a demonstration of his loyalty and love to Jesus. For our entrance into the kingdom of God takes place already now as we feed the hungry and satisfy those who are thirsty (Matt 25:34–37). We participate in the divine holiness by obeying the Lord God's decree to begin the eternal feast of love here and now in the midst of this present age.

Imperialistic Communion: Ongoing Expansion of Corporate Dominionship

Proponents of the global spread of modern capitalism argue that free markets, based on open competition and driven by the unfettered self-interest of both producers and consumers, are the most effective and democratic way of organizing the distribution of goods and services throughout a society. For "in a market economy, the decisions of a central planner are replaced by the decisions of millions of firms and households."[15] Whereas governments are overburdened by bureaucratic inefficiencies and corruption, and whereas centralized control stifles individual freedom, open markets, they claim, provide the conditions in which the innovation and creativity of free individuals automatically generates economic growth, growth that ultimately benefits the whole of society through the "invisible hand of the market."[16] Markets need to be freed therefore from all social restraints so that every aspect of society can be privatized and organized

---

15. Mankiw, *Principles of Economics*, 9–10.

16. "When the government prevents prices from adjusting naturally to supply and demand, it impedes the invisible hand's ability to coordinate the decisions of the households and firms that make up the economy" (ibid., 10).

according to the principles of unrestricted market exchange. For "economic freedom," as Milton Friedman maintains, "is an extremely important part of total freedom."[17]

There is no question that the free-market system, powered by unrestrained self-interested love, has produced enormous changes worldwide through innovative financial instruments, novel technologies, and new social configurations. Loosed from the wholeness of God's love, however, self-interested love inevitably leads not to individual or social freedom but to bondage, as profit-motivated individuals strive to draw everything and everyone within the grasp of their control. As such, the worldwide opening of more and more realms of existence to the logic of free markets has simultaneously allowed for the ongoing expansion of corporate dominionship over more and more aspects of social and ecological life on earth. "Capitalism is nothing if not vitally expansionist," Kloppenburg writes. "It constantly pushes against the barriers that restrain its advance, eroding them slowly, overwhelming them suddenly, or flowing past them and isolating them if their resistance is strong."[18] Precisely because the principal aim driving corporate producers within a capitalist economy is to increase financial profits, existing modes of production are constantly either overturned to increase productivity or expanded to extend the commodity form to new areas. Profits extracted by the exploitation of workers and nature are continually reinvested, therefore, in technological innovation, marketing, or novel product development. The result is the unremitting infusion of the processes of commodification into ever more social and ecological spheres.

The progressive invasion of the profit motive into ever-new spheres has taken place in three major waves. The first wave, as Vandana Shiva explains, happened during the five hundred years of European colonization of the Americas, Africa, Asia, and Australia. The second, postcolonial wave has occurred over the past five decades amidst the Western imposition of "developmentalism" on so-called "undeveloped" nations. The third wave of colonization, she asserts, is taking place today through patents, genetic

---

17. Friedman, *Capitalism and Freedom*, 9.

18. *First the Seed*, 10. Similarly, Harvey writes: "Precisely because capitalism is expansionary and imperialistic, cultural life in more and more areas gets brought within the grasp of the cash nexus and the logic of capital circulation. To be sure, this has sparked reactions varying from anger and resistance to compliance and appreciation. But the widening and deepening of capitalist social relations with time is, surely, one of the most singular and undisputable facts of recent historical geography" (*Condition of Postmodernity*, 344).

engineering, and intellectual property rights (IPRs). "The land, the forests, the rivers, the oceans, and the atmosphere have all been colonized, eroded, and polluted." In pursuit of new spaces to invade, enclose, and exploit for financial profit, she says, "the colonies have now been extended to the interior spaces, the 'genetic codes' of life-forms from microbes and plants to animals, including humans."[19]

Modern industrial agriculture represents the site of capitalism's most triumphant penetration into the processes of life itself. Traditional farming practices have always posed a set of barriers to the extension of capital, as Kloppenburg writes, because they are based upon the widely accessible means of production via the biosphere (i.e., soil, water), the free energies of the sun, and the re-generative capacities of living organisms. The transformation of farming in the modern world into "the most capital-intensive sector of the modern capitalist economy,"[20] therefore, required not only the colonizing enclosure of lands and the commoditizing of energy inputs (i.e., fuel-dependent machinery, petroleum-based nitrogen), but also the progressive insinuation of the profit-motive into the structures of plant and animal life.

In particular, the commodification of the plant seed in modern agriculture has commenced a tremendous revolution in the social and ecological relations constituting the modern political economy as a whole.[21] In traditional agricultural societies, the harvest of one year's crop provided both good fruits/grains to eat *and* the seeds for next year's crop. So, for thousands of years, as Shiva says, farmers saved part of each year's harvest to plant as seeds in the spring, while also sharing seeds with other farmers through seed exchanges based on the principles of cooperation and reciprocity. "A farmer who wanted to exchange seed," she writes, "would give an equal quantity of seed from his field in return for the seed he received."[22]

19. *Biopiracy*, 5, 4.

20. Kloppenburg, *First the Seed*, 31.

21. Kloppenburg quotes from a 1977 address given by University of California-Berkeley plant physiologist Boysie E. Day to the American Society of Agronomy (ASA): "I begin with the proposition that the agronomist is the moving force in many of the social changes of our time . . . He has brought about the conversion of a rural agricultural society to an urban one. Each advance has sent a wave of displaced farm workers to seek a new life in the city and a flood of change throughout society . . . Probably, no meeting in 1977 of politicians, bureaucrats, social reformers, urban renewers, modern-day Jacobins, or anarchists will cause as much change in the social structure of the country as the ASA meeting of crop and soil scientists" (quoted in *First the Seed*, 7).

22. Shiva, *Stolen Harvest*, 8.

Moreover, by selecting seed from those plants with the most desirable traits and/or by intentionally crossbreeding different varieties of plants, hundreds of generations of farmers around the world participated in the steady genetic improvement of food crops. Just within the United States, for example, prior to the commoditization of the processes of plant cultivation, "the development of the adapted base of germplasm on which American agriculture was raised is the product of thousands of experiments by thousands of farmers committing millions of hours of labor in thousands of diverse ecological niches over a period of many decades."[23]

Although the seed industry in the United States had already formed by the late 1800s, it was not until the sale of hybrid corn in the 1930s that the commercialization of seeds began radically to transform both farming and society. Hybrid corn is a vigorous, high-yielding variety developed from the direct cross-breeding of two pure inbred lines—i.e., two varieties that have been self-pollinated exclusively for several generations. Whereas yields from open-pollinated varieties are relatively consistent from year to year, hybrid corn yields at an appreciably higher rate the first year (F-1), but when its seeds are re-planted, shows a significant reduction the second year (F-2). Because individual farmers cannot maintain or recreate hybrid varieties themselves, if they want the yield advantage that corn hybrids (F-1) provide, they must buy hybrid seed from seed companies for each year's planting. As Kloppenburg writes:

> Hybridization thus uncouples seed as "seed" from seed as "grain" and thereby facilitates the transformation of seed from a use-value to an exchange-value. The farmer choosing to use hybrid varieties must purchase a fresh supply of seed each year. Hybridization is thus a mechanism for circumventing the biological barrier that the seed had presented to the penetration of plant breeding and seed production by private enterprise.[24]

In addition to increased yields, hybrid varieties could be bred for thicker stalks and stronger root systems, which enabled them to withstand mechanical harvesting, along with the capacity to absorb increased levels of nitrogen.[25] Although Harvard geneticist Richard Lewontin has shown that open-pollinated varieties, had they been developed, would be as good or

23. Kloppenburg, *First the Seed,* 56.

24. Ibid., 93.

25. For this reason, hybrid corn stands, quite literally, at the center of the Green Revolution's strategy of transforming agriculture in the modern world.

even better than hybrids by today, the combination of an immense infusion of capital, in particular from seed, nitrogen, and machinery companies, along with public policy decisions oriented toward those interests, meant that, by 1965, over 95 percent of U.S. corn acreage was planted with hybrid varieties. In other words, as Kloppenburg says, the dominance of hybrid corn in modern agriculture says much "less about biology than about political economy."[26]

Nature writer Michael Pollan, in his highly influential *The Omnivore's Dilemma*, describes the wide-ranging impact of commoditized corn on contemporary U.S. society. In 1920, for example, the Iowa countryside was populated with thousands of small to mid-sized farmsteads, each diversified with horses, cattle, chicken, hogs, apples, hay, oats, potatoes, cherries, and a great variety of other fruits and vegetables. Such diversity, he writes, provided the farmer with both food self-sufficiency and livelihood stability in the face of weather or market-related collapses in any particular crop. With the financial promise of increased crop yields and governmental guarantees of subsidies for hybrid corn, however, the vast majority of Iowa farmers began progressively focusing their farm operations on increasing their corn acreages. As production increased, of course, market mechanisms ensured that prices fell, so that farmers were successively forced either to plant more corn, requiring larger machinery, more land, and increased inputs, or to leave farming altogether. The result has been that the Iowa countryside is now populated by thousands of acres of monocropped corn produced by fewer and fewer farmers.

With the abundance of cheap corn, the industrial food system has developed innumerable ways to translate corn into various other commodities. For one, the glut of cheap corn has made it profitable to raise chickens in giant factories and cattle on massive feedlots rather than in farmyards or open pastures. "By far the biggest portion of American commodity corn (about 60 percent of it)," Pollan writes, "goes to feeding livestock, and much of that goes to feeding America's 100 million beef cattle."[27] Because cows are ruminants, however, and cannot digest grains without acute side-effects (i.e., bloating, acidosis, liver failure), the ground corn that feedlot cattle eat is mixed with heavy doses of antibiotics. In fact, "most of the antibiotics

26. Ibid., 101.
27. Pollan, *The Omnivore's Dilemma*, 66.

sold in America today end up in animal feed," a practice that Pollan says is "leading directly to the evolution of new antibiotic-resistant superbugs."[28]

The food science industry has also discovered many different ways of breaking hybrid corn down into countless processed products, such as cornstarch, glucose, high-fructose corn syrup, as well as adhesives, coatings, plastics, and now ethanol. In other words, "moving that mountain of cheap corn—finding the people and animals to consume it, the cars to burn it, the new products to absorb it, and the nations to import it—has become the principle task of the industrial food system."[29] The fact that nearly all of the food items sold in the modern U.S. supermarket are either directly or indirectly (i.e., corn-raised animal products) related to one commoditized plant, therefore, is not coincidental.[30] Likewise, neither is it an accident that the U.S. population is increasingly suffering from obesity, diabetes, and other weight-related diseases. The reality is that, despite repeated public health warnings regarding the over-consumption of processed foods, corn-sweetened sodas, and corn-fattened beef, both major political parties in the U.S. continue to enact farm bills subsidizing the over-production of hybrid corn. Not surprisingly, as Pollan points out, today only two agribusiness corporations—Cargill and ADM—presently dominate this entire process, including the shaping of food and agricultural policy.

> These two companies now guide corn's path at every step of the way: They provide the pesticide and fertilizer to the farmers; operate most of America's grain elevators; broker and ship most of the exports; perform the wet and dry milling; feed the livestock and then slaughter the corn-fattened animals; distill the ethanol; and manufacture the high-fructose corn syrup and the numberless other fractions derived from number 2 field corn [and] help write many of the rules that govern this whole game, for Cargill and ADM exert considerable influence over U.S. agricultural policies.[31]

Over the last three decades, the corporate drive to possess exclusive ownership over every aspect of the food economy has penetrated to the "inner space" of living organisms. With scientific "advances" in the capacity to

28. Ibid., 78.

29. Ibid., 62.

30. "Read the food labels in your kitchen," Pollan writes, "and you'll find that high fructose corn syrup [in particular] has insinuated itself into every corner of the pantry: not just into our soft drinks and snack foods . . . but into the ketchup and mustard, the breads and cereals, the relishes and crackers, the hot dogs and hams" (ibid., 104).

31. Ibid., 63.

understand and manipulate life at the genetic level, the commercialization of biotechnical research, and the extension of property rights to genetically modified life-forms, corporate interests have been able to commoditize the material elements of life itself. Unlike traditional breeding, which involves naturally crossing whole organisms within the same species (i.e., two varieties of corn), genetic engineering—also known as recombinant DNA technology or genetic modification/manipulation (GM)—involves directly transferring isolated genes across species (i.e., implanting a targeted salmon gene into a tomato).[32] The result, according to Norman E. Borlaug, who is often referred to as the "father" of the Green Revolution for his role in developing and promoting high-yielding crop varieties, is the "advent of a 'Gene' Revolution that stands to equal, if not exceed, the Green Revolution of the 20th century."[33]

Critics of genetically engineered crops argue that the primary motivation driving biotechnological research is not concern for the wellbeing of social or ecological communities, better nutrition, or even increased yields, but simply "the prospect of achieving a more complete commodification of the seed."[34] In fact, a gathering of the world's top molecular biologists at the Asilomar Conference in 1975 concluded that because genetic manipulation could prove to be enormously hazardous to human and ecological health, "it would be wise to exercise considerable caution in performing this research."[35] Subsequent legislative efforts in the late 70s to establish regulative guidelines on recombinant DNA testing were soundly defeated by the lobbying efforts of companies such as Eli Lilly, Monsanto, and Dupont. Not surprisingly, each of these companies has been a dominant player in the field of biotechnology. Monsanto, for example, has used "advances" in biotechnological research to dominate the agricultural commodities market with genetically modified (GM) seeds filled with fertilizers, pesticides, and other chemicals. In particular, Monsanto's "Roundup Ready" soy, cotton, and canola varieties are genetically engineered with bacterial DNA resistant to Monsanto's "Roundup" herbicide, which allows farmers to spray heavy doses of "Roundup" in fields planted with Monsanto's engineered seeds.

32. As Shiva writes, this process is usually accomplished through "a mosaic recombination of natural genetic parasites from different sources, including viruses causing cancers and other diseases in animals and plants that are tagged with one or more antibiotic resistant 'marker' genes" (*Biopiracy*, 34).

33. Borlaug, "Continuing the Green Revolution."

34. Kloppenburg, *First the Seed*, 243.

35. Quoted in ibid., 252.

Despite the fact that groundwater contamination, human cancers, and the overall degradation of the biosphere are all associated with herbicide use, the Monsanto Company, by coupling seed and herbicide in this way, has been able to monopolize both sectors of the agroeconomy and thus achieve enormous financial profits for its corporate managers and stockholders.[36]

Although the intellectual foundations of molecular biology and biochemistry that made genetic engineering possible were originally funded primarily through public monies given to research universities, biotechnology firms over the past forty years have managed to appropriate and "enclose" this knowledge for private commercial purposes.[37] First, as Kloppenburg points out, corporate firms like Agrigenetics, Monsanto, and Calgene have successfully convinced a number of publicly trained scientists to leave the academy for the private sector, thereby transferring their expertise from university to corporate laboratories. Second, biotechnology companies have forged a variety of linkages with university researchers by inviting them to assume managerial or ownership positions in private firms, while remaining on faculty or in positions of administrative leadership, or to serve as consultants on corporate advisory boards.[38] Finally, at a time when federal funding for universities has declined, university administrators have openly received massive financial "gifts" from corporations in the form of program grants, chaired faculty positions, and/or research facilities, in exchange for privileged or even exclusive access to resultant biotechnical knowledge. The result is that most biotechnological research today,

36. Although citizen and consumer groups in the United States have persistently raised objections to the imposition of genetically modified foods in the American diet, more and more acres of American farmland are being planted with GM crops. As Don West, a food and biotechnology consultant, has said, "the hope of the industry is that over time the market is so flooded [with GMOs] that there's nothing you can do about it, you just sort of surrender" (quoted in ibid., 318).

37. Kloppenburg quotes Jonathan King, who argues that "the public is being forced to buy back what the public itself initially financed," ibid., 198.

38. "The celebrated case of Dr. Raymond Valentine—University of California-Davis professor of biochemistry and founder of the new biotechnology firm Calgene—woke the academic community to the conflicts of interest that could emerge from simultaneously holding positions in business and academia. In his capacity as a member of the California Agricultural Experiment Station, Valentine received a $2.3 million grant from Allied Chemical for research on nitrogen fixation. Allied also purchased a 20 percent interest in Valentine's Calgene. Questions arose as to the distinction between Valentine's research for the station and his work for Calgene. There were also allegations of unethical management of graduate student research that was relevant to research projects underway at Calgene" (ibid., 227).

in corporate *and* university laboratories, is either owned or controlled by private interests.[39]

Corporate ownership of living organisms at the molecular and genetic levels has been made possible by a series of legal decisions allowing the patenting of "novel" life-forms. Prior to the 1980s, patents were not granted to seeds, plants or any part of nature, because it was deemed immoral by the courts for anyone to own an entire species of plant or mammal in the same way that one might own a car or a home. The pivotal governmental decisions that overturned this standard were the 1980 Supreme Court decision in *Diamond v. Chakrabarty* that ruled genetically engineered microorganisms are patentable; the 1985 U.S. Patent and Trademark Office (PTO) decision in *Ex parte Hibberd* that granted patentability to tissue culture, seeds, and whole plants; and the 1987 PTO ruling that declared animals to be patentable. As a result, "virtually all living organisms in the United States, including human genetic material, became patentable subject matter, just like any other industrial invention."[40]

> In what is frequently likened to a nineteenth-century style "land grab," vast tracts of the genescape and its products—DNA sequences, exons, introns, individual mutations, expressed sequence tags, single nucleotide polymorphisms, proteins, protein folds, parts of plants, whole organisms, whole classes of organism—are being appropriated via patents.[41]

Having acquired most of the major seed and biotech companies, and with exclusive intellectual property rights (IPRs) on patented life-forms, in particular seeds, giant agrochemical and pharmaceutical corporations now possess oligopolistic control over "the determination and shape of the *entire* crop production process."[42]

The patenting of genetically modified seeds, in particular, has allowed corporations like Monsanto or Dow to prohibit farmers from saving and reusing their seeds. Monsanto alone has filed over 500 lawsuits against

---

39. As Dave Henson points out, corporate control also extends over philanthropic organizations, since corporate foundations "fund many of the largest environmental, civil rights, arts, and other groups in the nation. The result of this 'corporate philanthropy' is that it gives control of much of our national culture and social movement agenda to these corporations through their decisions on which groups receive grants and which groups die on the vine for lack of funding" (Kimbrell, ed., *Fatal Harvest Reader*, 232).

40. Ibid., 243.

41. Ibid., 324.

42. Ibid., 201.

farmers for patent infringement. In a well-publicized Canadian case, the Monsanto company sued farmer Percy Schmeiser for infringing on a Monsanto's patent, because the genes of Monsanto's "Roundup Ready" canola seed were found in his canola fields. Although Schmeiser claimed never to have planted Monsanto's patented seed and defended himself by arguing that the presence of Monsanto's genes in his crops was due to pollen drift, Canada's Supreme Court held Schmeiser liable for patent infringement. "The justices held that how the genes had gotten into Schmeiser's field was immaterial," Kloppenburg writes. "According to the court, Canadian farmers do not have the right to knowingly 'use' patented genes even if they are incorporated into a crop through mechanisms over which the farmer has no control."[43] The profoundly troubling implication is that, if the genes of a corporate-owned organism cross with any other life-form—whether a tree, flower, vegetable plant—the resultant organism now belongs to the corporation. As Shiva writes, "it is not just the implanted gene, or one generation of animals, that is being claimed as intellectual property, but the reproduction of the entire organism, including future generations covered by the life of the patent."[44]

The 1994 TRIPs (Trade Related Aspects of Intellectual Property Rights) agreement of GATT, which is now administered by the WTO, globalized corporate control over seeds, plants, medicines, and even traditional knowledge. Shiva points out two examples in her home country of India—basmati rice and wheat. Although basmati has been grown on the subcontinent for centuries, developed and refined by generations of Indian farmers, the WTO Patent Office issued Texas-based RiceTec a patent on basmatic rice lines in 1997. As a result, Indian farmers were forced to pay royalties to RiceTec for growing varieties developed by their forebears. Similarly, Monsanto's patenting of wheat plants, grown in India for thousands of years, allowed them to claim exclusive property rights on Indian wheat harvests. More recently, under pressure from the World Bank, India passed the Seed Act of 2004, which prevents farmers from using traditional crop varieties. "The Seed Act," Shiva claims, "is designed to 'enclose' the free economy of farmers' seed varieties," thereby establishing a "seed dictatorship" in which "farmers are pushed into dependency on the corporate monopoly of patented seed."[45]

43. Ibid., 322.
44. *Biopiracy*, 96.
45. *Earth Democracy*, 151. Similarly, in 2004, Iraqi Order 81 made seed saving illegal

Perhaps the most disturbing technology patented in recent years is Genetic Use Restriction Technology (GURT), otherwise known as "Terminator Technology." Developed by the USDA and Delta Pine Land company in the 1990s, GURT terminates the reproductive capacity of seeds, so that grains harvested from such a variety would be incapable of germinating the following year. Although terminator genes are not yet commercially available, the purpose, Kloppenburg says, "is to eliminate once and for all the historical ability of farmers to maintain a degree of independence by short-circuiting the reproduction of capital through the reproduction of their own seed."[46] In late 2006, Delta Pine Land Company was acquired by the Monsanto Corporation.

The promise of the global economy is that unfettered, unregulated markets, which allow for the innovation and creativity of entrepreneurs to generate economic growth, are the most effective, efficient, and democratic means of organizing the distribution of goods and services in society. What an "awakened analysis" of our context (Herzog) reveals, however, is that the worldwide spread of free-market logic has made possible the imperialistic expansion of corporate control over more and more spheres of life. Seen in the light of God's holiness, an economy marked by the ongoing penetration of corporation dominionship over more and more spheres of personal, social, and biological life is oriented against God's creative love. Wherever Christians join together to share in the elements of an agro-industrial meal, therefore, they do so as participants in an unholy communion marked by imperialism and bondage.

Holistic Communion: Liberated Action Toward a New Economy

If Holy Communion, in obedience to the Lord God, is wholly liberated life together, how are citizens of God's kingdom to participate in the creative love of God in the midst of an economy dominated by the imperializing conquests of self-interested love? Specifically, in an agro-economy in which a few dominant agribusiness corporations now own the structures and organic processes of plant and animal life, how are Christians freely

---

for all Iraqi farmers.

46. *First the Seed*, 319. The very real possibility that "Terminator" genes could spread to other plants and life-forms, of course, portends a biospheric crisis of devastating proportions.

to celebrate the Lord God's joyous banquet as a festive manifestation of the new creation breaking into this present age? Those striving to obey the Lord God Almighty are called today to withdraw their cooperation with the dominant food system while participating in creative modes of economic life together that support the growth of a new economic order. Specifically, this requires the direct engagement of Christians in the emergence of a more liberated food economy, in which people are free to grow, harvest, share, and enjoy their daily bread and common cup.

By working toward a more liberated food economy, Christians affirm that the world is not bound to the imperializing powers of self-interest that rule this present age but is open to God's creative transformation. "The regime of God requires free people," as Christoph Friedrich Blumhardt affirms. "God needs flexible people" and "in the love of God we are uncommonly flexible."[47] In previous ages, singular allegiance to the Lord God has erupted in declarations of freedom from a host of captivities, including the rule of monarchs and dictators, repressive social practices and norms, and even the church itself. For "the Christian is independent of every human authority," as Leo Tolstoy writes, "by the fact that he regards the divine law of love . . . as the sole guide of his life."[48] In our time, those who have been set free by the sovereign love of God are called to declare their liberation from a global economic order governed by the unholy powers of self-love. At the very beginnings of our modern political economy—nearly five hundred years before transnational corporate entities would claim exclusive ownership over plant and animal genes—Thomas Müntzer openly declared that the source of "all usury, theft, and robbery" in society are the self-interested lords and princes "who take all creatures for their private property." For "the fish in the water, the birds in the air, the animals of the earth," he warned, "must all be their property (Isa 5:8)."[49] Although the modern age has seen Christian movements claim emancipation from various forms of repressive control, there have been few who have successfully declared freedom from the economic forces overruling nearly every aspect of contemporary life. The church, as Bonhoeffer says, "has not been able to make the loving care of God so credible that all human economic activity would be guided by it

---

47. Christoph Blumhardt, in Blumhardt and Blumhardt, *Thy Kingdom Come,* 95.

48. Tolstoy, *The Kingdom of God Is within You,* 137.

49. Müntzer, "A Highly Provoked Defense," in Baylor, ed., *The Radical Reformation,* 81.

in its task."[50] In working toward a new economic order, in which the perfect love of God guides our economic practices and decisions, Christians affirm their allegiance to the God whose transcendent freedom from the world is manifest in the power to bring about a new reality in and for the world.

There is perhaps no better starting point for those seeking to support the emergence of a new economic reality in our time than with the food economy. For the inbreaking of God's kingdom into this present age forces a decision about who or what truly governs our daily lives. That decision is clearly concentrated in two very different meal gatherings: the agri-business meal produced from the imperial conquests of self-love and the joyous banquet feast born of God's perfect love. The reality is that a few private corporations possess ubiquitous command over nearly every aspect of the production and distribution of most foods that we eat. As a result, unless we are willing to seek out and support the few alternative food sources that presently exist, as Marion Nestle says, "we support the current food system every time we eat a meal."[51] Nevertheless, having been liberated to begin the kingdom feast already here and now, Christians are free to support existing food alternatives, however small and imperfect, while helping to create models and systems that are even more closely aligned with the nature of divine love. Because the food economy is so foundational to any economic system, the eruption of new, more charitable ways of producing and distributing food has the potential to redirect the entire global economic order.

The sovereign love of the Lord God emancipates people, first of all, to "come out" and "be separate from" (2 Cor 6:17) the principalities and powers of this present age that are antithetical to God's reign. As citizens of God's kingdom of love, Christians are free to withdraw their participation in imperialistic economic practices. For "is there not, in Christian ethics," Berry asks, "an implied requirement of practical separation from a destructive or wasteful economy?"[52] Infused with the confidence of God's transcendent love, Christians throughout history have refused to cooperate with colonizing mandates to fight in wars, obey unjust laws, pay exploitative taxes, or labor under inhuman conditions. In our time, non-compliance with an economic order governed by imperialistic self-love will take many forms, including ceasing to purchase goods produced by the industrial agricultural system, withdrawing financial investments from agribusiness

50. Bonhoeffer, *Ethics*, 141.
51. Nestle, *Food Politics*, 374.
52. Berry, *Gift of Good Land*, 275.

corporations like Monsanto and Cargill, and boycotting specific food retailers and restaurants. The inbreaking of divine holiness into the world
also liberates citizens of God's kingdom to renounce certain professions
and occupational activities as being incompatible with the love of God.
The members of Christ's body are called, as Bonhoeffer says, to be "deeply
involved in all areas of life in this world." Yet in situations where they are
forced "to deny their Lord in exchange for every piece of bread they want
to eat," it becomes necessary that "complete separation remain visible, and
must become even more visible."[53] Not only as consumers and investors,
but also as professionals, managers, owners, and employees, Christians are
free to withdraw their participation in the imperializing conquests of an
unholy economic order.

The sovereign holiness of God, whose transcendent love radiates into
history for the sake of a new creation, also liberates Christians to engage
directly in creative alternatives to the economic system governing contemporary existence. Although critical opposition and non-compliance is
important, the creative love of God empowers us to be active participants
in the emergence of something new. "How can I hope for a new heaven and
a new earth," Christoph Friedrich Blumhardt asks, "unless I am conducting
myself in such a way that something more just, something better, *can* be
created on earth?" For along with the hope, which the inbreaking of God's
sovereign love creates in us, he says, "there also comes a certain strength:
'Now begin! The hope is there; so you can begin!'"[54] Unrestrained by neither the reality of ongoing market expansion into more and more realms of
existence, nor by the legal structures designed to protect corporate imperialism, Christians are empowered to engage freely in the creation of new
economic alternatives.

The creation of a liberated food economy that participates in the holiness of God's sovereign love begins at the most immediate level of self-
sufficient food production. True freedom, as Winstanley affirmed, "lies in
the free enjoyment of the earth" and the ability to receive one's "nourishment and preservation" directly from "the use of the earth."[55] For those with
access to a home yard, this means converting lawn space into productive
fruit, vegetable, and herb gardens. Master gardener John Jeavons has esti-
mated that, by properly preparing soil and using biointensive gardening

---

53. Bonhoeffer, *Discipleship*, 247.

54. Christoph Blumhardt, in Blumhardt and Blumhardt, *Thy Kingdom Come*, 93.

55. Winstanley, *The Law of Freedom in a Platform*, 66.

techniques, a family of four can meet all of its fruit and vegetable needs from a 1200 square foot garden.[56] Those living in apartments can grow on balconies and in indoor pots. In crowded urban environments, food can be grown on rooftops, up the side of trellised buildings, and in vacant lots. By engaging directly in the production and storage of our own food, we opt in favor of what Schumacher describes as the "life-giving and life-enhancing possibility, the conscious exploration and cultivation of all relatively non-violent, harmonious, organic methods of cooperating with that enormous, wonderful, incomprehensible system of God-given nature."[57] Although personal food production cannot address all of the global political problems bound up in our present food economy, nevertheless, "one must begin in one's own life," as Berry says, "the private solutions that can only *in turn* become public solutions."[58] For the creative love of God frees individuals to participate in the divine holiness in the small yet not insignificant sphere (Matt 10:29–31) of everyday life.

At the same time, emancipated citizens of God's kingdom are called to join together with others in grassroots food movements to create the broader social, economic, and political structures needed to support a new food economy. Although the Southern Agrarians urged American citizens faced with the perils of "industrial imperialism" to grow our own food, secure fuel from our own woodlots, "return to our looms, our handcrafts," and "take down the fiddle from the wall,"[59] they simultaneously hoped to ignite an alliance of southern farmers, western populists, and New England townships that would grow into a national movement. In our time, a profusion of food and agriculture movements have arisen around the world as a challenge to the global food economy—the Landless Worker's Movement in Brazil, the Zapatistas in Mexico, the Green Belt Movement in Africa, the *Confédération Paysanne* in France, and the international Via Campesina, to name just a few. One prominent example is the Navdanya (nine-crops) movement in India. Modeled on Gandhi's non-violent struggle against the British Empire, Navdanya is an interconnected network of small, cooperative communities that have rebuilt India's devastated rural economies at every level of production, processing, and distribution. By replacing chemically intensive, large-scale, monocultural farm-

56. From Shapiro and Harrisson, *Gardening for the Future of the Earth*, 99.

57. Schumacher, *Small Is Beautiful*, 135.

58. Berry, *Unsettling of America*, 23.

59. Lytle, "The Hind Tit," in Twelve Southerners, *I'll Take My Stand*, 244.

ing that is dependent on corporately sold, genetically modified seeds with small-scale, organic, and bio-diverse farming that practices seed saving and seed sharing, Navdanya has restored health to local farmers, ecosystems, and communities. According to founder Vandana Shiva, small-scale, direct responses like Navdanya are "necessary in periods of dictatorship and totalitarian rule because large-scale structures and processes are controlled by the dominant power." In particular, everyday essentials such as "our seeds, our rivers, our *daily food* are sites for reclaiming economic, political, and cultural freedoms because these are the very sites of the expanding corporate empire over life." [60] By participating in movements for food justice and sovereignty, Christians begin to engage in direct actions of creative love not in isolation or through fragmentary tactics but as an entire way of life together with others.

Whether individually or as part of broader movements, those set loose by God to participate in the emergence of a new economic order must do so by using technologies appropriate to the liberating purposes of God. The technological innovations that define modern economic life—including innovations in genetic technology—are primarily large-scale, capital-intensive, and therefore owned by the few rather than the many. Conversely, appropriate technologies, as Schumacher describes, are inexpensive enough that nearly everyone can access them, suitable for small-scale applications, and compatible with human creativity. He quotes Gandhi, in saying that "every machine that helps every individual has a place. But there should be no place for machines that concentrate power in a few hands and turn the masses into mere machine minders, if indeed they do not make them unemployed." [61] Examples of appropriate or liberating technologies in food and agriculture include rainwater harvest systems, outdoor solar ovens, composting barrels, chicken tractors, and biochar stoves. [62] By promoting the use of such appropriate technologies, Christians support the emancipation of workers, not from labor itself, but from the dehumanizing and enslaving dynamics of imperial control.

The ultimate aim of Christians involved in the creation of alternative economic models is not simply to fashion an economic sphere set-apart from the rest of the world but to challenge and transform the entire

---

60. Shiva, *Earth Democracy,* 183.

61. Schumacher, *Small Is Beautiful,* 31–32.

62. See Worldwatch Institute, *2011 State Of The World: Innovations that Nourish the Planet.*

network of political and institutional structures that constitute the global economy. "Because the life of the new righteousness cannot be restricted to the private sphere, but in the trend of its being presses towards the new creation or the new order of all things,"[63] as Moltmann affirms, citizens of God's heavenly kingdom are set apart not for their own private holiness but for the sake of the redemption of the whole creation. As such, participating in God's creative love in our economic life must include not only private and local efforts but public and political ones as well.

In the context of American history, the agrarian revolt of the prairie populists, which led to many of the legislative reforms of the "Progressive Era," is an instructive model. What began as a series of disconnected local struggles among small landowners and landless workers against monopolistic control of the land by financial elites led to a highly organized alliance that produced a national political platform that addressed, among other things, the corporate ownership of the media and transportation, the need for currency reforms, banking monopolies, humane work laws, and common access for all to the nation's fertile lands.[64] As Dave Henson, director of the Occidental Arts and Ecology Center, writes, many of the same struggles that the prairie populists engaged in against the corporate control of agriculture need to be fought again today.

> The fight against corporate chemical-industrial agriculture, against corporate control of the global food system, against corporate ownership of life, and against corporate control of economic decision making is the fight on this planet . . . In the 1870s to 1890s, American farmers built an anti-corporate movement that was clear about what it wanted. The Populists, Knights of Labor, Greenbacks, Alliance, and even the Grange worked to oppose the monopolizing consolidation of the banks and railroads . . . Times have certainly changed, but the fundamental struggle against rule by large corporations is much the same.[65]

Henson promotes a series of strategies to be implemented at the state and local level, including amending state constitutions to declare that corporations do not have the constitutional rights of an individual person, banning the corporate ownership of farmland, and restricting the financial

---

63. Moltmann, *Church in the Power of the Spirit*, 88.

64. See Goodwyn, *The Populist Moment*.

65. Henson, "The End of Agribusiness," in Kimbrell, ed., *Fatal Harvest Reader*, 233, 237.

influence of corporations on the political decision-making process.[66] For those who understand themselves to be citizens of God's kingdom, engaging in the legal and political struggles necessary to overturn the imperialistic conquest of our food system by monopolistic corporations is a participation in the creative love of God breaking into the world for the sake of a more liberated, just, and charitable world.

Conclusion

The transcendent Lord of heaven and earth invites us to join together in the joyous feast of redeeming love. From the realm of God's eternal kingdom, the divine holiness breaks into this present age as a creative power that frees us to participate in the emergence of a new world. In the midst of an unholy economy ruled by the imperial conquests of self-interested love, those seeking to obey the Lord God are called today to participate in the divine work of liberation by engaging in creative actions that contribute to the formation of a new economic reality. By participating directly in local food production, in grassroots movements for food justice, and in struggles to transform our global food system, Christians participate faithfully in the divine holiness that is redeeming all things in perfect love. Holy Communion is wholly liberated life together in which all are made whole. As we accept God's invitation to begin celebrating the banquet feast of creative love, including the ways we gather up and share the fruits of the earth in table fellowship, we obey the sovereign love of God who is making all things new.

66. Ibid., 238–39.

Conclusion

THIS IS A BOOK about food: about the economic, ecological, political, and philosophical contexts today within which we produce and consume our daily bread and common cup, as well as the ethical implications of how we are gathered together to eat. This is also a book about holiness: about the nature of God's perfect love and how it is we might participate more fully in the wholeness of God's life with and for the health of the good creation. Finally, this is a book about theology: about the context, tasks, and aims of theological reflection for the North American church.

In developing the claim that Christians in North America are called to participate in holistic modes of agro-economic life together as a faithful sharing in the holiness of God's love, I have attempted to engage four primary tasks for theology today. In the introductory chapter, I identified the following orienting methodological questions: 1) What is the nature of God's holiness at work in the world? 2) Are Christians faithfully gathering together in the context of the global market economy? 3) How might the church participate more fully in God's holiness? 4) What would constitute a truly *holy* communion meal gathering today? Within each chapter of the book, I drew from the holiness-communitarian and agrarian-ecological traditions to offer a theological interpretation of God's holistic love, a biblical account of the divine love manifest in holy meal practices, a critical analysis of the unholy meal prepared by a global market economy driven by sinful self-interested love, and practical agro-economic instructions for how Christians today might faithfully "come together to eat" (1 Cor 11:33) in the abundant communion of our Lord's Supper. Having done so, I can draw the following conclusions:

What is the Nature of God's Holiness at Work in the World?

I have based my holistic account of Holy Communion in the assertion that only God determines the nature of a truly holy communion, and I have argued that God's holiness is synonymous with God's perfect love, which is shared with the creation for the sake of its ultimate wholeness. Only God is holy, I have affirmed, and yet the God who is Father/Mother, Son, and Holy Spirit invites us to "be holy as I am holy" as we share *in* the perfect love that is *of* God. In doing so, I have provided a holistic and communitarian vision for our social, economic, and ecological life together that begins not with postmodern scientific claims about the interconnected nature of reality (McFague) or a strictly ecclesial understanding of the Christian life (Hauerwas) but with the being and work of the triune God.

With McFague, I have articulated a holistic understanding of the holy life that is oriented extensively toward the flourishing of all creation. Whereas McFague's "holistic paradigm" is ultimately based upon the findings of postmodern science, including especially those of biology and physics,[1] I have in contrast based my claims in the loving nature of God's holiness at work in the world. By doing so, I have avoided the Protestant Liberal tendency to translate the uniqueness of Christian doctrinal affirmations into a supposedly more universal or accessible framework for the sake of gaining public "relevancy" or "impact." Rather, I have drawn upon the scriptures and a vital tradition of the Christian church in affirming that God's restorative love is the only properly theological basis on which to embrace a holistic perspective and way of life. The result is a holistic account of the holy life that goes beyond categories like "unity" and "diversity"[2] in favor of the richer theological categories of grace, sanctification, incarnation, Trinity, and new creation.

In agreement with Hauerwas, I have articulated the ecclesial nature of holy living that is focused intensively upon the gathered life of concrete communities. Unlike Hauerwas, however, who ultimately bases his

---

1. See, for example, McFague, *The Body of God*. "Our focus for reconceiving the [holistic] model will be on the common creation story coming to us from the sciences," because "it is the view of reality current in our time. Theologies always have paid and always should pay serious attention to the picture of reality operative in their culture. If they do not, theology becomes anachronistic and irrelevant" (28–29).

2. Ibid., 27.

perspective in a set of philosophical-sociological concepts of community,[3] I have based my communitarian claims in a theological understanding of who God is as triune and what the love of the Father/Mother, Son, and Holy Spirit is doing in and for the creation. As a result, I have avoided the Protestant Postliberal tendency to constrict God's redemptive activity in the world to the church's performance of its liturgies, creeds, stories, and rituals. Rather, I have affirmed the importance of congregational life not because churches receive their mission, identity, and power from within themselves or by way of their ecclesiastical activities but because it is of the nature of God's holiness to assemble humans and nature within concrete, intimate, local communions. The result is a communitarian account of the holy life that grounds the meaning and purpose of ecclesial life together, including its central practices, in the depth and breadth of God's love for the world.

The contemporary theologian whose theological approach I have followed most closely is Protestant Holiness-Communitarian Frederick Herzog. In agreement with Herzog, I have articulated a holistic and communitarian account of the holy life that is rooted and grounded in the theo-praxis of God the Creator, Redeemer, and Sustainer. Herzog's call for theologians to begin not with metaphysical speculation concerning the nature of God or God's relationship to the world but with the unconcealed praxis of God that captivates us to follow, participate in, and co-labor with what God is doing in the world has guided my approach. Likewise, his affirmation that what the "divine agenda" is working toward is the "full communion" of all humans and nature, beginning with "bands and groups of people who communally seek to embody a new way of life,"[4] has shaped my assertion that God is calling the church to participate in holistic modes of economic life together that are aligned with the holiness of divine love. One of the ways I have built upon Herzog's work is by providing a more substantive account of the nature and shape of the "divine agenda." Although I agree

---

3. The key influence here, of course, is Alasdair MacIntyre's interpretation of the Aristotelian tradition. Hauerwas adopts from MacIntyre most of the key concepts that frame his entire project—"tradition," "practices," "narrative," "virtues," and "community." For example: "Christian convictions take the form of a story, or perhaps better, a set of stories that constitutes a tradition, which in turn creates and forms a community" (*Peaceable Kingdom*, 24). "To be like Jesus requires that I become part of a community that practices virtues," ibid., 76. "Practices make the church the embodiment of Christ for the world" (Hauerwas, *In Good Company*, 67–68).

4. Herzog, *Herzog Reader*, 283.

with Herzog that the praxis of God is marked by manifestations of love and justice within the dynamics of history, I have attempted to go beyond generic descriptions of God's "justice" and "compassion" in defining more clearly the holy nature of God's love. The result is a more thoroughgoing account of theo-praxis that draws deeply upon the holiness-communitarian traditions in affirming that the gracious love of Jesus Christ is the inclusive way that leads to peace, the convivial love of the Holy Spirit nurtures harmonious bonds of health, the enfleshed love of the Father/Mother is given for the flourishing of the earth, the mutual love of the Trinity directs us toward the service of our neighbor, and the creative love of the Lord God breaks forth in the eruption of all that is new.

What I have provided, therefore, are the theological foundations on which Christians ought not only to affirm but also contribute toward the contemporary search for holistic and communitarian alternatives—in economics but also in medicine, philosophy, the social sciences, and city planning, for example—as opposed to the atomistic, hierarchical, and mechanistic paradigm that has shaped modern life and its institutions.

Are Christians Faithfully Gathering Together in the Context of the Global Market Economy?

I have argued that the church is bound up in the unholy communion of the global market economy, a claim I have based in a theological examination of the unholy nature and impact of self-interested love. Whereas divine love leads to the fullness or wholeness of abundant life, I have argued, sinful self-interested love cut off from God's perfect love leads to numerous manifestations of life's diminishment. And because the modern global economy presently ordering nearly every aspect of our lives is ordered around the power of self-interest, I have deemed it both appropriate and necessary to describe the resultant worldwide web of social and ecological relationships to be an unholy communion. I have not denied that self-love is a powerful force or argued that the accomplishments of the modern market are insignificant, but I have claimed that an economy driven by self-interest is inevitably marked by contradiction and is ultimately unable to fulfill the promise of providing the abundant life for all.

In doing so, I am in agreement with McFague's assessment that the multiple threats to our planetary existence are ultimately rooted in our economic way of life, although I have focused my critique not upon the modern mechanistic worldview that she argues underlies many neoclassical economic presuppositions but upon the unholy nature of the concrete relationships that have been formed by the energies of myopic self-love. Similar to Hauerwas, I have argued that the modern social order presently governing the lives of North Americans, including Christians, is profoundly incongruent with the mission of the church. But whereas Hauerwas locates the problem almost exclusively in the ideology and practices of the modern nation-state, from which he imagines the church might be separated to the extent that it functions as an "alternative polis,"[5] I have located the problem in the dynamics of a modern political-economic order that are woven deep into the everyday lives of Christians and from which the church might be disentangled to the extent that it participates in alternative economic relationships. Here, I have followed Herzog's determination that North American Christians are captive to global economic "principalities and powers that own our lives"[6]—although I have argued not that we are "'money-woven' rather than 'God-woven'"[7] but that our captivity is, at an even deeper level, to the powers of self-interested love.[8] From Herzog, I have taken up the challenge that theological teaching must engage in an "awakened analysis of our context" that contributes to the smashing of the idol of the present economic system, which is ultimately rooted and grounded in a myopic, distorted form of love.

My "awakened" analysis of context has focused upon the agro-economy, not only because I affirm that God's invitation to participate in the abundant life of Holy Communion is a summons to share first and foremost in a wholly loving meal praxis in which we "taste and see that the Lord is good" (Ps 34:8), but also because the unholy nature of our modern economic life together is so tangibly pronounced in the relationships that are gathered up in the agro-industrial meal. What I have uncovered in my analysis of the global agro-economy is that nearly every stage in the planting, growing, production, distribution, sale, and consumption of our daily bread and common cup operates contrary to the holiness of God's

---

5. See Hauerwas, *In Good Company*. "I seek, therefore . . . for the church . . . to be a body constituted by the disciplines that create the capacity to resist the disciplines of the body associated with the modern nation-state," 26.

6. Herzog, *God-Walk*, 44.

7. Herzog, *Herzog Reader*, 292.

8. In this, I am following John Wesley's understanding that the problem is not money per se but the use of money in ways that are incongruent with the love and grace of God. See Wesley, "The Use of Money," in *John Wesley's Sermons*.

love. Whereas Jesus Christ welcomes all to the wholly inclusive feast of life, the agro-industrial meal is based in the exclusion of people from access to the land. Although the Holy Spirit joins all together within wholly loving communions, the agro-industrial meal contributes to the fragmentation of stable communities and complex ecosystems. Though the Father/Mother nourishes every body with the life-giving bread and cup of salvation, the agro-industrial meal depends upon the ravishing of earth and its many living creatures. Where the triune God arranges dinner guests as companions in wholly mutual communities, the agro-industrial meal serves only the select interests of a centralized elite. And while the Lord God grants permission for the festal reign of love to begin, the agro-industrial meal is bound up in the imperial expansion of corporate ownership over more and more spheres of life.

What this close analysis of a modern industrial food economy based in the violent, divisive, transgressive, unjust, and imperious energies of self-interest demonstrates is that the commonplace act of gathering to eat a meal in context of the global market economy entails a sharing in an unholy socio-political, economic, and ecological communion. For "unless we are willing to pay more for food, relinquish out-of-season produce, and rarely buy anything that comes in a package or is advertised on television, we support the current food system every time we eat a meal" (Nestle).[9] And if "how we eat determines to a considerable extent how the world is used" (Berry),[10] because "what we're eating is never anything more or less than the body of the world" (Pollen),[11] then the ongoing participation of North American Christians in a profit-driven agro-economy can only mean their ongoing complicity in an unholy use of the world. "We *are* the food we eat, the water we drink, the air we breathe" (Shiva).[12] For good or for ill, the eating of food *is* communion (1 Cor 10:20–21), which means that as Christians join together to eat as participants in the modern global economy, they do so as members of an unholy communion that is operating against God's love in and for the world.

What I hope to have demonstrated is the importance for contemporary theological reflection of attending not only to the internal and immaterial

9. Nestle, *Food Politics,* 374.

10. Berry, *What Are People For?,* 149.

11. Pollan, *The Omnivore's Dilemma,* 411.

12. Shiva, *Earth Democracy,* 5.

dynamics of ecclesial existence but also the external and material realities within which the church in our context is situated.

How Might the Church Participate More Fully in God's Holiness?

I have argued that Christians are called to participate in holistic modes of economic life together as a faithful sharing in the restorative wholeness of God's love, a claim guided by my methodological assertion that the work of theology is not ultimately fulfilled in reflection and analysis alone but must culminate in concrete proposals for the reformation of Christian life together in particular social contexts. My constructive proposals concerning how the church might participate in the emergence of economic alternatives to global capitalism should not be understood, then, as an attempt to prescribe a set of rigid ethical rules divorced from the being and activity of God. Rather, my assertion for concrete proposals for ecclesial reformation to be included as an integral part of the theological task is based in an affirmation that the God who is Father/Mother, Son, and Holy Spirit invites us not only passively to contemplate but actively to join in the divine holiness at work in the world.

Methodologically, I have been guided by McFague's insistence that theological reflection today be oriented toward the concrete particularities of our everyday lives such that our theological claims might "actually work in someone's life."[13] Whereas McFague is focused primarily on how *individual* North American Christians might transform the broader social structures of contemporary society, however, I have focused my constructive proposals on the reformation of ecclesial existence so that our *church communities* might become vitalizing centers from which alternative economic models of life together might emerge. In this, I have followed Hauerwas' claim that one of the most important theological tasks of our time is to contribute to the reformation of the church "as a body" whose practices offer an alternative to the violent practices constitutive of modern society. While Hauerwas' theological project is focused on a *recovery* of the traditional ecclesial practices of liturgy and sacrament, however, my approach is focused on the constructive *reformation* of the church's practical life together in light of its mission to participate in what God's love is doing in the world today. Once again, the contemporary Protestant figure whose theological approach

13. McFague, *Life Abundant*, 15.

I have followed most closely here is Holiness-Communitarian Frederick Herzog. My call for Christian communities to participate in the emergence of economic alternatives to global capitalism attempts to address Herzog's call for theology to be radically oriented in the concrete "where theology functions as praxiology"[14] while also discovering "how God's reality can break through to the people of God so that a new community will be built."[15]

My concrete proposals for ecclesial reformation should be understood, then, as the articulation of a congregational spirituality of participation in the divine life. I have not based my call for the involvement of Christians in holistic modes of economic life in general principles of "justice" or "sustainability" or "fairness" and neither have I presumed that the church can simply adhere more rigorously to its own established patterns of religious life. The church is called to reconcile those who have been excluded from access to the means of life and livelihood because this is what Jesus Christ is doing in the world. Congregations are summoned to heal the wounds caused by a divisive economy because the Holy Spirit is actively present wherever relationships that have been torn asunder are mended. Christians are drawn in to the work of caring for human bodies and restoring damaged ecosystems because the Father/Mother has sent Jesus Christ and the Holy Spirit for the salvation of all creaturely flesh. Church communities are called to lift up the oppressed poor and admonish the corporate mighty because the triune God is at work in the establishment of neighborly relationships of mutual service. And churches today are commanded to seek after creative social and economic alternatives that will liberate those enslaved by our present economy because the kingdom of God is already here among us in the eruption of new possibilities. In other words, the church is called to be holy as God is holy in the whole of life by participating in the holiness of God's love present and active in the world that it might be made whole.

What I have provided, therefore, is a spirituality for congregational life together that is grounded in the praxis of God, which I have affirmed is the gracious love of Jesus Christ whom we follow in peaceable communities of inclusion, the convivial love of the Holy Spirit within whom we abide in healthy communities of harmonious relationship, the enfleshed love of the Father/Mother whom we worship in earthly communities integrated with nature, the mutual love of the Trinity to whom we conform in neighborly

14. Herzog, *Herzog Reader*, 136.

15. Ibid., 70.

communities of cooperation, and the creative love of the Lord God whom we obey in new communities of liberation.

What Would Constitute a Truly Holy Communion Meal Gathering Today?

I have argued that the reformation of congregational life together ought to be particularly focused upon the participation of Christians in holistic agro-economic practices and movements, precisely because God's holiness in and for the world and the church's mission to participate in God's restorative love are both centrally embodied in the dynamics of a wholly loving meal gathering. I have based this claim in a theological account of the holistic nature of God's love and a biblical examination of the holy nature of Jesus' meals given by the Father/Mother and practiced in the Spirit by his earliest followers in anticipation of the coming reign of God. Rather than interpreting the Lord's Supper primarily as a metaphor from which we can glean a set of principles to be applied to the reformation of non-ecclesial institutions and structures, or primarily as a fixed religious ritual to be practiced in isolation from the world, I have offered a theology of Holy Communion oriented toward the reformation of how Christians understand *and* practice the Lord's Supper. In particular, in the context of a global market economy in which the everyday lives of North American Christians are bound up in an unholy communion woven together by sinful self-interested love—centered in what and how we eat—I have argued that a truly holy communion meal praxis will include the participation of Christians in a holistic agro-economy that fosters rather than damages ecosystems, supports rather than exploits workers, and up-builds rather than destroys human relations and communities.

In making this claim, I have held together McFague's holistic awareness of the economic and ecological relations within which we "live and move and have our being" with Hauerwas' ecclesial focus on the political nature of the material practices that constitute the holy meal. For while I agree with McFague that the "the feast of joy, the invitation to share the bread and wine" has important "implications for the holistic sensibility needed in our time," I have attempted to demonstrate that the Holy Communion meal is not just a "central symbol of this new vision of life"[16] but is the embodiment of the holistic life itself. For "eating is not merely a *sign* of something else,"

16. McFague, *Models of God,* 52–53.

as Andrew McGowan has affirmed, "but is among the most fundamental forms of social action there is; meals do not merely encode society, they *are* society."[17] In this regard, I have shown that Jesus' meals with tax collectors and sinners (Luke 7:34), his command to invite the poor and maimed to one's banquet feasts (Luke 14:13), his announcement that "whoever wishes to be first" must literally be a servant at the meal table (Mark 10:44), and the embodiment of this new social order in his own person (John 13:3–17) were not simply referential signs pointing toward a new society but a real and present manifestation of God's social order in the form of holy ways of eating together. Likewise, for the early churches, gathering to worship in the power of the Holy Spirit in and through communion meal gatherings (1 Cor 11:33) constituted not simply a symbolic but a bodily-material remembrance of Jesus in the form of a holy society of brotherly and sisterly love.

Hauerwas's characterization of the church as a social body and its eucharistic practices as "the essential rituals of our politics"[18] provides a helpful corrective to McFague's symbolic understanding of the Holy Communion meal. And yet, as McFague affirms, bodies qua bodies do not exist in isolation but are inextricably bound up in dynamic interconnections with a host of other bodies—both individual and social, human and non-human. What I have argued is that in the context of a global market economy, in which Christians share in agro-industrial meal practices marked by numerous forms of violence and domination—the ongoing loss of farmable land, for example, and sharp rises in asthma, attention-deficit disorder, fibromyalgia, and cancer, enormous waste and ecological damage due to long distance travel, the displacement of small landowners to urban centers and exploitative working conditions, and tremendous disparities in wealth and political power between migrant workers and the corporate executives of agribusiness corporations[19]—it is simply not accurate to say that the church's existent ritual meal practices embody a substantive social alternative set apart from the violent practices constitutive of modern society.

My proposal for the participation of Christians in holistic agro-economic practices as a faithful response to God's invitation to share in Holy Communion has been inspired by Herzog's call for the church today to discern how to confront the principalities and powers of this present age "in the political act of worship in the body language of the Eucharist"

17. McGowan, *Ascetic Eucharists*, 5.
18. Hauerwas, *Peaceable Kingdom*, 108.
19. Kimbrell, *The Fatal Harvest*.

in ways that manifest "a sociopolitical structure other than the world's."[20] I have attempted to articulate for our time the early church's holistic understanding of the eucharistic meal as "the realpresence of God in history in terms of Christian community"[21] by suggesting a contemporary ecclesial meal praxis characterized by "full communion, communion in every aspect of Christian life."[22] Although Herzog himself does not ultimately set forth concrete proposals for how the church might enact a "justice meal in which nature and neighbor receive their due,"[23] the holistic communion meal practices I have proposed are an attempt to fulfill just this vision.

The holistic communion meal praxis I have proposed for the contemporary church draws heavily not only upon the holiness-communitarian tradition that influenced Herzog but also upon the agrarian-ecological tradition. As I have demonstrated, the agrarian-ecological tradition provides concrete, livable proposals for a new agro-economy that are closely aligned with the holiness-communitarian understandings of the holy nature of God's perfect love. What I have argued, then, is that a truly holistic communion meal, in our context, will include following the way of Jesus Christ by ensuring common access for all people to the productive potentialities of the land; abiding in the sanctifying bonds of the Holy Spirit by weaving the diverse parts of our agro-economic life into a healthy whole; worshipping the Creator in the whole of life by integrating our agro-economic activities into the earth's economy; conforming to the triune God within local assemblies by cooperating together in worker-owned and democratically governed enterprises; and accepting the freedom to live now as citizens of God's kingdom by acting directly to create an agro-economy patterned after God's holy love. This is a justice meal (Herzog) embodied in the church's political act of worship (Hauerwas) and attentive to the host of human and non-human creatures gathered together in loving relationship (McFague). For as Wendell Berry affirms, "if the body is healthy, it is whole,"[24] and yet, precisely because our bodies are not distinct from the bodies of other people, of plants and animals, and of the earth—"for all creatures are parts of a whole upon which each is dependent"[25]—it is necessarily the case that

---

20. Herzog, *Herzog Reader,* 14.

21. Ibid., 110.

22. Ibid., 115.

23. Ibid., 5.

24. Berry, *Unsettling,* 103.

25. Berry, *The Gift of Good Land,* 273.

individual bodies cannot be whole alone. To be healed, he concludes, "we must come with all the other creatures to the feast of Creation."[26]

This is the abundant feast of God's holiness. Holy Communion is the feast of wholly loving life together in which all of creation is made whole, and the invitation is simply this: "Take, eat. Drink from this, all of you. Do this in remembrance of me."

---

26. *Unsettling*, 103–4.

Bibliography

Abrams, John. *Companies We Keep: Employee Ownership and the Business of Community and Place*. White River Junction, VT: Chelsea Green, 2008.

Arndt, Johann. *True Christianity*. New York: Paulist, 1979.

Arnold, Eberhard. *God's Revolution: The Witness of Eberhard Arnold*. Edited by John Howard Yoder. New York: Paulist, 1984.

Arnold, Gottfried. "The Mystery of the Divine Sophia." In *Pietists: Selected Writings*, edited by Peter C. Erb, 219–26. New York: Paulist, 1983.

Ayala, César J. *American Sugar Kingdom: The Plantation Economy of the Spanish Caribbean*. Chapel Hill: University of North Carolina Press, 1999.

Bailey, Liberty Hyde. *The Holy Earth: Toward a New Environmental Ethic*. Mineola, NY: Dover, 2009.

Barnet, Richard. *The Lean Years: Politics in the Age of Scarcity*. London: Abacus, 1980.

Barth, Karl, "Jesus Christ And The Movement For Social Justice." In *Karl Barth: Theologian of Freedom*, edited by Clifford Green. Minneapolis: Fortress, 1991.

Baylor, Michael, ed. *The Radical Reformation*. New York: Cambridge University Press, 1991.

Bellers, John. *Proposals for Raising a College of Industry of All Useful Trades and Husbandry with Profit for the Rich: A Plentiful Living for the Poor, and a Good Education for Youth. Which Will Be Advantage to the Government, by the Increase of the People, and Their Riches*. London: Sowle, 1695.

Berry, Wendell. *The Unsettling of America: Culture & Agriculture*. San Francisco: Sierra Club, 1977.

———. *The Gift of Good Land*. San Francisco: North Point, 1981.

———. *Home Economics*. San Francisco: North Point, 1987.

———. *What Are People For?* New York: North Point, 1990.

———. *Sex, Economy, Freedom & Community*. New York: Pantheon, 1992.

———. *Life is a Miracle: An Essay Against Modern Superstition*. Washington, DC: Counterpoint, 2000.

———. *Citizenship Papers*. Washington, DC: Shoemaker & Hoard, 2003.

———. *The Way of Ignorance And Other Essays*. Shoemaker & Hoard, 2005.

Bethge, Eberhard. *Dietrich Bonhoeffer: A Biography*. Rev. ed. Minneapolis: Fortress, 2000.

Black, E. *IBM and the Holocaust*. London: Little, Brown, 2001.

Blumhardt, Christoph Friedrich. *Action in Waiting*. Plough, 1998.

Blumhardt, Christoph Friedrich, and Johann Christoph Blumhardt. *Thy Kingdom Come: A Blumhardt Reader*. Edited by Vernard Eller. Grand Rapids: Eerdmans, 1980.

Boehme, Jacob. *The Way to Christ*. New York: Paulist, 1978.

Bonhoeffer, Dietrich. *Sanctorum Communio: A Theological Study of the Sociology of the Church*. Edited by Clifford J. Green. Translated by Reinhard Krauss and Nancy Lukens. Dietrich Bonhoeffer Works 1. Minneapolis: Fortress, 1998.

————. *Act and Being: Transcendental Philosophy and Ontology in Systematic Theology*. Edited by Wayne Whitson Floyd and Hans-Richard Reuter. Translated by Martin H. Rumscheidt. Dietrich Bonhoeffer Works 2. Minneapolis: Fortress, 1996.

————. *Christ the Center*. Translated by Edwin H. Robertson. San Francisco: HarperCollins, 1978.

————. *Creation and Fall: A Theological Exposition of Genesis 1-3*. Edited by John W. de Gruchy. Translated by Douglas Stephen Bax. Dietrich Bonhoeffer Works 3. Minneapolis: Fortress, 2004.

————. *Discipleship*. Edited by John D. Godsey and Geffrey B. Kelly. Translated by Reinhard Krauss and Barbara Green. Dietrich Bonhoeffer Works 4. Minneapolis: Fortress, 2003.

————. *Life Together*. Edited by Geffrey B. Kelly. Translated by James H. Burtness and Daniel W. Bloesch. Dietrich Bonhoeffer Works 5. Minneapolis: Fortress, 1996.

————. *Ethics*. Edited by Clifford J. Green. Translated by Reinhard Krauss, Charles C. West, and Douglas W. Stott. Dietrich Bonhoeffer Works 6. Minneapolis: Fortress, 2005.

————. *Letters and Papers from Prison*. Edited by Eberhard Bethge. Translated by Reginald Fuller, Frank Clark, and others with additional material by John Bowden. New York: Macmillan, 1971.

Bookchin, Murray. *The Ecology of Freedom: The Emergence and Dissolution of Hierarchy*. Oakland: AK, 2005.

Bové, José, and François Dufour. *The World is Not for Sale: Farmers Against Junk Food*. New York: Verso, 2001.

Brueggemann, Walter. *The Land: Place as Gift, Promise, and Challenge in Biblical Faith*, 2nd ed. Minneapolis: Fortress, 2002.

Buber, Martin. *Paths in Utopia*. Syracuse, NY: Syracuse University Press, 1996.

Canterberry, E. Ray. *A Brief History of Economics: Artful Approaches To The Dismal Science*. Hackensack, NJ: World Scientific, 2001.

Cavanaugh, William T. *Torture and Eucharist: Theology, Politics, and the Body of Christ*. Challenges in Contemporary Theology. Malden, MA: Blackwell, 1998.

Daley, Herman. "Economics in a Full World." *Scientific American* 293, no. 3 (2005) 100–107.

Daly, Herman E., and John B. Cobb, Jr. *For the Common Good: Redirecting the Economy Toward Community, the Environment, and a Sustainable Future*. Boston: Beacon, 1989.

Davis, Ellen F. *Scripture, Culture, and Agriculture: An Agrarian Reading of the Bible*. New York: Cambridge University Press, 2009.

Dayton, Donald W. "The Holiness Churches: A Significant Ethical Tradition." *Christian Century*. February 26, 1975, 197–201.

De Gruchy, John W., ed. *The Cambridge Companion To Dietrich Bonhoeffer*. Cambridge: Cambridge University Press, 1999.

Dosman, James A., and Donald W. Cockroft, eds. *Principles of Health and Safety in Agriculture.* Boca Raton, FL: CRC, 1989.

Douglas, Mary. "Deciphering a Meal." *Daedalus* 101, no. 1 (1972) 61–81.

Erb, Peter C., ed. *Pietists Selected Writings.* New York: Paulist, 1983.

Ellul, Jacques. *Anarchy and Christianity.* Grand Rapids: Eerdmans, 1988.

Flannery, Austin, ed. *Vatican Council II.* Vol. 1, *The Conciliar and Post Conciliar Documents.* Northport, NY: Costello, 1998.

Forrester, Duncan B. *Christian Justice and Public Policy.* Cambridge: Cambridge University Press, 1997.

Francke, August Hermann. "Following Christ." In *Pietists: Selected Writings*, edited by Peter C. Erb, 135–44. New York: Paulist, 1983.

Friedman, Milton. *Capitalism and Freedom.* Chicago: University of Chicago Press, 1962.

Goldsmith, Edward. "Feeding the World Under Climate Change." *Institute of Science in Society Website.* October 2012. http://www.i-sis.org.uk/FTWUCC.php. Accessed January 30, 2017.

Goodwyn, Lawrence. *The Populist Moment: A Short History of the Agrarian Revolt in America.* New York: Oxford University Press, 1978.

Green, Clifford J. *Bonoeffer: A Theology of Sociality, Revised Edition.* Grand Rapids: Eerdmans, 1999.

Grote, Geert, "A Sermon Addressed to the Laity." In *Devotio Moderna: Basic Writings*, edited and translated by John Van Engen, 92–97. New York: Paulist, 1988.

Gwynne, Robert N., and Critóbal Kay. "Agrarian Change and the Democratic Transition in Chile: An Introduction." *Bulletin of Latin American Research* 16 (1997) 3–10.

Halweil, Brian. *Eat Here: Reclaiming Homegrown Pleasures in a Global Supermarket.* Worldwatch. New York: Norton, 2004.

Hardt, Michael, and Antonio Negri. *Empire.* Cambridge, MA: Harvard University Press, 2000.

Harvey, David. *The Condition of Postmodernity: An Enquiry into the Origins of Cultural Change.* Oxford: Blackwell, 1990.

Hauerwas, Stanley. *The Peaceable Kingdom: A Primer in Christian Ethics.* Notre Dame, IN: University of Notre Dame, 1983.

———. *Dispatches from the Front: Theological Engagements with the Secular.* Durham, NC: Duke University Press, 1994.

———. *In Good Company: The Church as Polis.* Notre Dame, IN: University of Notre Dame, 1995.

———. *Sanctify Them in the Truth: Holiness Exemplified.* Nashville,: Abingdon, 1998.

———. *After Christendom: How the Church Is to Behave if Freedom, Justice, and a Christian Nation Are Bad Ideas.* Nashville: Abingdon, 1999.

Heinberg, Richard. "Fifty Million Farmers." Twenty-Sixth Annual E. F. Schumacher Lectures, Stockbridge, Massachusetts, October 2006.

———. *Peak Everything: Waking Up to the Century of Declines.* Gabriola Island, BC: New Society, 2007.

Hemenway, Toby. *Gaia's Garden: A Guide to Home-Scale Permaculture.* 2nd ed. White River Junction, VT: Chelsea Green, 2009.

Hendrickson, Mary. "Consolidation in Food Retailing and Dairy: Implications for Farmers and Consumers in a Global Food System." *A National Farmers Union Report*, Jan. 8, 2001.

———. "The Global Food System: A Research Agenda." Report to the Agribusiness Accountability Initiative Conference on Corporate Power in the Global Food System, High Leigh Conference Centre, Hertfordshire, UK, June 2005.

Herzog, Frederick. *Understanding God: The Key Issue in Present-Day Protestant Thought.* New York: Scribner's Sons, 1966.

———. *Liberation Theology: Liberation in the Light of the Fourth Gospel.* New York: Seabury, 1972.

———. *Justice Church: The New Function of the Church in North American Christianity.* Eugene, OR: Wipf and Stock, 1980.

———. *God-Walk: Liberation Shaping Dogmatics.* New York: Obis, 1988.

———. *European Pietism Reviewed.* San Jose: Pickwick, 2003.

———. *Theology from the Belly of the Whale: A Frederick Herzog Reader.* Edited by Joerg Rieger. Harrisburg, PA: Trinity, 1999.

Hill, Christopher. *The World Turned Upside Down: Radical Ideas during the English Revolution.* London: Penguin, 1972.

Horsley, Richard A. *Jesus and Empire: The Kingdom of God and the New World Disorder.* Minneapolis: Fortress, 2003.

Howard, Sir Albert. *The Soil and Health: A Study of Organic Agriculture.* Lexington: University of Kentucky Press, 2006.

Jackson, Wes. *New Roots for Agriculture.* Lincoln: University of Nebraska Press, 1980.

———. *Altars of Unhewn Stone: Science and the Earth.* New York: North Point, 1987.

———. *Becoming Native to This Place.* New York: Counterpoint, 1994.

Jefferson, Thomas. *Notes on the State Of Virginia.* New York: Penguin, 1999.

Kautsky, Karl. *Communism in Central Europe in the Time of the Reformation.* New York: Kelley, 1966.

Kimbrell, Andrew, ed. *The Fatal Harvest Reader: The Tragedy of Industrial Agriculture.* Washington, DC: Island, 2002.

King, Martin Luther, Jr. "Letter from Birmingham City Jail (1963)." In *A Testament of Hope: The Essential Writings of Martin Luther King, Jr.*, edited by James Melvin Washington, 289–302. 1st ed. San Francisco: Harper & Row, 1986.

Kirschenmann, Frederick. "The Future of Agrarianism: Where Are We Now?" *Leopold Center for Sustainable Agriculture Website.* April 25, 2002. https://www.leopold. iastate.edu/files/pubs-and-papers/2002-04-future-agrarianism-where-are-we-now. pdf. Accessed January 30, 2017.

———. "Reflections, Encouragement, and Inspiration for Iowa Agriculture." *Leopold Center for Sustainable Agriculture Website.* October 21, 2002. http://www.leopold. iastate.edu/content/writings-fred-kirschenmann. Accessed January 30, 2017.

Klein, Naomi. *No Logo.* New York: St. Martin's, 2000.

———. *Shock Doctrine: The Rise of Disaster Capitalism.* New York: Metropolitan, 2007.

Kloppenburg, Jack Ralph, Jr. *First The Seed: The Political Economy of Plant Biotechnology.* Madison: University of Wisconsin Press, 2004.

Korten, David C. *Community Organization and Rural Development: A Learning Process Approach.* New York: Ford Foundation, 1980.

———. *The Post-Corporate World: Life after Capitalism.* West Hartford, CT: Kumarian, 1988.

———. *When Corporations Rule the World*, 2nd edition. Bloomfield, CT: Kumarian, 2001

———. *The Great Turning: from Empire to Earth Community.* San Francisco: Berrett-Koehler, 2006.

————. *Agenda for a New Economy: From Phantom Wealth to Real Wealth.* San Francisco: Berrett-Koehler, 2009.

Kovel, Joel. *The Enemy of Nature: The End of Capitalism or the End of the World?* New York: Zed, 2007.

Lawson, Laura J. *City Bountiful: A Century of Community Gardening in America.* Berkley: University of California Press, 2005.

Lin, Brenda B., et. al. "Effects of industrial agriculture on climate change and the mitigation potential of small-scale agro-ecological farms." *CAB Reviews: Perspectives in Agriculture, Veterinary Science, Nutrition and Natural Resources* 6, no. 20 (2011) 1–18.

Lindblom, Charles E. *The Market System.* New Haven: Yale University Press, 2001.

Mankiw, N. Gregory. *Principles of Economics.* Mason, OH: South-Western Cengage Learning, 2008.

Marx, Karl. *Grundrisse.* Translated by Martin Nicolaus. London: Penguin, 1973.

————. *Capital.* Translated by Samuel Moore and Edward Aveling. Abridged ed. Oxford: Oxford University Press, 1995.

May, Roy. H, Jr. *The Poor of the Land: A Christian Case for Land Reform.* New York: Orbis, 1989.

McFague, Sally. *Models of God: Theology for an Ecological, Nuclear Age.* Philadelphia: Fortress, 1987.

————. *The Body of God: An Ecological Theology.* Minneapolis: Fortress, 1993.

————. *Super, Natural Christians: How We Should Love Nature.* Minneapolis: Fortress, 1997.

————. *Life Abundant: Rethinking Theology and Economy For a Planet in Peril.* Minneapolis: Fortress, 2000.

McGowan, Andrew. *Ascetic Eucharists: Food and Drink in Early Christian Ritual Meals.* New York: Oxford University Press, 1999.

McKibben, Bill. *Deep Economy: The Wealth of Communities and the Durable Future.* New York: Holt, 2007.

Meiksins Wood, Ellen. *The Origin of Capitalism.* New York: Monthly Review, 1999.

Mill, John Stuart. *Essays on Some Unsettled Questions of Political Economy.* London: Longmans, Green, Reader & Dyer, 1874.

Mollison, Bill. *Introduction to Permaculture.* Sisters Creek, Tasmania, Australia: Tagari, 1991.

Moltmann, Jürgen. *The Church in the Power of the Spirit: A Contribution to Messianic Ecclesiology.* Translated by Margaret Kohl. Minneapolis: Fortress, 1977.

————. *The Trinity and the Kingdom.* Translated by Margaret Kohl. San Francisco: Harper & Row, 1981.

————. *God in Creation: A New Theology of Creation and the Spirit of God.* Translated by Margaret Kohl. Minneapolis: Fortress, 1985.

————. *The Way of Jesus Christ: Christology in Messianic Dimensions.* Translated by Margaret Kohl. Minneapolis: Fortress, 1990.

————. *The Spirit of Life: A Universal Affirmation.* Translated by Margaret Kohl. Minneapolis: Fortress, 1992.

————. *Jesus Christ for Today's World.* Translated by Margaret Kohl. Minneapolis: Fortress, 1994.

————. *The Coming of God: Christian Eschatology.* Translated by Margaret Kohl. Minneapolis: Fortress, 1996.

————. *The Source of Life: The Holy Spirit and the Theology of Life*. Translated by Margaret Kohl. Minneapolis: Fortress, 1997.

Moore Lappé, Frances. *Hope's Edge: The Next Diet for a Small Planet*. New York: Penguin, 2003.

Morehouse, Ward, ed. *Building Sustainable Communities: Tools and Concepts for Self-Reliant Economic Change*. New York: Bootstrap, 1989.

Müntzer, Thomas. "A Highly Provoked Defense" (1524). In *The Radical Reformation*. edited by Michael Baylor, 74–94. New York: Cambridge University Press, 1991.

Nelson, Julie A. *Economics for Humans*. Chicago: University of Chicago Press, 2006.

Nestle, Marion. *Food Politics: How The Food Industry Influences Nutrition and Health*. Berkeley: University of California Press, 2003.

Nollert, Michael. "Transnational Corporate Ties: A Synopsis of Theories and Empirical Findings." *Journal of World-Systems Research* 11, no. 2 (2005) 289–314.

Oetinger, Friedrich. *Biblisches und emblematisches Wörterbuch*. 1776. Internet Archive. https://archive.org/details/biblischesundemb00oeti. Accessed January 30, 2017.

Ostrum, Elinor. *Governing the Commons: The Evolution of Institutions for Collective Action*. New York: Cambridge University Press, 1990.

Perkins, John. *Confessions of an Economic Hit Man*. New York: Penguin, 2004.

Polanyi, Karl. *The Great Transformation: The Political and Economic Origins of Our Time*. Boston: Beacon, 1944.

Pollan, Michael. *The Omnivore's Dilemma: A Natural History of Four Meals*. New York: Penguin, 2006.

Presbyterian Church (U.S.A.). "We Are What We Eat." A Report by the 214th General Assembly of the Presbyterian Church, 2002. https://www.pcusa.org/site_media/media/uploads/_resolutions/we-are-what-we-eat.pdf. Accessed January 30, 2017.

Robinson, John A. T. *The Body: A Study in Pauline Theology*. Philadelphia: Wyndham Hall, 1988.

Russell, Letty M. *Church in the Round: Feminist Interpretation of the Church*. Louisville: Westminster John Knox, 1993.

Ruusbroec, John. *The Spiritual Espousals and Other Works*. New Jersey, Paulist, 1985.

Schumacher, E. F. *Small Is Beautiful: Economics as if People Mattered*. New York: Harper & Row, 1973.

Shapiro, Howard-Yana, and John Harrisson. *Gardening for the Future of the Earth*. New York: Bantam, 2000.

Shiva, Vandana. *The Violence of the Green Revolution: Third World Agriculture, Ecology, and Politics*. Penang, Malaysia: Zed, 1991.

————. *Biopiracy: The Plunder of Nature and Knowledge*. Boston, MA: South End, 1997.

————. *Stolen Harvest: The Hijacking of the Global Food Supply*. Cambridge, MA: South End, 2000.

————. *Water Wars: Privatization, Pollution and Profit*. Cambridge, MA: South End, 2002.

————. *Earth Democracy: Justice, Sustainability, and Peace*. Cambridge, MA: South End, 2005.

Smith, Adam, *The Wealth of Nations*. New York: Barnes & Noble, 2004.

Smith, Dennis E. *From Symposium to Eucharist: The Banquet in the Early Christian World*. Minneapolis: Fortress, 2003.

Smith, Kimberly K. *Wendell Berry and the Agrarian Tradition: A Common Grace*. Lawrence: University of Kansas Press, 2003.

Sowell, Thomas. *Basic Economics*. New York: Basic, 2004.

Spener, Phillip Jacob. *Pia Desideria*. Edited and translated by Theodore G. Tappert. Minneapolis: Fortress, 1964.

Tasch, Woody. *Inquiries into the Nature of Slow Money: Investing as if Food, Farms, and Fertility Mattered*. White River Junction, VT: Chelsea Green, 2008.

Tauler, Johannes. *Johannes Tauler Sermons*. Translated by Maria Shrady. Introduction by Josef Schmidt. Classics of Western Spirituality. New York: Paulist, 1985.

The Theologia Germanica of Martin Luther. Translated by Susanna Winkworth. Mineola, NY: Dover, 2004.

Thomas, à Kempis. *The Imitation of Christ*. London: Penguin, 1952.

Tolstoy, Leo. *The Kingdom Of God Is within You: Christianity Not as a Mystic Religion But as a New Theory of Life*. Translated by Constance Garnett. Rockville, MD: Wildside, 2006.

Twelve Southerners. *I'll Take My Stand: The South and the Agrarian Tradition*. 75th anniv. ed. Baton Rouge: Louisiana State University Press, 2006.

Van Engen, John, ed. *Devotio Moderna: Basic Writings*. Mahwah, NJ: Paulist, 1988.

Volf, Miroslav. *After Our Likeness: The Church as the Image of the Trinity*. Grand Rapids: Eerdmans, 1998.

Wall, Derek. *Babylon and Beyond: The Economics of Anti-Capitalist, Anti-Globalist and Radical Green Movements*. Pluto, 2005.

Werhane, Patricia. *Adam Smith and His Legacy for Modern Capitalism*. New York: Oxford University Press, 1991.

Wesley, John. *A Plain Account of Christian Perfection*. Epworth, 1952.

Wheelan, Charles. *Naked Economics: Undressing the Dismal Science, Fully Revised and Updated*. New York: Norton, 2010.

Winstanley, Gerrard. *The True Levellers Standard Advanced: Or, the State of Community Opened, and Presented to the Sons of Men* (1649). In *Gerrard Winstanley Selected Writings*, edited by Andrew Hopton, 7–23. London: Aporia, 1989.

———. *The Law of Freedom in a Platform, or True Magistracy Restored*. Edited by Robert W. Kenny. New York: Schocken, 1973.

Wirzba, Norman. *The Paradise of God*. New York: Oxford University Press, 2003.

———, ed. *The Essential Agrarian Reader: The Future of Culture, Community, and the Land*. Lexington: University of Kentucky Press, 2003.

Worldwatch Institute. *2011 State of the World: Innovations That Nourish the Planet*. New York: Norton, 2011.

Zinn, Howard. *A People's History of the United States: 1492—Present*. New York: Harper Collins, 2003.

Zizioulas, John D. *Being As Communion: Studies in Personhood and the Church*. Contemporary Greek Theologians 4. Crestwood, NY: St. Vladimir's Seminary Press, 1985.

Index of Names and Subjects

Index of Scripture

OLD TESTAMENT

NEW TESTAMENT